"With his book, Scott Ferson delivers an intimate ethnography that will be the envy of political reporters and social scientists alike. In an age of caricatures and tribal polarization, Ferson sets aside his own ideology and does what many Americans won't: He steps out of his comfort zone, listens, and learns."

—**TIM ALBERTA**, *New York Times* bestselling author of *The Kingdom, the Power, and the Glory* and *American Carnage*

"Scott Ferson's *How the Democrats Lost America* isn't just a post-mortem on the 2024 presidential election. For all the hand-wringing about former President Joe Biden or fears of the rise of an autocracy under President Donald J. Trump, Ferson makes clear that the party that was once aligned with the needs and desires of the 'average' American forgot to listen and engage that 'average' American. If they had, as Ferson has done in thousands of interviews, they would have learned that the path to power is rather simple: it is about connection, about connecting with voters to remind them why government matters. The Democrats lost that capability, but Ferson—in a book that both condemns and tries to uplift the party—provides a practical path forward."

—**JULIETTE KAYYEM**, former Clinton and Obama Administration National Security Official

"Anybody who wants Democrats to win in 2028—or anyone still wondering why they lost in 2024—should read this book. Ferson treats the last election as a culmination, not a fluke. Drawing on a series of conversations around the country, he offers an unvarnished account of why Democrats struggle between the coasts and why those voters will be hard to win back."

—**JONATHAN MARTIN**, Politico columnist and *New York Times* bestselling co-author of *This Will Not Pass: Trump, Biden, and the Battle for America's Future*

"Scott Ferson has written flat-out the best book about contemporary electoral politics I've ever read. *How the Democrats Lost America* is so many things: part political analysis, part oral history, part travelogue, part cri du coeur for a different way of thinking—and not just our thinking about Donald Trump's victory in 2024, or about the Democratic Party's electoral prospects in 2028, or even about the lost art of personal civility between those on opposite ends of partisan spectrum. By documenting with such grace and wit eight years of coast-to-coast travels through the country's smallest towns and largest cities, in states blue and red and purple, Ferson wants us to join him in paying homage to the marvelous scale and scope of America—the multitudes it contains, the contradictions it embodies, the hunger for a better life shared absolutely everywhere. A sorely-needed and bracing reminder that politics still and forever happens one person at a time."

—SCOTT W. BERG, author of *The Burning of the World* and *38 Nooses*

"Scott Ferson is a modern-day political Kerouac, who takes readers on the road across America in search of what it will take to save our democracy. Ferson's keen political eye and quick wit make for a great read. From the football bars of Independence, Missouri, to the gun shops of Kennesaw, Georgia, and the coffee shops of Cathlamet, Washington, Ferson takes his readers on a listening tour like no other. Along the way, Ferson captures the voices of ordinary people from the forgotten main streets of America, and challenges us to build a democracy that works for everyone."

—CAROL ROSE, Executive Director, ACLU of MA

SCOTT FERSON

HOW THE DEMOCRATS LOST AMERICA

MAKING SENSE OF THE **2024 ELECTION** AND THE FUTURE OF **AMERICAN POLITICS**

TURNER
PUBLISHING COMPANY

Turner Publishing Company
Nashville, Tennessee
www.turnerpublishing.com

Cover design by William Ruoto
Book design by Ashlyn Inman

Library of Congress Cataloging-in-Publication Data
Names: Ferson, Scott, 1961- author
Title: How the Democrats lost Steve : making sense of the 2024 election / by Scott Ferson.
Description: Nashville, Tennessee: Turner Publishing Company, 2026. | Includes bibliographical references and index.
Identifiers: LCCN 2025032165 (print) | LCCN 2025032166 (ebook) | ISBN 9798887981857 hardcover | ISBN 9798887981864 paperback | ISBN 9798887981871 epub
Subjects: LCSH: Democratic Party (U.S.)—Public opinion | Presidents—United States—Election—2024
Classification: LCC E919.F47 2026 (print) | LCC E919 (ebook)
LC record available at https://lccn.loc.gov/2025032165
LC ebook record available at https://lccn.loc.gov/2025032166

Printed in the United States of America

CONTENTS

LOSING TRACK OF DEMOCRACY 7

    Prologue 9

1. The Des Moines Effect 15
2. The Electoral College Has Been Reaccredited 23
3. Democracy Is on the Ballot 31
4. The Coalition of the Disconnected 46

    Reflection 76

LOST COMMUNITY 79

5. Stuck in Place 81
6. Sticking With Place 96
7. Is It the Economy, Stupid? 121
8. Nobody Likes That Shit 132

    Reflection 142

LOST VISION 145

9. Greed 147
10. House Uncertain 156
11. The Border Giveth and the Border Taketh Away 163
12. Listening for God 173
13. The Very Online 184

    Reflection 192

BUILDING BACK 193

14. I Think I Can Swing It 195
15. Conspiracy Theories 200
16. Coin Flip 204
17. An Apprentice No More 211
18. They Hate Us 222
19. The Battle over Democracy 232

    Conclusion 237

    Acknowledgments 249

    About the Author 251

For Lucy

PART ONE

LOSING TRACK OF
DEMOCRACY

PROLOGUE

THE DEMOCRATS LOST STEVE

Steve Fischer—fifty-five years old, here in Georgia to supervise a crew of six who are replacing bridge supports on a rail line—knows why Donald Trump won. We're sitting in plush chairs in the lobby of the Hilton Atlanta/Marietta Hotel & Conference Center four days after the race was called. The Republicans are better for the economy generally, Steve notes, and Trump, specifically, for Steve's personal economy back at home in Toledo, Ohio. He got a bonus last year of $10,000 but netted $1,000 less overall. He watches his spending carefully, and it costs an extra $20,000 a year just to live since Joe Biden took office.

He's not fooled by Donald Trump. Steve knows exactly who Trump is, his many personal flaws displayed over his first term. But Steve is more wary of the forces arrayed against Trump, the elites, the liberal media, those pushing an agenda, those rigging the system.

If Kamala Harris had pulled it off—if the Democrats' "bait-and-switch from Joe Biden to Harris" had worked, and she had won—he wouldn't have wondered how that happened either. It would have proven his belief expressed to me in the same lobby, the day before the election, that "they" would never let Trump win.

"What happened to those seven million Biden votes from 2020?" The implication takes a minute to sink in for me. Steve doesn't think votes weren't counted this year, 2024, a smoldering narrative being stoked on social media in the post-election fog of defeat by baffled Democratic voices. He wonders if seven million votes from 2020 may have been manufactured to elect Joe Biden. He isn't telling me so much as asking, as someone who works in politics, and more importantly, someone who is having a civil conversation with him, and he wonders why people can't be civil more often. He feels talked down to on the subject of politics by people who disagree with him and who seem hostile, but we've gotten to know each other this week while we are both anchored here, and we can ask questions without being judged, either one of us.

Steve works for a construction firm contracted to repair those bridge supports for Norfolk Southern railroad. He usually rents a house for monthslong assignments but prefers the Marietta Hilton when in this part of Georgia: Robert the bartender knows his drink; the breakfast buffet is pretty good; and it's located close to the robust variety of village restaurants, just past the *Gone with the Wind* Museum and the Confederate Cemetery across the street.

He's a member of the laborers' union, one of several bargaining units at his company, and can retire in four years, maybe even "double-dip" with another job in addition to his pension as he's still a young man. His daughter is a deputy sheriff married to someone Steve likes very much—not like the high school boyfriend. Steve's girlfriend of eighteen years bartends, but you can't really make a living doing it today in Toledo. When they first met, more people went out and she could pull down a thousand dollars in tips on a shift.

He asks me why "they" hate Trump so much. They "won't let it go." "He's not even in yet." CNN and MSNBC, two networks he checks on regularly, flipping from Fox to keep an eye on the liberals, will pound the forty-seventh president relentlessly for four years, Steve is certain. It reinforces Steve's belief that Trump is fighting "the system," the one that takes $100,000 of his earnings in taxes each year. "Where does that money go?" It's not as if Trump needs the money. He's joining this battle not to enrich himself, even if he is ham-handed in his leadership style, in Steve's view.

I resist the urge to explain where tax money goes, but Steve wouldn't be surprised if I had schooled him, as he would expect that from a condescending Harris-voting member of the coastal elite. But where one might hear ignorance of how tax money pays for programs approved by Congress, I think Steve has a more basic question: Where does *his* money go? And who determines where it goes? Does it go to the right places, in a way that he trusts?

He voted for the first time in his life in 2016 when he began both questioning where his money went and why things always seemed to revolve around racial identity, why we were in foreign entanglements—some of our own creation. He wondered how we had gotten away from what the government should be doing, like back when he wasn't as engaged in politics?

And it hits me. The Democrats lost Steve—not just the one sitting with me in this hotel billed as "the Mansion of the South" with its English gardens and rocking-chair veranda opening onto its 120-acre golf course—but a lot of Steves, too many Steves, enough Steves to swing an election and tilt history's trajectory. This one happens to hail from Toledo, enjoys full health-care coverage, belongs to a union at a company where they compensate him well and treat him accordingly. A generation ago, he would have been a Democrat, by tradition or community or through union organizing, though maybe a Reagan Democrat. But Reagan Democrats, at that time, were still Democrats. Steve was never connected to a party. He worked and raised a daughter and left the concerns about governance to others.

He was impervious to messaging about how Biden has delivered for people like him, how Trump is a fascist, how our democracy is at stake. When Steve started to question how his tax dollars were being spent, when he became politically curious back in 2016, looking for answers to what he was seeing and wondering how things were being run, in his forties at that time and secure in his life's position, the Democrats were yet again absent. Steve is lost to them now, and, for those in disbelief over how what happened in 2024 happened, the hard lesson is *the Democrats never tried to win over Steve.*

From the formerly pivotal (see: Kerry, John, 2004) but no longer swing state of Ohio, Steve was not a target in their voter file, so they never listened to him. Broadly, in the past decade or so, there has been no desire among the base of the Democratic Party, or the Beltway-centric consultant class, to listen to someone like Steve. If he doesn't realize his life is built on hard-fought Democratic wins, well, thirty-five million more votes have been cumulatively cast for the Democratic nominees since Bill Clinton was elected in 1992 than for the GOP standard-bearers.

And that's true, but the Democratic base continues to erode to the coasts, even as the coasts erode, piling up big totals in California, New England, and other blue strongholds. And even there along the oceans, places like Fall River, Massachusetts, rejected Harris outright, while Trump tamped down the crucial margins in Democratic vote gushers like Philadelphia and Illinois's Cook County (which encompasses Chicago).

Donald Trump didn't win the presidency in 2024 so much as the Democrats lost it, having lived off a Clinton-era economic posture that no longer works for those neither wealthy nor dwelling along the coasts nor in concentrated liberal enclaves. In those places, they don't think of Steve. In those places, the fight for democracy means something to them, and they don't get why it doesn't to the rest of the country. In these wealthy places, there is no need to move past Clinton's North American Free Trade Agreement. Maybe Trump's tariffs will be better for the Steves.

SQUIRREL AND THREE

Up the road from Marietta, at the Old Fort Restaurant on 25th Street in Cleveland, Tennessee, Amanda and Don Willoughby, who are in their early seventies and semiretired, represent tiny blue dots swimming against the current in a Tennessee River of MAGA red.

"Can't get these every day," Don says after spying the chicken dumplings special on the menu, adding wryly, "Could be squirrel." Don's bimonthly Texas Hold'em tournament gang comprises bricklayers and lawyers, county officials and painters, insulation guys, cops, and two former prisoners. They don't talk politics much, but it's a safe bet that Don, who started voting consistently Democratic in the Trump Era, would be in the partisan minority.

Bradley County, of which Cleveland is the county seat, went for Trump by more than 78 percent, and voted Republican at almost precisely the same clip all the way down the federal ticket, even heavier at the state level.

Don's wife, Amanda, who eschews the restaurant's panoply of meat-and-three offerings in favor of a salad, praises him for steering clear of the political chatter as her husband only goes so far as advising one interlocutor, "You need to check where you're getting your news." Don—who has strong Sam Elliott energy right down to the mustache, the droll humor, and the drawl—allows, "We don't talk politics, but every now and then, someone will slip."

A gathering place, in a country whose citizens can't talk to one another, let alone new arrivals, is a rarity. A community built around a recreational activity shared in enjoyment where partisan acrimony does not infest and metastasize is a prize to be cherished and celebrated.

Trump vs. Harris was the first presidential election Don has ever called wrong, and Amanda was surprised by the results too, "because I didn't think people were that stupid." They are big-hearted people who open their home to folks down on their luck or in need of a place to stay for the time being. When Amanda thinks about the "vile, disgusting" victor of Tuesday's election, she displays double middle fingers, thrusting them in the air left and right, and says, "I want to vomit every time he comes on TV."

If the obscene gestures are noticed in the packed diner—with Bible verses in cursive on the walls and crosses dotting the shelves—I'm sure they are perceived as directed to her companions at the table. Amanda is careful to state her opinions of the election results sotto voce. And it hits me again. Democrats have abandoned Amanda and Don too—true-believing, Harris-backing guerrilla warriors with neither hope nor expectation that the billions of dollars Democrats spend each election cycle, including midterms, will ever cross their horizon.

Folks around here work hard, and the Willoughbys recognize that not everyone has time to consume a diet of high-quality news, and that the broader, fragmented media landscape is perhaps not the most hospitable ecosystem for a well-informed citizenry to flourish.

"Just the massive flow of garbage," Amanda says. "And I think that won the election for Trump, and I think the news media won the election for Trump. They'd just focus on anything he did." She hasn't watched the news since election night. Don says he seeks news sources "in the middle" but that it is a vanishing middle. "I looked at the Internet, but you can't believe anything that's on there."

In addition to being the Bradley County seat, Cleveland, Tennessee, is a jewel on the Bible Belt. The Church of God, which counts around 6,000 churches across the nation, is headquartered in town. Don likes to say that every time a building becomes vacant around here, it becomes a church, even briefly, and estimates about 300 churches stand across the county of a little over 100,000 residents. Amanda says, like the media, the local religious infrastructure lined up behind Trump, leading the faithful to believe "God appointed Trump and he's the savior."

Leaving Cleveland to drive back to Marietta, I'm struck by the reality on the ground in the reddest parts of this country and the coverage of a seemingly different reality as seen on the preferred channels of those in the bluest parts of this country, where an anomaly is wished into a trend. You can leave the diner buoyed by your conversation with the Willoughbys, but to do so, you'd really need to ignore the political reality in the rest of the restaurant.

CNN coverage showed the sophistication of the Democrats' ground game, the microtargeting in the seven swing states. The get-out-the-vote (GOTV or "go-teevee" in political operative argot) effort, unmatched and unchallenged by the Republicans, to vacuum up votes, rendering the swing states Harris lost—all seven—agonizingly close.

Democrats will search, perhaps for years, for answers to what went wrong and who is to blame, the circular firing squads assembled even before Trump was declared the victor. Famed writer H. L. Mencken is reported to have said, "For every complex problem there is an answer that is clear, simple, and wrong."[1]

Kamala Harris did not lose Steve, and she could not have won him over either. He was lost long before she took the torch from Biden. Kamala Harris proved a better candidate than most pundits expected, and her campaign did come within two points of winning the popular vote, but she encountered an ossified political landscape that limited her avenues to an electoral majority.

Steve's been lost to the Democrats for years, and the Democrats never even noticed—or if they did, they evinced little to show they cared. They have a complex problem to work out and now have the luxury of time to do so. Steve's right there, sitting in a plush chair, happy to engage with someone who doesn't talk down to him, because he has questions, and they shouldn't be answered only by Tucker Carlson.

Democrats have a choice. Steve can be lost and forgotten or lost and found. And Trump isn't some savior for Steve. He just won Steve's vote in a binary choice determined by others. Steve knows exactly who Trump is. But when one side offers you nothing, you will take a promise from the other side every time and hope it won't prove false.

If it does prove false, Steve, his political voice found, will speak again in four years.

---

1   Alastair Dryburgh, "The Problem Is Not The Problem, But The Solution Is," Forbes, February 10, 2015.

CHAPTER ONE

THE DES MOINES EFFECT

Inside a high school gymnasium on the west side of Des Moines, Iowa, on the first night of February 2016, Republican caucus-goers stood one at a time in a proud tradition of the Republic, making the case to their neighbors for their preferred candidates. The moderator moved alphabetically through the twelve candidates on the ballot, starting with Jeb Bush, until finally arriving at Donald Trump.

Campaigns had lined up speakers to make their best case for their candidate, but not, apparently, the candidate who would quickly scorched-earth march through the primary season. The moderator called a second time for a Trump advocate to speak. Nothing.

The voting by secret ballot was completed, the clerks tallied the results, and the moderator announced the winner: Donald Trump. I found this hilarious. Until election night.

I first traveled to Iowa in 1988 to work on the presidential campaign of Missouri Congressman Dick Gephardt and have worked in politics for more than forty years, at all levels and in any number of capacities. I am a go-to source on all things political, predicting what the voters will do or concluding why they have done what they have done.

Thankfully, political pundits cannot be sued for malpractice, but, still, I try to be thoughtful, my punditry grounded in my experience, and I stand by my reasoning when I look back on what I have said might happen over the years, even if I ended up being wrong. Politics is not a science, if that wasn't obvious after 2016. And it has been unalterably affected by that year's outcome, the forces that drew momentum from it, and the changes both wrought and revealed in our country. The election of 2024 further confounded the norms that have governed our politics even through our most turbulent times.

I should have listened to the silence after the moderator's call for a testimonial for Donald Trump on that cold caucus night in Des Moines, Iowa. I should have listened some more after the votes were cast and the results announced. I should have heard. But for me, this epiphany revealed the harder truth: This wasn't a singular event. The political sands had been shifting under my feet for some time, and I was oblivious, comfortable in my own assertions of the immutable truths of the business of politics, checking my assumptions against those I agreed with politically and those I didn't, who would provide reliable validation inside the pundit bubble.

My travels since have been a journey for redemption for a capital sin committed by myself and most of the political consulting class: not listening to voters.

After the election results of 2016 proved I had missed the lesson of Des Moines, I set out to *listen*, determined to check my assumptions about what voters want. Since then, I have visited every corner of the lower forty-eight to engage people where they live, never leading with politics but following when they do, mostly just intent on listening to them talk about their lives.

I've been fortunate to enlist other listeners in this journey, men and women I know from my professional life as well as personal friends from different backgrounds, willing to take trips in the spirit of the project and report their findings. What follows draws from their encounters, traveling in pairs mostly, as I did, to more accurately reflect our interactions with people. Save one, we are not trained reporters, and our reflections were recorded after our discussions. Because of this, some names and identifying details have been changed to protect the privacy of individuals. While the vast majority of the text reflects my own experience, I've transposed the first person voice into the entirety.

A lot of what we heard is confounding to the way I think about what I want in my elected officials—which is why listening must lead to questions and hopefully to discussion. I already took high blood pressure medication, so I wasn't looking to argue. When I told someone in my progressive hometown outside Boston that I was traveling around some red states chatting with voters, she replied, "Good. Maybe you can explain to them why they're so wrong."

Asking questions respectfully, as people given equal agency in our democracy to voice our opinions, tempers political pronouncements—particularly if you're engaging people about their daily lives, struggles, hopes, and fears. I have also learned a lot about a country I'd already thought I knew well. I hope the voices collected here might speak to you in some way as well.

This book is not titled *They Were Right and You Are Wrong*. It is also not titled *You Are Still Right and They Are Still Wrong*. I think Kamala Harris proved to be a good candidate but that the outcome was determined the day she was elevated to the top of the ticket. I heard, "I've got nothing against her," a lot. The book will also argue that this election was not about Donald Trump's manifold personal flaws and self-evident political talents. I heard, "I know exactly who he is," a lot.

Beyond the veneer of the binary choice of 2024, there is a rot that's eating at the core of our politics—a purposeful disconnect between the bipartisan power elite in this country and we the people, who, after all, were featured prominently, right at the top, in the Constitution that still governs us. William H. Hastie, the first African American governor of the US Virgin Islands, once called democracy "a process, not a static condition. It is becoming, rather than being. It can easily be lost, but never is fully won, its essence is eternal struggle."[1]

In this book, you will find the American people's thoughts on this struggle of becoming and discover the answer to the question of what the outcome of the 2024 election was really about: a deep disconnect between what the Democratic Party was selling in much of the country and the constituencies it was losing.

Beyond the surfeit of advertising that precedes any election, most of the people I talked to for this book have never been directly contacted by a campaign of any kind or a political party of any flavor. They mostly don't live in the hyper-targeted counties in the seven so-called swing states. No one ever knocked on their doors. The voices in this book were purposely ignored. If they got political mail pieces, no one mentioned it to me. They see the campaigns only in TV commercials and crowding their social media. They knew way before George Clooney that Joe Biden was too old to serve another four years. But the Democrats weren't listening until Nancy Pelosi, Mr. Clooney, and other big donors

---

1   Famous Quotes, "William H. Hastie – Famous Quotes," accessed May 25, 2025, https://
    www.famousquotes.com/quote-author/william-h-hastie/#google_vignette.

determined for themselves he was too old to run, the money dried up, and that was the tipping point—Biden was out.

I get asked, all over the country, what the answer is, why so many voted for someone so manifestly unqualified to be president, someone who tried to overthrow our very democracy. This book is also not titled *I Have Answers*.

But I *do* have thoughts.

If you are concerned about the threat to democracy, ask yourself if democracy has worked for you. My experience tells me it might have. But what if our democracy, checking and balancing things since the Founding Fathers launched the experiment almost 250 years ago, *doesn't* work for you? Of course, at the time, it wasn't meant to work for anyone other than propertied white males.

The history of enfranchisement should not and cannot be viewed through rose-colored glasses. Former Congressman Barney Frank once quipped, "A rising tide lifts all boats, but if you are standing on tiptoe in the water because you cannot afford a boat, the rising tide is not good news."[2]

I will make the case that those in the rising boats need to pull those on tiptoe in the shallows on board. It's not enough for the Democrats to throw life preservers at them and hope they thank Democratic candidates with votes every four years. And it's a cynical take to believe that when Donald Trump tries to drown them, as Democratic voices predict, that they will suddenly remember they had been tossed something to keep them afloat and will be eager to go back. They're not going back. And we might then be honest that there are a lot of people in the seaworthy boats of democracy, particularly of the Democratic variety, who didn't really want to bring others on board anyway.

Opening a dialogue on the state of our democracy requires that we start with a willingness to listen. I was talking to a Democratic political operative who spoke of the deepening disconnect between voters in a growing number of states and his party. He said righting the ship will not happen in a single election cycle, and I agree. Some Democrats think they don't need to listen. Voters may be in a different place in two or four years. The razor-thin national margin—less than 1.5 percent—may cut the other way. This is true, and it's not an invalid strategy for 2026. Power through, fight the administration at every turn, raise a record

---

2   Barney Frank, Ford Hall Forum, November 13, 2008, Boston, MA. https://dc.suffolk.edu/fhf-av/100/.

number in contributions, wait for Trump to fumble, and if the political ball pops in your favor, employ the midterm equivalent of the NFL's "tush push" into the end zone of a majority in the House.

Republicans have the same problem of a different stripe. The cult of personality that is Donald Trump may not translate to JD Vance, who appears not to have one, to some observers. The GOP may push hard on their own social agenda, rolling back rights federally that Trump only feints at, and it may be all too much for "swing voters," resulting in blue splotches to pop up in unexpected places.

This book IS titled *How the Democrats Lost America*, and I will make the case that Democrats should look to expand their own map, not by telling people what the coastal elites think they should hear, but by hearing what everyone thinks is important. This is not a quick fix, and it's bigger than getting better messaging. The Democrats have a near-term problem: How to flip the 1.5 percent. It may be a combination of what they do and what Trump does that answers that question. Back in Boston, fretting Democratic friends ask me who should be the nominee in 2028. I understand the desire to find a savior who will lead them out of the wilderness, an Obama, or maybe a Michelle Obama. Personally, I have a poor track record backing winning presidential nominees. Obviously, Dick Gephardt did not become president. I was with Hillary Clinton in the 2008 primary but not her husband in 1992. So, I'll let others speculate on the messenger for 2028.

This book deals with the Democrats' long-term problem, and it has very little to do with Donald Trump. If the near-term is a "who" problem, the person best suited to lead the party forward, the long-term is a "what" problem.

Historically, our politics have been governed by a succession of party systems as the country grew and changed, from the thirteen original states, through growth and Civil War, and explosive growth and battles over enfranchisement. The Republicans' "Southern Strategy" ushered in our present system, and the map has bubbled and hardened and shown cracks over the past four decades. It was not that long ago that Barack Obama won Iowa, Florida, and Ohio, states that seem well out of reach for any Democrat now. And in 2024, Republicans softened Democratic strongholds. The Democrats must now decide what kind of leadership they should offer, and to whom, so the party can determine how welcoming the boat it will rebuild is to those who are treading water, or worse. As Frank pointed out, not everybody has a boat.

One need not look further than deep-blue Rhode Island. How blue? It is the only other New England state Massachusetts Governor Michael Dukakis carried in 1988. But in 2024, if you live in a town that cannot see the water in this Ocean State, your town voted for Donald Trump; fourteen of the state's thirty-nine municipalities broke his way.

On March 1, 2025, an email update from the Democratic National Committee to their subscribed list summarized the Democrats' response to Trump's first month back in office: They've "held town halls, attended roundtables, rallied with federal workers, and protested Musk's shameful layoffs." Lawsuits have been filed, and "every single Democrat" voted against confirming Kash Patel as FBI director. Newly elected Democratic National Committee Chair Ken Martin has been traveling the country. "Florida lawmakers filed legislation to overturn the state's six-week abortion ban, and Democratic attorneys general won a lawsuit temporarily blocking Elon Musk's Department of Government Efficiency from accessing sensitive data from the Department of the Treasury systems." [3]

The resistance to Trump is strong but already exhausted, according to the people I've talked to scant months into his second term. It makes sense to fight what you think is being lost, reversed, or dismantled. But it's important to know that a lot of the country is not fatigued and is giving the second Trump Administration, with a different vibe from the first, some breathing room to succeed, or not. Voters in 2016 took a chance on him, gave him room to prove himself, but thought he didn't by 2020 and voted for a reprieve. However, voters get to weigh in every four years, and he got a second chance because when voters aren't happy with the status quo, whichever flavor of status, they will vote for change.

Exhaustion is a symptom. And if there is no time for rest to address the effects of a barrage of assaults on the norms of democracy—not only by President Trump and his administration, but by his partners in Congress and often on the high court—efforts must be devoted to finding new allies, to building one's own base, to pulling people in, to expanding the map of possibilities. The gap is so small. Trump and the Heritage Foundation know this. They know public sentiment is not on their side. They know that while they have the power, they have to dismantle as many democratic safeguards as possible and make access to

---

3   Democratic National Committee, email, March 1, 2025, to subscribed distribution list.

the ballot, both as a candidate and as a voter, as hard as possible for traditional Democratic voters.

There are ideologues on the right who believe you cannot leave decisions in this country to the majority. They loved the Electoral College until 2020, when they didn't, and this fact—the love-hate-love-again-in-2024 relationship with the super-majority check on the popular vote—shows that they will rely on it as long as it goes their way. But they cannot guarantee the College won't betray them again, in their eyes. This is what they envision the Founding Fathers wanted. When a majority looks like a mob to the minority in power, the preferred outcome by the chosen, those who know better, must win out.

So, this book hopefully serves as a call to pivot and fight for what was once quaintly called "the loyal opposition" in our democracy, to offer a positive alternative, because I believe that's what the people I listened to truly want.

If the voters think Donald Trump's second administration is succeeding, the Democrats' focus on resistance is not a winning alternative. But it is necessary, and urgent, to provide a vision of democracy's next chapter—beyond simply hoping Trump fails—if they hope to succeed in time to affect the midterms in 2026.

The future of the Democratic Party is not in the hoped-for failure of Trump, but in what the party—that of FDR and JFK and LBJ and Obama and Kamala Harris—offers instead. Only then can the people who are left out and left behind, who had options in November foisted upon them, participate as full members in the exercise of American democracy.

People I have talked to want things that will sound familiar, including a democracy where the majority rules. But more fundamentally, they want to be secure in a home. To make enough money to raise and support a family. To have some sense of work-life balance that includes a decent education for their children, regardless of how they decide to do that, and health care when needed.

They want their kids to have a better opportunity in life than they had. Most want to be left alone, to worship as they wish, to associate with those they wish to spend time with. They do not need government—and that includes school boards, the trench warfare *du jour* of America's civil cold war—at any level, telling them how they should live their lives. FDR defined his agenda in the four freedoms: Freedom of speech and expression. Freedom of worship. Freedom from want. Freedom from fear.

His agenda (a word he wouldn't have used) meant something to people and connected with them at a time of profound hardship. Want and fear spoke to their condition, one Roosevelt would fight to relieve them from, and the positive focus on protecting speech, expression, and worship reminded them of the core values of the Republic.

Exhaustion can lead to a reawakening. It's time for an alternative to MAGA and Project 2025, one that doesn't fulfill some fantastical idea of what God wants in a Christian society, but one that "the people" want in a democratic country.

CHAPTER TWO

THE ELECTORAL COLLEGE HAS BEEN REACCREDITED

EVERY TOWN HAS A BILL

The remains of a Shaker village stand within the walls of the medium-security prison, MCI-Shirley, just off Route 2, fifty miles west of Boston, Massachusetts. The Shakers established the village in the 1870s as a pacifist utopian community. Committed to celibacy, it logically did not last long, and it now houses a thousand or so prisoners. If you drive by at 3 p.m., you get caught in Shirley's rush hour: shift change at the prison.

The preserved New England picture-perfect town common is two miles north. The meeting house and the old town hall face each other at angles, and the cemetery is still in use from the founding of the town, named for the sitting Royal Governor, William Shirley, in 1753. The position itself would hang on for almost another two decades before a rambunctious bunch of colonists decided, well, that was that.

I'm talking with Shirley's sixty-five-year-old town clerk, Bill Oelfke (pronounced Elf-key), to ask him about a story an election volunteer told me that seemed to be a perfect metaphor for the 2024 election. A man in his sixties waited in the line to vote in the after-work rush to the polls. His small leashed poodle squatted and pooped, as astute an election commentary as any. Another volunteer, there to direct voters to one door or another depending on their street addresses, noticed and alerted Bill, who confronted the man walking back through after voting and asked him to clean up after his dog. The man replied, "That's not my dog's."

I wonder if Bill thought he would be cleaning up poop when he woke up that morning. He chuckles at the recollection. The dog was small and so was the deposit, and it wasn't the biggest deal, even if the owner thought it wasn't his to deal with at all.

Bill knows the poodle owner. Town clerks know everyone in small towns. In the seven years of elections he's run here, this one went pretty smoothly, with one non-poodle-related exception. As cars were turning into the Town Hall parking lot, someone was offering each car a Trump flag, which, whether you rolled down the window to take it or not, was causing a back-up of cars. Someone, presumably one of the 2,028 souls who voted for Kamala Harris in Shirley, called Massachusetts Attorney General Andrea Campbell's office to complain. If Bill was frustrated by this escalation, he didn't say.

But he had added a second police detail just in case, and he asked the officer to check outside. She thought the activity was beyond the 150-foot buffer and therefore allowed, which Bill explained to the person who called from the AG's office. A second call, from a more senior official, asked Bill to put a stop to it, which he did, after explaining that the officer had attended the attorney general's own training on election laws.

The worry that 2024 would be a repeat of 2020—when the seemingly simple act of tabulating votes and certifying them fell prey to a hyperpolarized era, ultimately ending the tradition of a peaceful transfer of power on January 6—fell to town clerks and election officials everywhere. Would it lead to riots or just leave a bad taste in their recollection?

In Marietta, Georgia, a day before votes were cast, I'm discussing predictions of the outcome with two people in town for a conference. They both agree there will only be riots if the election goes one way. I nod, then hesitate, unsure whether we're in agreement. I ask, "Which way?" "If Harris loses," comes the reply. With the thought that there would be riots if Harris lost but not Trump, I leave alone, swallowing a bad taste of my own.

On election day, when we reconnect in the lobby of the hotel after the workday, one of the pair, echoing Steve Fischer, asks, "Where did those seven million Biden votes go?"—with the implication that they didn't go away at all, but instead were not even real in 2020. That comment I choose to not let alone and offer that maybe voters who hadn't voted in 2016 were energized to vote in 2020 and reverted to nonparticipants in 2024.

Back in Shirley, where Harris won by 500 votes, I ask Bill if he encounters voters who question the integrity of the process. He tells me no, and that a voter told him, "Bill, we trust the system here because you're running it." Bill, with a touch of exasperation, replied, "But every town has a Bill!"

I STILL TRUST IN THE PEOPLE

The framers of the Constitution of the United States knew that every town had a Bill, though they probably would have called him William. The federal government they conjured into being had no capability to run a national election. Local officials had been running them under the Crown for more than a century. In a newborn country with its umbilical cord freshly cut for the sake of independence and local control, who better to conduct the first election for the White House and Congress than the locals in each hamlet, city, and town? And so it has been ever since for elections at all levels of government. The system, until purposely shaken recently, had proved remarkably resilient.

January 6, 2021, weaponized this simple but effective construct, questioning the integrity of the system and then attempting to halt and alter the counting of the Electoral College vote itself, which had until then been sacrosanct, even when the winner of the popular vote differed.

In 1860, Abraham Lincoln won with barely 40 percent of the popular vote, but the southern representatives couldn't affect the electoral count—though some tried. When their efforts failed, they lobbed cannonballs into Fort Sumter, and thus the Civil War began.

How long the mistrust of our elections' integrity lasts, or lingers, remains to be seen. I wonder if those I spoke with in Marietta were surprised that Kamala Harris supporters didn't riot. If so, it didn't come up. We settle into this unhappy stalemate of remembrance of a race that many believe was rigged by the Democrats in 2020. Others are still aghast and angry that the January 6th assault on the Capitol and democracy itself wasn't considered treason—and ultimately pardoned by Trump within hours of retaking office. The air in the bubble of conflict was released by the 2024 results, maybe or maybe not with a booming flatulent sound, depending on your position. The Electoral College lives!

But for those of a certain age who protest this hypocrisy, which it is, how do they remember the presidential election of 2000? A majority of Democratic voters urged Al Gore not to concede the election to George W. Bush well into four weeks after the election, which was ultimately decided by a five-to-four vote of the Supreme Court. Ask yourself if that election was legitimate. If Trump had won the popular vote but not the Electoral College in 2024, would things have progressed as smoothly as 2016, when Hillary Clinton did so? Or would it look more like a repeat of 2020?

The corruption-busting corporate lawyer Samuel Tilden can be forgiven for shaking his head from his perch overlooking the Berkshire Mountains to the east of New Lebanon, New York, his final resting place. The twenty-fifth governor of New York, he was nominated to lead the Democratic ticket in 1876, and he won the popular vote by 250,000 votes.

But on election night, he found himself one electoral vote shy of majority. The outcome stalled, and both party machines got to work to influence the count in the remaining states. The Republicans, who controlled Congress, eventually appointed an Electoral Commission to sort the whole thing out and award the remaining twenty disputed votes. All were awarded to the Republicans' Rutherford B. Hayes of Ohio.

In return, Hayes ended Reconstruction. The Republicans maintained their sixteen-year streak occupying the White House while the Democrats returned to power in the southern states.

Tilden remains the only candidate for president to win more than 50 percent of the popular vote but lose the presidency (Hillary Clinton came close in 2016, with more than 48 percent). Etched into the granite of Tilden's impressive but tasteful monument are the words "I Still Trust in the People."

NIKKI HALEY WAS RIGHT, BUT NOT PRESIDENT

On February 14, 2023, former UN Ambassador and South Carolina Governor Nikki Haley announced her bid for president in an upbeat, optimistic celebration of South Carolina, American exceptionalism, faith, and a feel-good American success story. In it she pointed out her party's Achilles' heel: "Republicans have lost the popular vote in seven out of the last eight presidential elections. That has to change."

Before 2024, George W. Bush and his father, H. W., were the last Republicans to win the popular vote. But that vote has shifted. In 1988, Michael Dukakis won Iowa and West Virginia, two states where Democrats no longer compete. But he lost California, Illinois, New Jersey, Maryland, Connecticut, and Vermont, all solidly blue today. Republican dominance in states with smaller populations gives them an Electoral College advantage, even when losing the popular vote by a percentage or two.

A decent case could be made that Nikki Haley might have outperformed Donald Trump this time—if she had made it out of the primary. The unifying thought I encountered, in red and blue states, prior to Harris's *de facto* coronation, was a dislike of both candidates. On the Democratic side, Harris was rarely mentioned as an alternative before Biden's catastrophic June debate; nor was anyone else, as most senior Democrats were resigned to a superannuated nominee seeking a second term. On the Republican side, Nikki Haley's and Ron DeSantis's names came up all the time.

The Democrats, in addition to losing the popular vote in 2024, have painted themselves into blue electoral corners both ideological and geographical; though rich in votes, they are—in national elections—potential dead ends. California is a powerhouse, but your vote is worth more in Wyoming, if you divide the total number of voters by the electoral votes they wield. For every one Californian electoral vote, there are 707,087 Californians. In Wyoming, the ratio is 195,495 voters for one Electoral College tally. Extrapolated across the map, fourteen red states cumulatively match California's population, but together account for thirteen more electoral votes than the Golden State's fifty-four.

It's hard to imagine that Donald Trump would say he had listened to Nikki Haley and adjusted his campaign strategy accordingly. But Donald Trump did, in fact, win the popular vote. Nikki Haley identified the Republicans' popular vote problem, and Donald Trump solved it. The ball is now in the Democrats' court. I think we can all agree that Trump doesn't play by the rules, but in 2024, he won the election by the election rules.

Do the Democrats have the ability to turn the tables, or will they run with the same playbook? We find ourselves watching the Democrats, in the spring of 2025, struggle with what to do, while in complete agreement that something needs to be done.

Two months into the second Trump Administration, Speaker Mike Johnson's House moves a spending bill to keep the government running through September, the month President Trump has pegged as the key to turning things around. And while I was driving from Ohio to Texas, I heard no clear Democratic response that addresses the real-life concerns of those in the heartland. I hear worry about tariffs, and the reports of the stock market dips and dives get attention, but no one is pointing to a Democratic alternative, which makes sense, since none has been offered.

The Democrats have become solely the resistance without an obvious pro-active policy agenda. In April 2025, they got bogged down in the question of whether they should vote to keep the government open.

Progressive voices in Congress urge members to vote "no," arguing that Trump would own the shutdown, and it's a through-the-looking-glass moment. Republicans vote to keep the government open. Democrats, who think Donald Trump is set on dismantling much of the government, urge a vote that would force a shutdown of the government.

On March 13, 2025, Minority Leader Chuck Schumer says he will vote to keep the government open and persuades nine other Senate Democrats to do so as well, which is just enough. A reporter asks House Minority Leader Hakeem Jeffries if he has lost his confidence in Schumer. He replies, "Next question." A few days later, he is asked the question positively: "Do you have confidence in Schumer?" To which he replies, "Yes." It shouldn't be surprising that voters are confused.

The political calendar continues at a breakneck pace through the spring of 2025 with the echo of January 6th. Trump supporters are happy with the full-on assault on democratic norms, and those who believe democracy was validated with the prosecution of the January 6th insurrectionists are back to full-on panic that the foundations of our republic are in imminent peril.

The assault on the Electoral College count itself, not the physical assault on the Capitol building, but the disregard for Constitutional provisions that led to the counting, seems ancient in 2025. It is allowed to return safely to its obscure slumber, the assault on it a vague memory for most, and the physical act, the attack of the building and the hunt for Nancy Pelosi and Mike Pence, becomes a rallying cry, like Bloody Sunday, for what has become the resistance. The focus on the figurative ivy gates of the Electoral College have given way to the string of executive orders targeting the actual ivy gates of the top colleges in the country.

The reality is that the Electoral College was always an unlikely rally cry, a mechanical vestige of colonial times, not even igniting the passions of the nerdiest political scientist. Some historical touchstones do, though, still inflame, long after the fact.

On a tour of the Lincoln homestead in Springfield, Illinois, in 2022, the guide asked if we had been to other presidential homes. Half of the dozen of us raised our hands. He asked where. One late-to-middle-aged man happily said, in a clear voice, "Jefferson Davis." Some historical memories endure; some do not. The website for Beauvoir, Davis's home, promises a "Legacy of History, Resilience, and Southern Heritage." Words such as "slavery" and "treason" are less prominent. Trump's orders to reinstate the names of Confederate generals to US military bases still strike a chord with some.

The reality, with the distance of four years from the very real assault on the Capitol, is that the Electoral College has always been subject to political forces. Its mere existence was a compromise, and today those small states that benefit from that artificial construct are today rural, white, older, and vote Republican.

The argument years ago was that if you abolished the Electoral College, candidates would ignore those with the fewest residents, being too small in population to matter much. But they are, in fact, ignored today, seemingly not in play for one party or the other, mostly to the Democrats, but also for the Republicans ignoring the small blue states such as Vermont and Delaware, as none of them are swing states.

But in 2025, when the Electoral is seemingly the only prominent college not under assault, the Democrats have a chance to reengage with all fifty states, and new party chair Ken Martin makes plans to do so, while Bernie Sanders fires up the Socialist renewable-energy-fueled Kill the Oligarchy Greatest Hits Tour of red states.

The Democrats know they are disadvantaged in the Electoral College vote distribution. A fifty-state strategy is smart if it's real—it would be an investment in time, maybe significant time—or would it be just for show? Do the Democrats who control the party and the money behind the party and who come from the coasts even get it? Or is it a feint to demonstrate to the blue base that the party is making the effort? Are they listening? Because if they *say* they're listening, it's almost as good as actually listening, right? As right as a company that has a poor safety record saying that safety is their number one concern.

The sitting president heads his or her party. For the party not holding the presidency, the void in leadership is amplified, the factions exposed, and it leaves the voters wondering what it stands for or where it is headed. Rudderless while it waits for a leader or leaders to emerge, the campaign for the midterms and control of Congress must ramp up. A new chair of the Democratic Party cannot say, "Altering the electoral map will take a long time" without saying, "But I have an immediate plan to help win congressional seats next year." But a transformative chair would know that the hard work of transforming the party into a more inclusive one should be the work, because one can't expect to lead the country only from wealthy enclaves on the coasts. Kamala Harris said that Democrats like hard work, and the first step is accepting that hard work isn't the easy path.

CHAPTER THREE

DEMOCRACY IS ON
THE BALLOT

Clichés fuel politics, the apocalyptic phrasing that partisan crowds devour, while the millions watching at home hear mostly the hyperbolic pronouncements shouted by the TV journalists—many of whom strain the bounds if not the definition of the profession—who cover it all as if each will determine the fate of the Republic. Two banalities that cause my temples to throb every election cycle: "Democracy itself is on the ballot" and "This is the most important election in our lifetime."

In the modern hyper-partisan reality, there has been a recent violent uptick among those who declare that democracy is under siege; yet each side of the political looking glass reveals a different assailant. From the outset of the 2024 campaign, both presidential candidates acknowledged the stakes, and hyped them in their own easily satirized styles. "2024 is our final battle,"[1] Donald Trump told supporters more than a year before the vote. At his first reelection rally of 2024, Joe Biden, following a not-so-subtly-symbolic stop at Valley Forge, admonished, "Is democracy still America's sacred cause? I mean it. This is not rhetorical, academic, or hypothetical. Whether democracy is still America's sacred cause is the most urgent question of our time, and it's what the 2024 election is all about."[2]

---

1   Kate Plummer, "Donald Trump Sends Ominous Warning About 'Final Battle' Ahead," *Newsweek*, November 9, 2023.

2   Joe Biden, AP transcript of speech delivered in Blue Bell, Pennsylvania, January 5, 2024.

When Biden exited the stage and passed the baton to Kamala Harris in his valedictory speech on opening night at the Democratic Convention in Chicago, he also gave her the keys to the vault protecting democracy, constructed for her to defend in the fight against Trump. She acknowledged the gift, and out of the gate echoed that democracy was worth defending but quickly traded that rhetoric in for a fight for "freedom," something that perhaps better fit her as a woman, person of color, and a former prosecutor, someone with a role in deciding who is granted personal freedom and at what cost.

A slight rhetorical shift, perhaps, to the casual observer. But to those schooled in political messaging, this was beyond a tactical nip and tuck; it represented a profound strategic change in direction, more than a few degrees on the electoral compass. And the fact is that Biden's heartfelt defense of democracy wasn't hitting home.

Democracy is always on the ballot, and this has been true throughout the nearly two-and-a-half centuries of our American experiment. One person, one vote—though, in practice, that rhetorically blanketing principle has evolved significantly with time. We exercise our democratic rights every time we pull the lever or fill in an oval or when "X" marks the spot and we place our trust in a person to govern at the local, county, state, or federal level. In each election before this one, stretching back to 1788, we have collectively digested and accepted the results regardless of how much it roiled our stomachs or those of our neighbors.

Five times, the winner of the popular vote has lost to the winner of the electoral vote, and yet five times we accepted the results of this quirky barrier against our direct exercise of democracy in the end. The first instance came in 1824 when Andrew Jackson earned the most votes but watched John Quincy Adams take the presidency thanks to soon-to-be Secretary of State Henry Clay, the odd man out in the electoral count when it was a free-for-all but who had enough votes to determine the winner and bargain for his appointed post. The Jacksonians regrouped, surged to power in the next contest, and remade the country, not for the last time.

FOLLOW THE RULES

The last time the winner of the popular vote didn't win the electoral vote was in 2016.

We Americans have historically been rule followers when it comes to elections. We never before stormed the US Capitol to protest an electoral count that went against the popular will, let alone the hopes of a losing minority of voters.

On January 6, 2001, several objections arose from the floor of the House Chamber to the tallying of Florida's vote. Vice President Al Gore, not yet psychologically recovered from his razor-thin loss (literally grew a beard during the months immediately following) of an office he had first sought a dozen years earlier, stoically and patiently let his supporters talk themselves out and, hearing no second to the stated objections that Republicans might have taken for grandstanding, dismissed them and called the election for his opponent, George W. Bush.

A majority of Democratic voters didn't want Gore to concede, holding fast to the notion that the election had been stolen from him by officials in Florida, where Bush's brother happened to be governor, and ultimately by the slim majority of Republican appointees on the Supreme Court.

Precisely two decades later—though several ice ages in the ever-quickening and expeditiously warming hothouse of American politics—partisans of Donald Trump stormed the Capitol on January 6, 2021. In its wake, there were three more years of escalating rhetoric and political convulsions in the democracy that was once the envy of the world.

The shock having long since worn off for most who watched events unfold that day, the judicial process having dealt with most of the offenders, and with Republicans remembering it as a passion play of patriotism that caused minor damage and no real harm, it had—as Campaign 2024 began to simmer—become convenient for some to think of the siege of the Capitol as "just" a day.

One day. An ugly anomaly even in a political world where "unprecedented" is normalized with unsettling frequency. A day to note, certainly, but to fade as the battle over the 2000 results did, or 2016, or 1861, and all the others.

But it wasn't just a day. It was a turning point in the life of the country. In the same way we took for granted that we removed our shoes going through airport security before the restriction was recently lifted, and are surveilled in a way not possible before 9/11, we may grow accustomed to questioning the administrative infrastructure that manages our elections every two years.

Nevertheless, the reality remains that a ballot—a physical, tangible ballot, filled out by voters and fed into a machine or slid into an envelope—is not partisan. The document itself contains no agenda, though the options it proffers certainly do. It is paper or a counting mechanism inside a machine. It is a vessel for conveying an individual's act and beliefs. But questioning the ballot's neutrality, casting its validity into doubt, has been normalized, even if the flavors of the questions differ by party and each is certain the other is tampering with the results.

If Harris had won the popular vote but not the Electoral College, I am certain there would have been an effort from November through January 6, 2025, to encourage electors to change their expected votes, as there was—aggressively and, in some cases, illegally—in 2020.

The administration of elections in this country, simply spelled out in the US Constitution as a power given to the states to suss out, should be remembered by that date, January 6, 2021, and whether the election happened before it, when we trusted the process, or after, when this trust has been broken. This country has been physically attacked, large-scale, on its own soil by foreigners—remarkably, given our size and manifest willingness to tinker on others' shores—on just three occasions: the War of 1812, Pearl Harbor, and 9/11. January 6th wasn't an attack just on a building, the Capitol, or on an official election procedure. It was a domestic attack on the mechanics of our election system, the historically mundane nuts and bolts that have ensured the continuity of government for 240 years.

And that is why the hackneyed clichés and tired hyperventilating that made me, as a political professional, want to cower under my desk have finally found their mark, square in the middle of the Constitution and all that we've taken for granted. In 2024, democracy was, in fact, on the ballot, and this one was, in fact, the most important election of our lifetimes to date, not because of who won but because of the destabilization of our democratic institutions, and both parties are at fault.

Democracy's survival may not have depended on a reelected Donald Trump, and it wouldn't have been had Harris won; neither can it be a savior of our democracy when the trust in the mechanics of the system has been so badly broken. If there is a person out there who alone can do so, that name did not appear on the 2024 ballot.

Former House Minority Leader Gerald Ford, upon gamely assuming the presidency in August 1974 while elected neither to that job nor the vice presidency to which he had been elevated by a president suffering from fatal and self-inflicted wounds, said "Here, the people rule."[3]

No one would conjure a scenario in which our current Congress is up to that job. The people rule and, thus, can save democracy. In fact, it's the only way it can be saved, with all due respect to Mr. Trump and whoever succeeds him. The question plumbs deeper, though, past what a restoration to the historic "small d" democratic norms would even look like, or who could achieve such a feat, and it's much more fundamental than how we would go about resuscitating democracy as it has come to be understood through the generations: Do we, the people, even want to? Or have we changed so much from Ford's day that we are willing to cede the birthright that made us the envy, and the military, economic, and cultural power, of the rest of the world?

PRO-DEMOCRACY

This seems an obvious question to those for whom saving democracy sits top of mind when entering the voting booth. But the reality is, one thing you learn when you engage people across the country is that the urgency of saving our democracy does not sit highly on the majority of priority lists. People are "for" democracy, if you ask it that way. But the imminent threat to it is evident and urgent only to a minority of voters. Many don't notice. Many don't mind.

To be clear, our historic version of democracy wasn't meant to be nimble, dealing quickly or efficiently with competing interests and visions. The Founding Fathers weren't big on fast moves, and their "rapid response" operation functioned at the pace of a transatlantic sail, which could take three months, given the vicissitudes of the winds and currents. While James Madison likely would have mastered it with silver-tongued aplomb, there is no record of his tweeting. Perhaps John Hancock's TikTok presence would be as outsized as his signature.

Adrenalized by the Enlightenment, they broke from Great Britain but not from the elite station they believed to be their birthright, and their version of

---

3   Gerald Ford, "Gerald Ford's Inaugural Remarks: August 9, 1974," CBS News, accessed May 25, 2025, https://www.cbsnews.com/news/gerald-fords-inaugural-remarks-august-9-1974/.

democracy was paternalistic, at best, to those disenfranchised from the vote. They enshrined slavery, our nation's original sin, in the Constitution, a devil's bargain that haunts this country to this day in ways both psychological and physical. The sainted framers baked a sour foundational ingredient into the American zeitgeist. Today's elite, those who run the government in elective office or from C-suites, are heirs to this slow-moving balancing act where it is easier to kill progress or even simple movement on the issues of the day. And even when they don't succeed in slowing things down, hasty decisions like many of Elon Musk's DOGE forays are reversed almost as rapidly.

And while the election of Trump or Harris would not save what is broken or at risk in our democracy, neither can they be blamed for the disconnect most Americans feel, viscerally, from what has become of the only country that was, to borrow another cliché, founded on an idea. The fact is that the ruling political class, in a variety of ways, has fostered the disconnect between individuals and the federal government, and they've grown fat and happy doing so. This was done deliberately and systematically, by law and practice. The results have left no one happy, save perhaps the plutocrats. Even our most sacrosanct institutions suffer from deep distrust among the public, and many in the populace are so jaded that they either rage blindly against some perceived unfairness or don't make the effort to care much at all.

Donald Trump didn't have to destabilize our democracy so much as take advantage of how destabilized it had become, how the people had been detached from its grounding in a money-fueled political process, and how the people living in their devices, cloistered in digital rooms with fellow travelers, could be co-opted for his personal benefit.

And, boy, did he take his opportunity.

It's easy, and a bit lazy, to look at politics before this destabilization with nostalgia. Politics is a rough-and-tumble sport, and the stakes given federal elected officials under our Constitution could not be higher. It may be, though, that the rules of engagement were clearer in the pre-Trump past, having been established over time, and adhered to by combatants of both sides.

JUST THE FAX, PLEASE

When I worked for Senator Ted Kennedy of Massachusetts before the invention of modernity, back in the 1990s, I had to fax him "the clips" early every morning so he could "read" the Boston papers first thing while in Washington or at his home on Cape Cod. After I cut the clips, I would drive from my house in Belmont, Massachusetts, to Senator Kennedy's Boston office, where I worked, and fax them down to DC or Hyannis Port. I did this every day for five years. I did other things, but this was usually how I started my day.

On weekends, not wanting to drive into Boston and not having a fax machine at home, I walked up to the local pharmacy, which did have one. It was an old-fashioned affair in a low-slung building on Belmont's business thoroughfare, Trapelo Road, across a side street from a shop that sold wedding dresses next to Rancatore's Ice Cream parlor.

The pharmacy had been in one family for generations, the window boxes were award-winning, and it was the type of traditional place that had built up an inventory of what people wanted—a little bit of everything. The fax was behind the pharmacy counter, and on my first trip, I handed the pharmacist the Kennedy-relevant clips and a phone number on a slip of paper and paid for the service. I did this again on Sunday. And the following weekend.

There isn't a lot to do when you're feeding things into a fax machine, except notice what it is you're sending. I don't remember how long he contained himself before making glancing comments about them, the news in them, and the reports about Ted Kennedy, good and bad. I would look blankly at him and then gaze at the display of plastic toys, waiting for him to finish and hand back the originals. I really didn't want to get in my car and drive to downtown Boston on a Saturday just to complete this task.

He was never directly confrontational. He never refused my business. I don't know if he would have liked to debate there at the counter of his throwback shop, lotions and boxed candy and dime store toys and sunscreen in all seasons and bottles and bottles of pills and concoctions. He clearly didn't like aiding and abetting Ted Kennedy.

I never had a conversation with him about anything. He never asked me who I was or why I was underlining things in articles about Ted Kennedy and sending them on weekends to a Hyannis, Massachusetts, number. He did not seem worth getting to know.

If we hadn't been introduced to one another in this way, might we have had a different relationship? I might have asked him what sunscreen he recommended. We might have talked about how he got such results in his window boxes. Maybe we'd progress to asking about each other's families. We may never have talked politics. I might have learned what challenges he faced in operating a family pharmacy with the explosion of chain pharmacies, how our shared town had evolved in the decades since his family had first set up shop there.

This was not possible with him then. Because of our transaction, he knew he didn't like me and my politics, and I knew I didn't like him or his.

THE LION IN WINTER

I was born the year Ted Kennedy's brother became president. A year later Ted assumed his brother's Massachusetts Senate seat. Not quite thirty years later, I came to work for him out of his Boston office. By then he was knocking on the door of his role as "Lion of the Senate," his own presidential run a decade past and his reputation as legislative juggernaut, leading with his expansive vision backed by the incredible work of brilliant minds in his DC office, taking hold.

This lion roared; his booming voice could command any space he occupied. Staffing him was always an adventure. He was the center of attention the minute he walked into a room. Occasionally, someone I don't think I know will remind me we met years ago, and I'll realize that it's because they met Senator Kennedy and I was handed their camera to take a photo. My handiwork adorns offices throughout Massachusetts.

Some politicians absorb the energy radiating toward them, the adulation emboldening them, but I came to understand that Ted Kennedy managed his attention differently. He would take time at events to assess the lay of the land. He would want to speak later in a program, not to hear the praise for him, though there was that, but to listen and maybe adjust his words to speak to those present, or to the issues they introduced. When he listened to a constituent talk about an issue, personal or policy, he was instantly on the same page, thinking about how to address what they were discussing.

He was the youngest of nine children of very demanding parents, and I would think of him at the family dinner table, history questions being fired off by his mother. The littlest can charge into the breach, or absorb by listening, and it's a lesson he took to the Senate to great effect.

It was his superpower, I think, this ability to understand where people were coming from and what they were trying to achieve. He could meet them in compromise on legislation he cared about, or bank it for future negotiations. He had access to the best health care money could buy but spent his career trying to secure the same for all.

He understood that his family gave him a head start, but listening and understanding others, his colleagues in the Senate from different states, backgrounds, and agendas, was the key to getting what he wanted: to notch a win for his constituents in Massachusetts and for his vision for the country.

Leaving a penthouse meeting in downtown Boston one day, the elevator doors opened on a lower floor and a young man in a business suit stepped in. He seemed to freeze as the doors closed behind his back, but he didn't turn around. After an awkward beat, he said, "You're Ted Kennedy." The senator let out a laugh and placed a hand on his shoulder. "Yes, I am."

WE'RE NOT GOING BACK

Politics has its own rules, and Ted Kennedy mastered the intricacies of them, both the political theater of it and the complicated ones governing the legislative process. "Outsiders" run for office pledging to shake things up in Washington, but in reality, the institutions shape the outsiders more than they are shaped by them, at least at the legislative level. The Executive wields a different power entirely.

The United States Senate operates under arcane rules that sweep up newcomers and veterans alike in the cadence of the deliberations. Kamala Harris's campaign for the presidency in 2024 was historic and also unprecedented in the way the nomination was secured. But Harris, the first woman to serve as Vice President of the United States, came up through the ranks of elected office adhering to the rules of the road. Her short campaign for the presidency was no different. She inherited a political infrastructure that also grew up in the rule-following world of political play.

On the first night of the Democratic National Convention in August 2024, inside Chicago's United Center, Kamala Harris takes the stage to deafening applause and visible emotion among some delegates to eulogize briefly the presidency of Joe Biden, who will speak later. She presents a different strength than Reagan or Carter or Obama and certainly Trump. A week before, she had displayed the same quiet confidence in shutting down a heckler in a moment that quickly went viral. And seventy-eight days out from an election when democracy will be on the ballot, the face of leadership that confronts Trump's version changes from slow, steady, thanks-for-your-lifetime-of-service Joe Biden to the prosecutor from Oakland, California, who already shattered several thickened glass ceilings by becoming the first woman and first person of color to serve as vice president.

The confidence builds through the short campaign, and she presents a forward-looking, optimistic—even "joyful," in running mate Tim Walz's words—version of the country's future. "We're not going back." It's a hard pivot, from Biden's "Democracy is on the ballot" to "Freedom," with little time to sell voters on the updated message. Again, political professionals notice the mid-flight course adjustment.

Her sudden candidacy didn't elicit the same visceral reaction in some voters that Hillary Clinton did or that Donald Trump continues to do. Voters in the swing states I spoke with, and who kept an open mind, made a point of this; they had nothing against her. Few people pointed to something she or her campaign did that disqualified her for them. She took an electoral hit for saying she couldn't think of a policy where she differed from Biden. And some thought she was "pushy" or "hypocritical" for changes in her positions. Some thought her "arrogant" in a coastal elite way. Most who were truly open to an alternative to Trump, who had voted for him once but not twice, thought she was just not given enough time to close the deal, with them personally and with the country.

They weren't buying the "bait and switch." The old salesman, Joe Biden, peddling his quaint notions of Democracy, then told them that his vice president, whom he entrusted with relations in Scandinavia and saddled with the impossible task of jump-starting something at the southern border, all of a sudden had been instrumental in the administration's biggest accomplishments.

Kamala Harris needed more time, and too many questions were left unanswered. One was central to the question of our Democracy. To wit: If Donald

Trump is such a threat to it, what are you going to do about it? Biden could implore voters all he wanted, but he controlled the Justice Department. If someone has broken into your house and is holding your family hostage, you don't post an appeal for help on Facebook; you call the police (or should). Aggressive prosecution of Trump would have had serious political consequences, but Biden's dire warning not only packed no punch but left the impression with voters that it was hyperbolic political gamesmanship.

ARE YOU KIDDING ME?

One week after the election, I'm in Miami, talking with Irina and Marc, both management consultants in their late thirties. They're expecting their first baby soon and looking for an affordable place to buy a home in greater Miami, one that's more suitable than their Midtown high-rise rental, which has a view but also limited space. The Harris proposal to help with first-time homebuyers' down payments was intriguing to Marc but ultimately not enough to win his vote, all things being equal. Irina was a Harris voter even without the dangled subsidy.

Marc is sick and tired of the "politician" who strikes a certain pose that seems not to exist in daily human interaction. This is the candidate who holds their hand just so, not quite a closed fist, one knuckle pointing forward for emphasis. The rules of how to look have been refined over time, limiting human expression to fit on the "small screen" of television, a contained and manufactured sincerity. Today we have candidates who speak in poll-tested sound bites and look like they have a graduate degree in looking the part. Someone whose focus is on the election, and winning it—but on what beyond that?

And Marc speaks for a lot of voters who weren't happy with the choices on the ballot. What they saw was the bullshit and the exaggerations, like politicians think "people are stupid." A candidate, Biden, said the sky would fall and democracy would end if the opponent were elected, and then welcomed that person, Trump, with open arms after the election to the Oval Office. "Are you kidding me?" Marc concludes.

If the threat to democracy wasn't moving votes, the dire predictions of Project 2025—the Presidential Transition Project—didn't close the deal with undecided voters either. While voters weren't buying that Donald Trump had never heard of it, as he claimed, they also weren't convinced of the horrors Democrats promised would rain down on them.

From the first days of the transition, it became clear that the Trump administration would move forward on Project 2025, almost page by page. By April, he had issued over one hundred executive orders, more than half those of his predecessor's full term, and began dismantling the Department of Education, USAID, and a host of long-established agencies. He moved to end birthright citizenship and ignored lower court orders to return detainees to the United States that his administration was in the process of sending to El Salvador. By the beginning of April, Senator Patty Murray, Democrat of Washington state and former chair of the Senate Veterans' Affairs Committee, reported that the Trump Administration had "fired" 2,400 employees at the Department of Veterans' Affairs, an agency already not widely renowned for high performance or rapid delivery of services to its constituents.[4]

Trump moved swiftly to populate the Executive Branch with those who would carry out his will, which increasingly looks like the doomsday predictions of those who said, before November, that this would happen. Democratic vice-presidential nominee Governor Tim Walz said in his convention acceptance speech, and at almost every stop after, "Their Project 2025 will make things much, much harder for people who are just trying to live their lives. They spend a lot of time pretending that they know nothing about this. But look, I coached high school football long enough to know, and trust me on this, when somebody takes the time to draw up a playbook, they're gonna use it."

The plays are being run in the first months of the administration when I drive in April from Cincinnati to Dallas, via Indianapolis, Indiana, then Missouri through St. Louis, Jefferson City, Springfield, to Tulsa and Oklahoma City in Oklahoma to wind down in Denton to, technically Grapevine, near Dallas-Fort Worth Airport in Texas. By the time I get home to Massachusetts, the mood has shifted from extreme anxiety to outright fear of the preservation of the rule of law, with a healthy dose of "What the fuck are the Democrats doing?"

---

4   Ashley Murray, "Vets Worry Trump Cuts to VA Workforce Will Interrupt Benefits," *KTTN-FM 92.3 and KGOZ -FM 101.7*, March 12, 2025, https://www.kttn.com/vets-worry-trump-cuts-to-va-workforce-will-interrupt-benefits.

But through dozens of interviews along the road trip with Trump and Harris voters living in red states, mostly with those who pay only casual attention, I realized there is relative calm. It's early, and though there is recognition of the frenetic pace, there seems no reason to jump to conclusions. And what if it works? What if the government gets trimmed, even if deep cuts hurt? No one I spoke with read the Project 2025 document. Neither had I at that point. And if this stuff was in there, and they seem okay with it, well, what's wrong with that?

SHARING THE PAIN

Back home, people in my circle of friends tell me that at some point it *will* affect them, and perhaps that's true. But I'm left wondering how exactly this will manifest for most of those I talked with, and will they both like and dislike the effect? Certainly, a hit on Social Security or Medicare will rattle senior voters. Or perhaps most senior voters. Billionaire Commerce Secretary Howard Lutnick said on March 21, 2025, "Let's say Social Security didn't send out their checks this month. My mother-in-law, who's ninety-four, wouldn't call and complain." But Social Security recipients with billionaire sons-in-law are a tiny subset.

Those on Medicaid see the states, which administer the federal program, as providing their services, and how will they respond? And if Trump finds a way to mete out his cuts to blue and not red states, will his voters rise up in protest? Will they notice at all? As Trump revokes the visas of international students at colleges in the northeast, or targets Harvard and Columbia University, will Trump voters care enough to change their overall opinion? Have the people who have willfully turned away from the political tumult care?

But for a lot of people I talk to—working to get a paycheck, focusing on housing and raising kids—I'm hard-pressed to connect Trump's actions in May 2025 with their lives. What about cuts or elimination of USAID, aid to Ukraine, Voice of America, or research funding to universities with enormous endowments, the Institute of Museum and Library Services, the Minority Business Development Agency, the US Interagency Council on Homelessness, the Woodrow Wilson International Center for Scholars in the Smithsonian Institution, the Maine Sea Grant program? Most initial cuts deeply affect those who are connected to them but taken together dent only a small percentage of the general population.

There is virtually no direct connection to any of these eliminated programs and services for most of the people I talk with. And aid to Ukraine has never been popular in talks I've had since the invasion. I'll confess to being taken aback initially because I'm a Cold War baby, but while people may support Ukraine in the war, the majority have never warmed to the idea of US military aid, in money or equipment. While Volodymyr Zelenskyy is a more sympathetic leader than Vladimir Putin, Zelenskyy has been weaponized politically, from the very first "perfect" phone call that led to Trump's very first impeachment to the very not perfect Oval Office dressing down by Vice President Vance five years later.

Our youngest generation of adults reached the age of eighteen having lived their entire lives while the US was engaged in a foreign conflict, the first generation to do so in the history of the country. Older generations have wondered since the end of the Cold War—an easily recognizable, if often shadowy and far-flung global conflict between two superpowers, with the United States being the one left standing—when regions will take care of their own affairs and fund their own interests. The fatigue is palpable and the desire to turn off the international lights and live under a golden dome is strong, and Trump's early actions respond to this desire.

Trump 2.0 is not the beta version the Electoral College bought, maybe off Amazon in 2016, only to be returned as unsatisfying and headache-inducing when used in 2020. But, and this is a big "but," he is still Donald Trump. He remains as impulsive as ever, perhaps more so returning to an office with emboldened powers, courtesy of his appointees to the Supreme Court, plus Clarence Thomas and Samuel Alito, who have been pining for just the opportunity to do so for years, empowering an executive to their liking unafraid to move boldly to undo decades of federal policy. He has also been handed some of the legislative branch's powers by their own active neglect as well. Not to mention slaloming seemingly effortlessly through two impeachments and a dizzying array of felony convictions.

What *does* penetrate voters' minds at this early stage of the Trump Restoration and has people concerned, some deeply, is the tariff strategy—if it is, in fact, a strategy. If voters hope for peace under the golden dome of security, then pissing off easy friends like Canada and the European Union while prices rise at home is a head-scratcher. Supporters of Trump think, or hope, he knows what he's doing. He is, after all, a businessman.

In a presidential term, there are sixteen quarters. At the end of the first quarter in 2025, the Democrats aren't doing anything legislatively about tariffs, which might seem odd to the authors of the Constitution, who gave the right to do so to Congress. But long before Donald Trump took negotiating tariffs as a personal cat toy, both Democratic and Republican Congresses have been happy to cede the task to presidents of both parties. And beyond tariffs, they aren't doing much of anything else, except for suing in court.

FROM THE ASHES

In July 2025 I'm in Iowa when a *Wall Street Journal* poll shows the Democrats with their highest unfavorability rating since 1990, two years before Bill Clinton and his New Democrat strategy had delivered their party from its twelve-year wilderness. Two quarters down in Trump 2.0, I'm back on the road to take voters' temperature.

At the Source Book Store in Davenport, Iowa, just blocks from the Mississippi River, I chat briefly with the owner, Stephen, while paying for a 1928 campaign biography of Herbert Hoover. Stephen bought Iowa's "oldest and largest used bookstore" just seven months before, a bit of a fulfilled dream for him and his wife. The Hoover book is a quick read, as campaign biographies are meant to be, and offers a fascinating snapshot into the political marketing at that time, touting the Republican's extensive resume and promising with his election that the good times of the Roaring Twenties will continue. Of course, I know, we all know, what happens: In two years, one in four Americans would be unemployed.

Stephen's excited about my book. He's excited about all books, of course, especially his 100,000. We talk briefly about the political climate, but he's less sanguine about the state of the body politic. "The masses are in ashes," he says.

CHAPTER FOUR:

THE COALITION OF THE DISCONNECTED

The election outcome wasn't a surprise to Jamie Chandler, a thirty-year-old electrician from Lookout Mountain, Georgia. He expected Donald Trump to win. He first registered to vote in 2016 because "something needed to happen." He thinks Trump did a "decent" job in the first term. "I think he was the first president since Reagan that other countries were a—I don't want to use the word—but scared of. Trump stood by what he said. I do think he needs to shut up some. He talks out of his ass a lot."

Ronald Reagan left office five years before Jamie was born, but Jamie's a student of history, taking his learning into his own hands after walking away from high school to become a firefighter. "I knew I needed some extra help with a couple of classes. I was getting A's and B's in some but was struggling a bit in others. But when I spoke up, they placed me in a remedial room that didn't even have a teacher, so I walked out."

This year, he thought, "The Democratic Party fell short. Nobody really knew Kamala. I think they were banking on the popular vote." But he and his buddies "sitting around watching football and drinking beer and talking politics" have a game where they debate their ideal candidate. Jamie believes "it needs to be someone from the middle class, someone that actually knows what it's like to work forty hours a week and not make ends meet. Someone that actually knows what it is to work, whether it's blue collar or, well, someone that doesn't make six figures a year, someone with a family, who has a [real] job."

Without that ideal on the ballot, he voted for the "lesser of two evils." "Remember when North Korea launched that missile at Guam, remember what Trump said? 'Hellfire the likes of which the world has never seen.' And you know what? North Korea ain't never done it again." (While North Korea hadn't targeted Guam again, when Jamie and I spoke, they had conducted scores of missile tests since Trump's admonition.) "I don't care if you're a Democrat or a Republican. I want what's best for me, my family, my country. I don't believe our political parties are really what our Founding Fathers had in mind. I think it's more career-based than it was meant to be. They should make minimum wage."

He belongs to the first generation he thinks that really cares about work-life balance. He doesn't want to work sixty hours a week. It's one of the reasons he switched jobs from being a first responder. "Also, too many DOAs." He sums up his generation this way: "We want to work forty hours a week, go home, and not get taxed out the ass."

He may have voted for his lesser of two evils, but he voted for the candidate who he thinks will deliver for him and his family. "The Democrats never had a plan. Trump has a plan." Harris's slogan, "We're not going back," didn't resonate with Jamie. He voted for his future and for his schoolteacher wife and their two children, one four years old and the other seven months.

A full week after the election was called for Trump and control of the Senate for the Republicans, votes were still being counted in California, narrowing the popular vote margin, which proved to be the closest since 2004, a lifeline to Democrats wishing to make the case that the outcome wasn't a colossal loss.

But it was, and not because of the numbers. The big loss for the Democrats was in the reality of the results stacked against their expectations, their certainty that the country would reject a twice-impeached, felony-convicted, and disgraced former president. If Trump voters were focused on change, Democrats cannot understand why people want to go back.

THE COUNTER VIEW FROM THE DOG PARK

While Jamie in Georgia knew that Trump was going to win, then a cybersecurity analyst I spoke to, a Doodle parent, Bailey's mom, in her early forties, was equally sure Harris would, and her focus was on what Trump might do to overturn it. A dozen Doodles, products of crossbred poodles, of various sizes and colors romp around Town Field in Belmont, Massachusetts, taking advantage of the new "off-leash" program in designated spots around the wealthy suburb, dense with turn-of-the-century homes, close to Boston. I've lived here for more than three decades, through ever-increasing housing prices, and have watched how its pronounced exclusiveness has influenced the local political discourse.

Harris would take almost 80 percent of the vote here, so Bailey's mom is in safe company with the other dog parents, all confident but nervous about Harris's chances at finally breaking the glass ceiling. They don't understand how anyone could vote for Trump except the racists.

I keep an eye on my Willa, happily chewing on another dog's squeak ball, and say that I don't think the people I encounter are racist, and that they come to their support of Trump for various reasons. But generally, the parents in the dog park, echoing others I speak to in this liberal enclave, aren't buying it.

"Do you ask them where they get their news?" "They've all been poisoned by Fox and worse." I do say that in a recent conversation, a young man, who said he didn't like mainstream media, including Fox, got his information from InfoWars, Alex Jones's website that peddles conspiracy theories and miracle cures that have not earned glowing reviews from the Food and Drug Administration, Trump's included. "See," I'm told, "they're brainwashed."

Some Trump voters I speak with can't understand the hate directed his way. They see his flaws, I'm told, and they don't, in fact, hate Kamala Harris. But the voters in my blue bubble do hate Trump, more than before if possible, and their opinion of Trump voters has hardened here as well. They may never understand why, and you get the sense that there is no desire to understand. They figure that Trump will be so horrible in his second term that the scales will fall from his supporters' eyes and they will come to regret that they ever fell for it. Those old enough here could then dust off their "Don't blame me, I'm from Massachusetts" bumper stickers from 1973. This, of course, may still prove true.

Town Field is in the shadow of the Senior Center, which doubles as a polling location—Mitt Romney's during the years he lived here. He lost this precinct and the town the three times he was on the ballot, as aspiring senator, governor, and president. But now the Doodle dads and moms pine for the day the Republican Party had more Mitt Romneys than Donald Trumps.

The percentage of the white vote nationally has steadily declined, shrinking from the time it could ensure Ronald Reagan a landslide to where it couldn't carry a John McCain or a Romney over the popular vote finish line to where Donald Trump, who lost the popular vote twice, would need to find voters of color, or younger voters, or wealthier voters, to make the math work. Since 1992, thirty-five million more votes have been cast for the Democrat nominee than the GOP's.

And that's why 2024 was such a monumental, foreboding loss. Democrats took for granted the actual base of the party, the working class, the geographic bulk between the coasts, rural voters, those without a college degree, Black and Latino voters. While the party spoke to slices of special interests and in broad economic terms to wealthy voters, the Republicans spoke to the voters Democrats assumed they had in their pocket. And those voters listened.

Prior to the election, Democrats watched, with some glee, the traditional Republican coalition fracture and retreat to a seeming ugly corner of isolationism and hate. It stood by, ready to accept fleeing Republicans, maybe not with quite open arms.

But the results put the reality in stark relief. The Republican Party has staked its new claim: to shake off the plodding bureaucracy, to retake our borders, to be unconventional and bold and unpredictable, and to remake the rules of governance.

The Democrats are now the ones who must decide a path forward, to reconnect with the voters it has not been listening to and perhaps were talking down to. Or it can be the party that retreats into what a lot of swing voters deride as its self-righteous corner (one I live in geographically), where we're fat and happy and our states ensure our rights are protected and we think we are right. A place where it's safe to ask, "What kind of a dog is that?" because it's never just a mutt, or "Where are you spending the summer?" or "Will you be touring colleges with your daughter this fall?" Or we can open up the democracy we say we care about so much—and, let's face it, democracy is working for anyone who says they care about preserving it—to those it isn't working for.

The Democratic Party lifted people into the middle class. But where is the middle class now? And, from a political standpoint, where is the party in relation to the middle class?

POLI-TICKS

In February 2024, I am sitting in the dark behind a one-way mirror in Braintree, Massachusetts, just south of Boston—and, coincidentally, John Adams's birthplace—with a few other professional political operatives watching a moderator ask a series of questions to a mixed group of voters. It's a focus group, an exercise common in both politics and other branches of the marketing and sales industry to elicit on-the-spot, low-stakes feedback that can then be extrapolated and used to ply broader public opinion with much more on the line.

This session happens to deal exclusively with a pending ballot initiative that would empower Massachusetts's executive branch to audit the state legislature. The focus group participants know we're there, behind the slightly creepy police-procedural glass, though not *who* we are. They are paid a modest sum and provided a chicken dinner to participate. When asked if they know anything about the workings of the state legislature, there is silence.

Finally, a man in his early forties, arms folded and sporting a worn Bruins cap, says, "I know the governor appointed her girlfriend to a judgeship." The previous day, Governor Maura Healey appointed her former romantic partner to the state's highest court, garnering a lot of media attention.

The moderator gently tries again: "That's the executive branch, but what about the legislature? Does anything come to mind?" Finally, a woman in her fifties ventures, "Maybe I should have done some homework before tonight."

It's not surprising that Healey's elevation of an ex-girlfriend to the Supreme Judicial Court would come up, as the city's tabloid covered it with alacrity. Further, an act of apparent cronyism is far more easily understood than the dry and anachronistically opaque budget deliberations wending their way through the legislature, so predictable and routine that lawmakers and lobbyists can often predict to the hour, months in advance, when their vacations will begin.

The making of laws is not always mundane nor predictable. When Newt Gingrich was elected Speaker of the House following the Contract with America sweep of 1994, he weaponized the House of Representatives. Until that point in history—even through high-profile House speakers like Tip O'Neill of Cambridge, a colorful personality not afraid to mix it up, gleefully at times, with President Ronald Reagan—the House tended the spadework of our republic: passing appropriations to keep it running as well as acting as a check on the other two branches, the judiciary and the executive, to say nothing of the Upper Chamber across the Capitol.

Gingrich sought, and largely succeeded, in making the House a power center. It punched well above its historical weight, with little regard for the checks the Constitution placed on it. It operated from its own newly expanded and empowered bully pulpit fueled by the cable network C-SPAN with talk radio fanning the flames, quickly passing the Contract with America agenda and exerting its oversight authority, ultimately impeaching President Bill Clinton.

About fifteen years later, the third branch of government, the Supreme Court, weaponized money in politics by declaring it "speech" in the watershed 2010 *Citizens United v. Federal Election Commission* decision, opening up the floodgates of dark money, or more accurately, reopening the spigot. Before reforms implemented in the wake of Watergate, money flowed into campaigns sometimes, literally, in cash-packed suitcases. And when obscene amounts of money are there to be made, greed is sure to follow, if not steer. The portion of the populace that pays attention began to question whether the motive behind any discrete political action was to serve a cause or acquire a windfall.

Perhaps a major reason the folks sitting on the other side of the glass from us, tucking into their chicken dinner, are apathetic is that they've recognized this dysfunction, greed swamping service as a motive to run for office, shrugged it off because there is little they can do to combat it, and accepted it as business as usual instead. That is, from an objective and nonpartisan point of view, both true and dreadfully disheartening. And it speaks, in stentorian tones, to our national disillusionment.

Politics is big business. Campaign spending in the United States—at least that which was reported publicly—hit more than $30 billion in 2024, more than double spent at the election cycle just four years earlier and higher than the GDP of Jamaica in 2021, according to World Bank data.[1] That doesn't count the $3.53 billion spent on lobbying—again, these are the numbers that were actually reported—according to OpenSecrets, a nonpartisan organization that tracks political finance.[2]

---

1   GDP (current US$) - Jamaica | data, accessed May 25, 2025, https://data.worldbank.org/indicator/NY.GDP.MKTP.CD?locations=JM.

2   OpenSecrets, accessed May 25, 2025, https://www.opensecrets.org/elections-overview/cost-of-election.

Such gaudy sums, and the actions they bankroll, have corroded our trust not just in elected officials who seem to later leave office far wealthier than when they arrived—a list that spans and reaches deeply into both parties—but our confidence in the institutions of the federal government to address our individual concerns. People don't think that the government can solve their problems. They don't believe that our elected officials in Washington can affect their personal economy, and certainly not in any helpful direction—or that those officials are much invested in doing so, at least in any positive way.

And even then, it would just be for the votes, wouldn't it? To gain power? Across the thirty-five states my research team and I have toured—diners and bars, yes, but also quirky bookstores, military souvenir shops, big-box stores, antique emporiums, hotel breakfast rooms with bleary-eyed tradesmen in fluorescent yellow hoodies far from their families because that's where the jobs are that morning, the homes of folks kind enough to invite us in—the resounding consensus is that greed governs.

The ruling class inside and outside government—big business, big Pharma, big banks, big tech, hedge funds, private equity, telecom, and the billionaires controlling both legacy and new media—colludes with a political culture that enriches itself on the billions raised and spent every election cycle.

The average person, who once viewed democracy as a ladder, whether Republican or Democrat or independent, now feels that democracy works for "those people," the elites, removed from Main Street and certainly the backstreets and, therefore, from the reality as it persists for the vast majority of Americans. A Gallup poll in 2022 found that Americans were the least optimistic they had been in almost thirty years about young people's chances of achieving greater material success than their parents. Only 13 percent thought it very likely that "today's youth will have a better living standard, better homes, a better education"—not the sentiment of a confident nation.[3]

And, of course, those in elected office in either party don't want to be replaced, so the deck is purposely stacked against the people on the outside. If most individuals are disaffected and disconnected from the political process, the

---

3   Megan Brenan, "Americans Less Optimistic about Next Generation's Future," Gallup.
     com, October 5, 2022, https://news.gallup.com/poll/403760/americans-less-optimis-
     tic-next-generation-future.aspx.

power is free to pursue its own agenda, pushing ever more extreme policy positions that speak to each party's base, further putting off those who feel left out, ever narrowing the circle of influence that wields power. When the politically powerful stare through the looking glass to find who to blame when things take a wrong turn, they might be surprised to see themselves.

People all over this country agree, from the packed Sunday football bar in Independence, Missouri, to the barbershop in Oakland, Maine: Greed fuels politics.

James Rabun, thirty-six, runs a family-owned gun shop in Kennesaw, Georgia. He's not ready to give up on democracy, and he thinks his vote for Trump counts, but he does think politics is rigged, the whole thing. "Capitalism for cronies." He asks if I know the Latin origin of the word "politics." I play along. "'Poli' meaning 'many' and 'ticks' as in blood-sucking insects." It's an old joke, but jokes survive for a reason.

The vast majority of voters don't like the choices foisted upon them by the narrow bands of activists and influencers who decide the nominees—which, one could argue, is exactly what the powers that be intend. Nothing to see here, folks. Those who do, or profess to care about saving democracy, share a commonality. Democracy, generally speaking, is working for them. The Founders' construct—codified in the Constitution, built to prop up propertied white men and later expanded to include disenfranchised populations, women, people of color, non-landowners—still protects those with property, wealth, status, or advanced education. I'm one of them.

ARE YOU LARRY?

In May 2024 at the Walmart in Beloit, Wisconsin, I'm told that I cannot get a new phone until Larry gets in at 7 a.m. If you hold on to your phone long enough, it seems eventually it will give up on you. Built-in obsolescence is an economic driver in today's economy.

Needing the internet in the meantime, it's back to the hotel and the laptop, past the Popeye's, Taco Bell, Wendy's, and Starbucks to the Quality Inn and Baymont by Wyndham.

"They want to silence me because I will never let them silence you," Trump is saying from the corner TV in the breakfast room, the sound bite from a rally held in Waukesha, not far from here, the day before.

The Hormel Foods production plant is against the skyline, a horizon relic, the oversized replica of the universally recognizable chili can. It's a local landmark in this city of 36,000, where Illinois militia officer Abraham Lincoln made camp during the Black Hawk War in 1832, and twenty-seven years later delivered a speech about slavery. Products that are consumed by people are made at the Hormel plant by other people—more than 300 of them. In fall 2023, Hormel installed a new five-story hydrostatic cooker for chili. Hormel chili has a very long shelf life. Some things last.

Not having a phone is isolating in today's world, but at least with a car, you're not dependent on the dedicated bus route, the "Walmart Line." And there's time to check on the local offerings: $2.98 for a gigantic canister of parmesan cheese; $0.97 for enough paper plates to cover several church suppers; $0.90 for an avocado. Inflation has not fully encroached on the Beloit Walmart, it appears.

The roadside tableau—the Walmart next to the Arby's next to the Taco Bell—is replicated across the country, splayed out along highways dotted with chain hotels and chain gas stations. Regional identity is hidden at a Starbucks. It might be Beloit, Wisconsin, or Marietta, Georgia, filled with people who can pay $4.15 for a grande latte. Just as feeling existentially unempowered because a small lightweight device carried in one's pocket beckons the loneliness of postmodernity, so too does the same corporatism that has enveloped much of America. And there's not a hell of a lot we can do about it, best efforts notwithstanding.

Larry, who appears to be in his late twenties but might be older, gets in a little past his scheduled time by my watch—maybe the Walmart Line was late—but is given space to settle and set up. A personal peeve of mine is jumping on salespeople the minute they arrive, something learned behind the sock counter at Jordan Marsh at the mall back in my hometown of Burlington, Massachusetts. "The lady isn't here," Larry says when he's settled behind the counter, mentioning for the first time that there is another person who it seems is in charge of addressing this type of issue. I have pinned my hopes on Larry, my savior, and now find it was misplaced. "Yeah, she said they sent her to the other store. They might send her here this afternoon." And so, I remain personally silenced until "the lady" arrives.

There is a helplessness in the disconnect, exacerbated by technology, which at times can prove so frustrating—especially for those of us not raised in the Digital Age—that it prompts retreat. Even given my demographic advantages mentioned above, the feeling of alienation makes sense to me.

SEARCHING FOR CONNECTION

When "Real ID" was mandated and I needed to bring my documents in person to the Massachusetts Registry of Motor Vehicles, I brought a book to hedge the hope for a mid-morning lull and that I wouldn't be there long. I wasn't there long because we were all told that the machine that verified passports was down and we would have to come back. I weakly protested that I thought the actual passport was verification of citizenship but decided to simply return the following day.

Clearly, others had to plan this chore, taking time off from work or relying on childcare, and returning would be twice the hassle. It's a bit of a catch-22. Services are stretched or hard to access, not only for the big things like health care and education, but also the little daily hassles like getting a Real ID or replacing a cell phone. So the frustration builds, and we feel more helpless and disconnected. Give us your date of birth, address, last four of your social, membership ID, password, first pet's name, and prepare to sit on hold.

Feeling alone at the Beloit, Wisconsin Walmart, with no one to commiserate with, either in person or electronically, at least at the Registry, we were all frustrated with the technology breakdown together, even if we communicated it only through side glances and eye rolls.

In my travels, I look for the gathering place that still favors human interaction. In Mount Vernon, Illinois, which sports a replica of Washington's manse of the same name at a local car dealership, I try out several local independent coffee shops, one run by an Amish family, in hopes of engaging locals, but I have very little success. On the last day I'm there, with the local shop closed, I pop into the Hardee's next door; $1.99 a coffee. Bingo. Several local retired farmers are discussing the Ukraine war and the effect on gas prices in the US. The consensus is that if it hurts Putin, then bearing the cost increase temporarily is worth it.

In Doral, Florida, home to one of the president's golf clubs, I ask where I might find the center, or what I would call the downtown, the place where I can find people. I'm directed to the Town Center, which on my map looks like an outdoor mall. It is, I'm told, chock full of eateries interspersed with dentists, urgent care, and all manner of personal care. I grew up in a town with a huge indoor mall—quite the paradise when it opened in the early '70s, as I had never seen a palm tree before. I would never consider it the town center. But if you aren't from Burlington, Massachusetts, and only know the town for its mall, you might think that's where the pulse of the town is.

In Millcreek Township, Pennsylvania, next to Erie, the mall *is* the heart of the town, providing the lifeblood to all other commercial organs in the vicinity. It is the nation's fourteenth largest mall, a complex of leviathan proportions that seems to have been calculated into being by a planner perfectly fine with trading charm for scope. The JC Penney building alone looks like something we built in the 1950s to incubate the military industrial complex and serve as a stern, hulking warning to the Soviets. Imagine how many small mom-and-pops disappeared into this Death Star for modern commerce.

In a lot of towns across this country, they've literally lost their center, the place where people were sure to gravitate. This leaves us with the idea that control over our own immediate fate no longer lies in our own hands, and we can't get it back. What's worse is the feeling that there's nothing we can do about it.

It could be Larry, dealing with his own stuff, running a few minutes behind and tweaking a person's day, or it could be the Fed keeping interest rates high and preventing someone from buying a home. There's not really much to do about either, until it goes too far. Two-and-a-half centuries ago, that's why people painted their faces and hurled tea into Boston Harbor.

THE PELICAN TAKES FLIGHT

Pensacola in January is lovely, a secret gem of Florida to those of us from up north who think of that quirky state strictly as Disney World or a favorite destination of hurricanes. The Panhandle jewel is unpretentious and affordable, and the people are friendly; also, the sun shines there, a climatic unicorn for New Englanders.

On New Year's Eve, they celebrate with a "pelican drop" but fortunately not a real one. The pelican is said to represent the ultimate sacrifice of Christ, piercing its own breast to feed its blood to its young, an ensanguined tribute to the cruci-fixion that appears on many Catholic altars.

Tracy, thirty-five, works shifts at the upscale restaurant across the street from the open-air bar where a lot of servers have gathered after work. She hails from Indiana but loves it in the Sunshine State and loves her governor, Ron DeSantis. Her eleven-year-old daughter, who needs additional learning services at school, gets them; her health care is affordable; and her apartment, close commuting distance from work and spacious enough for the two of them plus her one-year-old, costs $750 a month. And, she says, thumb and forefinger rotating her shot glass of tequila slowly back and forth, "If I have to cook dinner for the landlord once in a while, frying chicken with one hand with a baby on my hip, I'll do it."

It's a precarious arrangement, if you ask me. If the rent goes up, her world is upended. Her situation is safe at the moment, but is it secure? And is there anything a nominee of either party can do to change that?

Her eldest, who can be a "handful," has taken to helping with the baby. The magic of Christmas has not faded with age, and she strongly felt the baby needed her own Elf on a Shelf. At the dollar store, Tracy found a cheaper, more creative answer: a one-dollar reindeer they named Cornflake. Cornflake follows the more seasoned elf but does everything backward and wrong. It never sits on the shelf. It bakes cookies upside down and with the wrong ingredients. Rudolph before the career advancement.

Tracy can see the services the state provides, and DeSantis has been governor for most of the time she's been paying attention to politics. His is the face of the health care she receives, though it was in place before he took office. But the federal government is distant and not in her thinking. She is not familiar with her local congressman. I mention one of the more recognizable members of Congress, prominent on Democrats' list of most pernicious congressional villains: I prompt, "Matt Gaetz?" She shakes her head to signal her lack of recognition but tells me Pensacola's new mayor comes into the restaurant often, and he is nice.

From the Gulf Coast to the Gulf of Maine, the political apathy, or perhaps fatigue, echoes in cooler climes. Four months after my meeting with Tracy in Pensacola, on the last day of May, Donald Trump is convicted of all counts by a New York jury.

The dinner crowd has gathered at a markedly different venue, the Sunset Grill in Belgrade Village, Maine, where the sun shines less. But they've not convened to take in a milestone in American political history. Mostly regulars, they assume their usual configuration, a line of bearded men in front of beers at the small bar, couples and families at tables and under umbrellas on the patio. The grilled chicken is heavily seasoned with a lemon rub, I'm guessing in substitution for any tenderness or flavor present in the underlying bird. The baked potato is top notch. This has to be a Maine potato, and even without special request, it arrives with sour cream and two pats of butter.

Two of the four corner TVs show amateur hockey, the third a show about Maine nightlife, which is portrayed as more robust than it probably is. NBC's Lester Holt pops up on the fourth screen at 6:30 to report on the scene in Manhattan, where a former president of the United States has just been convicted of a crime for the first time in history—even more remarkable when one reflects on the miscreants and scalawags who have occupied the office across the centuries. The sound is off, no closed caption, but the story Holt is reporting is unmistakable. And there is the former president speaking to reporters outside the courtroom. You need neither sound nor closed captioning to know what he is saying.

No one in the Sunset Grill takes notice. I overhear no conversation about the historic events. Reports the next day include person-on-the-street interviews where they say the verdicts won't affect their votes; Trump has been such a ubiquitous public persona for so long that opinions are fairly well-baked. But listening to the everyday chatter over dinner in central Maine reinforces what I see across this country. The constant bombardment of partisan vitriol and unceasing drama that whirls around Donald Trump's person have caused most to actively tune out.

Between Maine and Pensacola, Mary Ellen sits at the bar at the Hilton Atlanta/Marietta hotel and conference center, sipping a vodka soda while waiting for a takeout dinner order for her daughter and friend upstairs in the room. They're in town from North Carolina for a softball tournament. She wonders if Robert behind the bar would premix her a Bloody Mary for her to pick up for tomorrow at 6 a.m. before they hit the road for the first of four games. Knowing Robert, I'm sure he would. A lifelong Republican, she's pro-life and an admirer of what Trump was able to accomplish as president. She wishes, though, that he would "just shut up." The regional inspector for municipal water systems from Alabama, sitting three stools down, nods in agreement. The Alabamian is voting for Trump but pines for another option. Mary Ellen says she hasn't decided.

There is nothing Donald Trump can do, even suffer a felony conviction, that will cause Alabama to change colors. Voters are solid red there in the same way there is nothing that will paint Massachusetts, my lifelong home state, anything other than blue—although Trump made inroads, purple splotches blooming on the state's South Coast, where I got my undergraduate degree, and up through the central spine of the state. The last GOP presidential candidate to win the blue-collar city of Fall River, which Trump carried by 3 percentage points in 2024, was former Massachusetts Governor Calvin Coolidge exactly a century prior. Trump and Harris might not be the candidates that folks in neighboring Westport (Trump by 6.5 points) or Somerset (Trump by 4) wished for, but if we choose to walk into the voting booth in November, we are presented with a multiple-choice decision, not a wish.

In Pensacola, Tracy is scraping by in our democracy, but an unlucky event or two—loss of the apartment, a layoff, a serious health issue—will hurl her delicate economic equilibrium into disarray. The checks and balances inherent in our system aren't designed to keep Tracy afloat; they are meant to slow and stifle the changes needed to benefit those not doing well. Money makes money, as the saying goes. The rules and practices of our capitalist system are greased by our founder's construct of government.

This disconnection from democracy might hit differently for African American men and women, or Native Americans who only got the right to vote one hundred years ago. For them, what the slave-owning George Washington termed "the great experiment" has had less time in the lab, but many trials and many errors.

Polls tell us that young voters don't think the slow slog of democracy works for them, and it's understandable. Faced with existential threats of climate change, crushing debt that puts the American dream out of reach, and a seemingly unsustainable entitlement superstructure built up over decades from New Deal through Great Society policy, not to mention the expansion of health care through the Affordable Care Act—all issues that preceding generations have repeatedly punted—they may want more decisive action than our Founding Fathers envisioned. Like those who boarded British merchant ships in Boston Harbor in the dead of night, they've got some tea of their own they'd like to spill.

Trump gained votes among African American men, Native Americans, younger millennials who mostly weren't paying attention to what their older siblings regard as the halcyon days of the Obama Era, and the youngest voters, Gen Z. In the absence of a specific plan that speaks to cohorts of voters left out of the political conversation—and I'm talking about the oft-contentious post-election debate within the Democratic Party—there is an appeal to a message of strong leadership. The "elites" on the coasts may mock that as chimerical, a false promise.

But I found in my travels that people who feel left out will grab for a promise, even if it sounds improbable or proves false, over nothing every time. Trump realized that the shrinking percentage of male white voters meant he needed to expand his vote, and he appealed to what I've come to think of as The Coalition of the Disconnected, and it worked.

As part of my team's research, Lila Guzkowski, a junior at Clark University in Worcester, Massachusetts, and Connor Murphy, a sophomore at Tufts University in Somerville, Massachusetts, surveyed a cross section of young voters over the final months of the campaign. "People were angry with the political climate," says Lila. "Joy" sounded naive in their post-pandemic anger. Young voters have seen things taken away from them and face mounting crises: the pandemic, climate change, global security, school shootings, women's rights, the cost of college, the "American Dream." "Court rulings threaten our rights. Young people thought the talk of democracy, which resonates with our grandparents, was an elitist take."

THE LOST ELECTORAL COLLEGE-LESS WORLD

The 2022 Dobbs decision ruling that the Constitution does not confer abortion rights has exposed a weakness in our system, a system that purports that equal justice is central to democratically elected governments. The last time a Republican presidential candidate won the popular vote before 2024 was George W. Bush in 2004. Before that, it was his father, George H. W. Bush, in 1988. Following logic and historical precedent, if the Electoral College did not exist, there would be only three Republican-appointed Justices: Chief Justice Roberts (a Bush 43 appointee), Justice Thomas (Bush 41) and Justice Alito (43). Without the Electoral College, Justices Gorsuch, Kavanaugh, and Coney Barrett (all Trump appointees) would likely still be presiding over lower courts and Democratic presidents would have tilted the bench. Were the popular vote recognized as the deciding tally, it's highly likely that a 6–3 conservative majority would be flipped to a 6–3 progressive majority, and Roe, not Dobbs, would still be the law of the land. The myriad other differences in countless other national policy arenas are sobering to calculate.

Roe's reversal has unleashed an assault on reproductive rights. On February 16, 2024, the Alabama Supreme Court ruled that embryos have rights, sparking chaos at IVF clinics in the heart of Dixie and putting Republicans on the backpedal across the nation. Later, Republicans in Congress blocked a Democratic attempt at codifying contraceptive rights in federal law. Imperiled reproductive rights infuses meaning into democracy for large numbers of voters. A theoretical Harris victory would have hinged on women, millions of them motivated by the notion that abortion, regarded as settled law for generations, was on the ballot.

Of course, the votes of women helped Trump win. And in some of the states where he won, reproductive rights were indeed codified or restored through ballot questions. Harris made the case that she would protect such rights. Trump argued that he was putting the power directly in the people's hands by the federal repeal of Roe. In states where reproductive protections were on the ballot, women could vote for what they perceived as a strong Trump on the economy while voting directly on restoration of reproductive rights. One might suggest that this is democracy in action, voters deciding what works for them on the state and federal level.

And there is a historic appetite for muscular executive agency in this country. Abraham Lincoln suspended the writ of habeas corpus, an enumerated power of Congress, during the Civil War, requiring Congress to validate the action after the fact. During a meeting in Warm Springs in February 1933, journalist Walter Lippmann told President-elect Franklin Roosevelt that, given the country's dire economic situation, he "may have no alternative but to assume dictatorial powers."[4] When Eleanor Roosevelt suggested the same, that "the country might benefit from a benevolent dictator who could force through reforms," her husband replied "that one could not count upon a dictator staying benevolent."[5]

But consider this: Would Bernie Sanders govern in a style different from

---

4   Robert Dallek, *Franklin D. Roosevelt: A Political Life* (Viking, 2017), 133.

5   Dallek, *Franklin D. Roosevelt: A Political Life*, 134.

Trump? Or would he have come to the White House, had he been elected in 2016 or four years later when things seemed even more dire, cheered on by his passionate and Internet-savvy supporters, intent on flipping the tables of our political status quo? Trump and Sanders are rule breakers. Well, Trump has actually broken rules, and laws, but part of Sanders's appeal is his urgency of action.

Sanders, just a day after the election, does indeed break a party rule, taking the loss on directly while decorum would have allowed time to "heal," saying Democrats need to get back to basics, asserting a program that speaks to the traditional Democratic coalition. Different tables, certainly, or at least flipped in different directions, but it makes sense that around 12 percent of Sanders's primary voters in 2016 voted for Trump that November. Those 12 percent want to see tables flipped, the contents scattered, and to watch as those who presumed their tables were sturdy and immovable scurry to salvage the detritus. "Wraparound coalitions" occasionally crop up during foreign policy debates; the righty America Firsters don't want us spending blood and treasure overseas, while the lefty peaceniks want less global conflict generally. But rarely do the far left and far right fall into step when it comes to foundational principles like the idea of the structure and animating spirit behind our nation.

We may craft a new understanding of how to make our democracy work today and for the next generation. Or we may move toward concentrated power in the executive branch. Perhaps a benevolent dictator, perhaps not; Americans have not dived to these depths of introspection about their own self-governance since those doing the diving wore powdered wigs.

We should recoil at the notion that we, as a nation, would embrace a strongman as leader. But historically, strongmen, by definition, present themselves as decisive and forceful leaders, which resonates with Americans.

We also love an outsider, though with hope that fresh thinking isn't of the dictatorial bent. Actor Reagan, one-term Georgia Governor Carter before him, Arkansas Governor Clinton, Illinois State Senator Obama, businessman and reality show host Trump, martyr Trump 2.0—all outsiders. If we don't believe the institutions of government work for us, we look to the branch of government consolidated in one person to manifest what we wish for: change. The critical question of our time is lost when people feel that the federal government cannot possibly—or actively chooses not to—affect their lives in a positive way, so they look for a leader who can.

The Founders were concerned about this when one branch of government is vested in one individual. They all loved George Washington, and thought of him when drafting Article II, but there was only one Washington. They placed Congress first in the Constitutional lineup to ensure it would provide a collective check on an executive who might be tempted to run amok. But over two and a half centuries, the power of the presidency has only grown, the bully pulpit for everyone to see, now 24/7, satisfying our need for that successor to Washington. As Congressman Byron Daniels of Florida said of Trump on Inauguration Day 2025: "Daddy's home."

PADDLING OUR OWN CANOE

In Carson City, Nevada, Hanifin's, the antiques store a few blocks from the state capitol, is vast but has a going-out-of-business sign in the window. With the landlord asking for such a steep rent hike, the antiques connoisseurs, passionate and knowledgeable about their trade, will be gone soon after more than a quarter century in business. And they are happy to offer a deep discount on the wooden canoe they catch me looking at. For a moment, I wonder how I might get it up to my camp in Maine. The Nevada legislature is not in session, and I ask the pleasant older woman behind the counter, amid the ornate grandfather clocks and vintage jukebox displays, if things are noticeably different when the lawmakers are in town. She says no. "They keep to themselves so they can get back home and do nothing. Just like Congress."

Another hurdle for democracy fans out there. If conservatives are running against the woke elite huddled on the coasts and selective hamlets dotted from one to the other, progressives' dismissiveness (or utter ignorance) of the broad swath of red real estate comprising the majority of the nation's landmass comes through loud and clear. One person, one vote. In Massachusetts, in Alabama. And there may be less difference in the perception of the federal government than one might think between the solid red and blue states.

Whether voters knew it then or not, whether they'd thought about it deeply or intuited it in their bones or just didn't see it because of its enormity, democracy was on the ballot in 2024, and it will be for the foreseeable future. Donald Trump will not, and Kamala Harris could not, save it. Believing so is an act of collective political narcissism, convenient for campaigns to rally support for a candidate. But the January 6th attack was aimed at something much more fundamental than any one candidate. The attack was meant to, and did, undermine the concept of one person, one vote.

Once trust in an institution is badly broken—let's take the one of marriage—the union may repair itself and move on, but it won't be as it was before. Our trust in the integrity of our elections, the foundation of our democracy, has been broken—violently ruptured—the compound fracture jutting through our American skin and nerve endings just as the throngs forced their way into the symbolic and fortified compound of the US Capitol. There is no turning back.

The postmortem finds the Democrats gobsmacked by the results. I confess I too was surprised. I saw no way Harris would lose the popular vote, though I was not surprised by the Republican takeover of the Senate or the Electoral College outcome. I've been traveling for years talking to voters all across this country—across three presidential elections, with four different Speakers of the House wielding the gavel, plus a global pandemic—and they were telling me what they were going to do in 2024. And yet all the evidence, both qualitative and quantitative, couldn't pierce my bubble with my Doodle in the dog park in Belmont, clinging to my love of our democracy as it is.

There is a quote from Dylan McKay, a character in the TV show *Beverly Hills, 90210*, that goes, "May the bridges you burn light your way." The Democrats lost big in 2024; the narrowness of the popular vote notwithstanding, Trump swept the seven swing states, as he will remind us more than once or twice in the coming years. In the Democratic tent—which ballooned under duress last year to include both AOC and, for the purposes of ballot-marking but evidently to limited persuasive effect among the electorate, Dick Cheney—there will be endless donnybrooks over messaging and vision and who gets a voice. Some of these fracases will prove productive. Others will not.

People who are disconnected from politics deserve to be listened to. If we don't listen, they will be heard nonetheless, and in the face of nothing from one side, will accept a promise, even if it proves false, from the other side every time.

The flames of the Democrats' burnt bridges of 2024 should illuminate the words "We the People" that have crackled across this land for almost 250 years, sometimes as smoldering embers and—at our best—as righteous wildfire.

And that means *all* the people. You can spend another billion dollars three years from now on ads, polls, digital and DC-based consultants, or you can go out—as I did for my peripatetic and often wonderfully serendipitous project— to places like Pensacola, Florida, and Independence, Missouri, and Lookout Mountain, Georgia, Marked Tree in Arkansas, and the Clevelands in Tennessee and Ohio both, and the manifold Springfields around the country, and then you can propose a way forward that works for all of them, or at least most of them.

Because here, in this country founded on an idea, the people still rule.

AN INDIVIDUAL DEFIANT ACT

On September 11, 2001, a special election was held in Massachusetts to fill the unexpired term of Congressman Joe Moakley, who had died. My candidate, State Senator Stephen Lynch, was the front-runner. If you're old enough, you probably remember the day: how brilliant and clear it was, the crispness of the air in the northeast. Stephen and his wife, Margaret, walked down the hill in South Boston to vote—yards from where Washington fortified Dorchester Heights to chase the British out of Boston and change the course of the American Revolution—holding their small daughter, Victoria, dressed in red, white, and blue.

We had proceeded to the western part of the district that morning, a car of reporters in tow, when the planes hit the Twin Towers, and by the time we abandoned the schedule and got back to the Boston campaign headquarters where there were TVs, the Pentagon had been hit. Two of the planes had left from Logan Airport, with a number of Stephen's constituents on board. So while Stephen focused on the needs of his district, the Secretary of the Commonwealth, Bill Galvin, halted the voting. A short time later, Attorney General Tom Reilly and Governor Jane Swift overturned the decision and reinstated voting, ending at the usual 8 p.m. despite the terroristic interruption.

A little after ten, Stephen made his way outside campaign HQ and without fanfare of any kind, spoke of the day, what it meant for the nation, and thanked the constituents of the 9th District for the faith they had put in him. *The Boston Globe* editorialized that he had "assumed the sage mantle of his predecessor, Joe Moakley."

Working on a campaign, you become a sort of family in the way one does with a group of people who have collectively taken on a harrowing task. We would share this experience on this day, but the day would live in infamy.

In the car on the way home, a friend called and suggested I meet him for a drink at a Cambridge bar that was still open, since it was midnight already. When I opened the door, I walked into a scene of normalcy—warm lights, people playing pool, TVs turned to the destruction in New York, the unbelievable now becoming surreally familiar.

My phone rang, and Yvonne Abraham of *The Boston Globe* asked me to comment on the fact that turnout was higher than predicted, even with the chronological gap in voting. I said, looking around the paneled bar of a certain era, at the patrons of a certain era, that every American on some level understands the power that has been given them. In the face of an attack on American soil, the first since Pearl Harbor, stuck at home watching the towers collapse, casting a vote was a defiant act, and more people came out to vote than was predicted. Americans were motivated to vote, in a special election they might have taken a pass on, as an expression of defiance.

ALL POLITICS IS LOCAL

There is an inverted pyramid at play in politics. National politics gets the most interest and attention and media coverage, but most of our interaction with the government is local: property taxes, zoning, education funding, trash pickup, street cleaning, and, in certain climes, snow removal or wildfires or hurricanes.

If you aren't involved in your local government for whatever reason, the decision-making process flies under the radar, particularly with the gutting of local news. I met a retired pastor in Springfield, Ohio, who attends every county council meeting just to show support—a governance unicorn, of sorts. A generation ago, most city council meetings would have a reporter or two attend, and you would be informed through the local paper about the goings on. Not so today.

In some places I visit, people talk about big decisions their town or county has taken, and they shake their heads in wonder that such a thing could happen. Rarely does someone tell me they were part of the debate or knew they could participate. This disconnection locally can cause an overreaction sometimes. An issue introduced by national groups pushing an agenda can flare up locally, and there is an effort to ban books or trans athletes. And of course, Trump's questioning of election integrity leads people to question their own election officials, especially if you don't know your town's Bill Oelfke.

I have yet to meet someone unaware of who Donald Trump is, though more people than you might imagine are neutral about him. One female supporter, in Illinois, says she's not voting for a best friend, so she looks past the personal traits. Another voter in New York explains it to me this way: "A lot of people who vote for him would march over to his house if he moved in next door and tell him 'never step foot on my lawn!'" And the neutral disconnected aren't sure it matters who's elected to the federal legislative offices. Most people I talk to have no idea who their elected member of Congress is and often confuse members of the House with the Senate—even people who vote regularly. Certain members have national profiles and break through the disconnect, even to the point of being identifiable by initials; Alexandria Ocasio-Cortez (AOC) and Marjorie Taylor Greene (MTG) are two that are frequently mentioned, usually negatively.

Marjorie Taylor Greene is a lightning rod for the political left. In her district, most people I talk to might know who she is, but they couldn't identify her as their particular member of Congress. There are lots of factors that contribute to this disconnect, and for House districts, the redistricting process can wildly swing who represents whom at least every ten years. Ticket splitters, those who vote differently for Congress than their choice for president, are an endangered species. While a blue state might have a Republican governor (or the reverse in red states), down the federal ballot, voters show little appetite for rewarding even outstanding representation of a different party. This absolves voters of even having to know who the person is behind the party affiliation.

A county official I speak with in Greene's district in northern Georgia, on primary election day in 2022, does know her and he likes her, but he wishes she were a little more attentive to directing federal money back home. I ask how she will fare in what CNN tells me is a competitive primary against a number of challengers, but most notably Jennifer Strahan, a CEO with a doctorate in healthcare leadership, a race watched closely by Democrats raising significant money for her eventual Democratic opponent. He tells me, "She'll be fine." This proves true, Greene getting 70 percent of the primary vote and 65 percent in the general election. Neither a stellar resume nor a ton of out-of-state blue money could penetrate the local disconnect. And for her district, which went heavily for Donald Trump three times, her reliable vote for Trump's agenda is all they ask.

"I'M JUST A BILL, AND I AM ONLY A BILL AND I AM LIVING HERE ON CAPITOL HILL"

It's convenient to blame a lack of civics on this disconnect, and as someone who has taught Introduction to American Politics at the collegiate level, I can hardly disagree that we need to do a better job well before students go off to college, but it's a small part of the problem. I took algebra in high school, and today I'm not sure I could identify an algebra equation if you stuck one in front of me.

The teaching of civics has to have an experiential component for people to understand it. If you reach adulthood and haven't familiarized yourself with the political process at any level, you'll look at it the same way I look at math: impossible to understand.

The difference, of course, is I can muddle my way through life with a calculator, and now AI. The stewardship of our democracy should be a full participation effort, and that requires those who are active in it to find ways that include everyone. It's a lazy and unacceptable excuse to only blame the disconnected.

A century and more ago, when people landed on these shores, it was the political parties that were likely to reach out, or their family members who were already here and affiliated with one or the other party, and the parties stuck with them. Politics was a team sport, and the platforms of each were tied directly to the interests of its members.

A growing part of the problem is an individual political campaign's disconnection from personal interaction. The microtargeting of voters who are then bombarded with digital communication has become the whole effort, crowding out a robust field effort – boots on the ground, obsolete machine politics for better or worse. This is particularly damaging for Democratic candidates. The instinct for Democratic Party leaders might be to focus on matching the Right's communications platforms – including podcasts and premeditatedly controversial comments, and that is certainly part of the solution. The Right appeals to those who want to be left alone by government. The Democrats' appeal is one best presented in community, particularly to those not microtargeted.

But as technology platforms proliferate and our lives get sucked further into them—taking us further away from human interaction, ultimately calcifying the skill to communicate with each other—the disconnect from politics will further widen, a death spiral that encourages tyrants.

TEACHING BY DOING

The Blue Lab, a political incubator I started in 2012 to train college students on how to run campaigns at the local level, has graduated hundreds who have gone on to staff campaigns across the country. The students work on actual campaigns for state representative or city council, supervised by political veterans teaching from a developed curriculum.

Every election cycle technology takes us further away from human interaction. COVID gave us a glimpse into where we are headed. In March 2020 when everything shut down, Stonehill College, where I teach classes in the Political Science Department as an adjunct, went online, and the loss of classroom back-and-forth was impossible to overcome over Zoom.

In 2024, the lab concentrated on the New Hampshire House of Representatives, the largest legislative body after the US House, with four hundred members. The Blue Lab employed several dozen college and post-college students to work directly with Democratic candidates, most of whom had no other staffing. In early 2024, there was optimism that the razor-thin margin separating the Republicans and Democrats could be closed.

That November, New Hampshire voted for Harris and the Democratic candidates for Congress at the federal level, but the red tsunami swept down the ballot for state offices, from governor to the state legislature. It's a weak argument, I know, that it would have been worse if the party didn't invest in the Blue Lab. They had, and the storm swept from the Massachusetts border to Dixville Notch in the north, where the first presidential votes are cast every four years.

So it's not a surprise that some wondered if the money that went to pay the Blue Labbers would have been better spent on digital. I would counter that we're increasingly reaching voters on digital platforms, and far less so in person, and the tsunami came. But when you lose, the instinct is to do something different next time, and digital platforms are popping like corn, a new and exciting prospect for any operative hoping to right the wrongs of the last election. Certainly, 2026 will be the AI election, run by a generation of operatives who were practically born with a device in their hands.

I remember wondering, while teaching not that many years ago, if it was OK to ask students to close their laptops when they started showing up in the classroom. Now, of course, I make an obscure reference—familiar to me, but further removed from them chronologically as I was from FDR—to Tip O'Neill or Newt Gingrich maybe, and in seconds everyone has googled them.

And people-fueled campaigning is so analog, so torch-lit parade, so nineteenth century. The reality is that the elections in 2026 and 2028 will see even less human interaction.

But I would argue you are better able to capture hearts and minds in person, and not just by knocking on their doors late in the game. The charged political atmosphere makes people reluctant to say anything to anyone, but that's why political parties need to connect, listen, and encourage participation in the political process. People need to be coaxed out of their devices and invited to participate in democracy.

Democrats would like to think the person who answers the door can be persuaded, and each election cycle, social media is full of anecdotes of just this. The Pennsylvania voter who had no idea that Donald Trump was going to cut her Social Security and would now vote for Harris. But if that voter consumed a steady diet of information from ideological news sources of any kind, the hypnotic spell of her belief, one would argue, cannot be broken by seeing a stranger once at her front door.

APRIL FOOL

April Fools' Day 2025 is election day in Florida. Two congressional vacancies will be filled—created when Trump tapped Mike Waltz to be his National Security Advisor, and Matt Gaetz, briefly the nominee for Attorney General—in a first test of Trump's performance to date, we're told by CNN.

The 6th district, which runs from St. Augustine to Daytona Beach, and the 1st district, centered around Pensacola, are solid red, full stop. Trump took them both in a landslide, as did Waltz and Gaetz. The Democratic Party would be forgiven if it ignored the races entirely, foregoing the expense of races where loss is a foregone conclusion. Or it might recruit a young activist to learn the ropes, planting seeds that might eventually bear electoral fruit.

To contrast, Joe Biden won the Massachusetts 4th congressional district in 2020 by about the same margin that Trump won the two in Florida, and easily reelected its congressman, Jake Auchincloss. Before Jake, it sent his predecessor Joe Kennedy III with very comfortable margins, if he pulled a Republican opponent at all. If a special election were held to fill a vacancy in the 4th, the Democrat would win, full stop, and would be happy to have the Republicans burn millions of dollars trying to flip it.

But the Florida races presented too ripe an opportunity not to be exploited by the media, the Democratic Party, or the consulting class. Democrats Josh Weil in the 6th and Gay Valimont in the 1st were fine candidates, but the fundraising machine kicked into high gear as if they had a snowball's chance in Florida in the spring of 2025.

The money poured in from wealthy donors up north, where snowballs are real and pipe dreams might be possible, ten million dollars or so for each. The referendum on Donald Trump, which shouldn't have been a referendum at all, left the Republican majority exactly as it was before the vacancies and left the Democrats to crow into the void about the reduced winning margins in both from the November 2024 results, a $20 million waste, an expensive distraction if your urgent calls to put forth a winning strategy are to be believed.

Minority Leader Hakeem Jeffries spoke the truth about the situation on election day, but too late to slow the money spigot spewing obscene amounts at consultants and for media buys, while the media relentlessly teased the possibility that Florida voters would smack Trump for his outrageous behavior with, perhaps, fingers crossed, an upset win for Democrats that would upend Trump's presidency.

Just two days before, *The Washington Post* opinion writer Shadi Hamid wrote about how Trump had "squandered his moment" in a piece titled "The beginning of the end of the Trump era."[6] Hamid wasn't predicting wins in Florida. He was writing about a doomed trajectory for the administration, but such headlines are catnip for Democrats looking for any indication that the Trump regime will magically come to an end, or be thwarted by a robust Democratic opposition, or at least slowed.

Jeffries said, "This is the functional equivalent of Republicans running a competitive race in the district that is represented by Representative Alexandria Ocasio-Cortez. Kamala Harris won that district by 30 points. Do you think a Republican would even be competitive in that district in New York, currently held by Alex? Of course not."[7]

All politics is local, Tip O'Neill said, but today you can spend tens of millions of dollars in a congressional race in Florida and have very little impact. Many congressional races are now national races. After voting, two voters spoke to a reporter from the Associated Press: "Teresa Horton, 72, didn't know much at all about Tuesday's election—but she said she didn't need to. 'I don't even know these people that are on there,' she said of her ballot. 'I just went with my ticket.' Brenda Ray, 75, a retired nurse, said she didn't know a lot about Patronis (the Republican, and winner in the 1st) either, but cast her ballot for him because she believes he'll 'vote with our President. That's all we're looking for,' she said."[8] For Democrats in states like Florida, money cannot solve what has been lost long ago. An early-term message that things are already broken, nationally, and Donald Trump is to blame for it, didn't resonate.

This combination of huge amounts of money raised with the reality that money alone is not enough exposes a mechanical problem facing the Democratic Party and its leaders. In an April 2025 *New York Times* story about the Florida specials, reporter Shane Goldmacher profiled how "a 23-year-old law student and dungeon master—in Dungeons & Dragons" raised millions as a fundraising consultant for both Weil and Valimont.[9]

---

6   Shadi Hamid, "The beginning of the end of the Trump era," *The Washington Post*, March 27, 2025.

7   Jill Colvin, "Wisconsin and Florida elections provide early warning signs to Trump and Republicans," AP News, April 2, 2025.

8   Colvin, "Wisconsin and Florida elections," 2025.

9   Shane Goldmacher, "Meet the 23-year-old student who raised $25 million in Democratic losses," *New York Times*, April 4, 2025.

While the article focuses on the profit made by the young gamer, and his percentage take of the money raised is impressive, it's important to remember that the Supreme Court decision in *Citizens United* granted that this money, and the raising and spending of it, represents free speech. Democratic consultants of all ages have taken to the task, which must seem natural to a generation of fundraisers who were under ten years old when *Citizens United* was decided. This assumes that the path to victory in red districts is not to engage on the ground but to bombard them from the air with money raised from out-of-state blue districts.

The Goldmacher article continues: "It's an adage of online political fund-raising that you have to spend money to make money. The question is if quite that much needed to be spent. Records show the advertising blitz overwhelmingly went to raising more money rather than persuading Florida voters. Both Mr. Weil and Ms. Valimont's campaigns spent far more on ads in California than in Florida, records show."

The young fundraiser went where the money is. Knowing nothing of Dungeons & Dragons, I ask an expert, my nephew Jason Robbat, middle school teacher at St. John's Prep in Danvers, Massachusetts, and the faculty advisor Dungeon Master to the school club. He says applying a Dungeons & Dragons skillset of collaborative storytelling to craft a message works for his sixth graders by engaging them in what they want. "They want a castle and a dog," he says. The equivalent, for anxious Democrats in far-off California, is of hope for upsets in ruby-red lands, and the thought of it makes them open their wallets and hand it over.

CALLING ALL HUMANS

It is only sustained human interaction—augmented, not replaced, by communication on the various technology platforms—that I think will prove effective for Democrats.

Is this different for Republicans? I think so. I hear a lot about the uncle or parent who watches Fox "all day long." I rarely hear of the person who watches MSNBC all day long. The focused news diet builds a strong base for MAGA voters who reinforce this with personal interactions at work, home, or in the booth at the coffee shop. Maybe the Dungeons & Dragons consultants could start clubs focused on red states and use their skills to rebuild the brand, but it doesn't seem that the Democratic establishment is recruiting Dungeons & Dragon masters, as maybe they should. It's a lot easier to persuade rich coastal Democrats to hit the "donate" button.

Should Democrats build out their own media platforms? Of course. But that alone won't suffice. Democrats are selling a different product, which is more nuanced and needs time and eye-to-eye communication to sell. It's not enough for Democrats to snap their fingers with limited face time, hoping to break the hypnotic devotion to the other side. The key to selling a product, in this case a version of democracy, is knowing what people are buying.

By focus grouping and polling, you may not get to the heart of the matter. Donald Trump is a successful salesman by knowing exactly what people are buying—even if he doesn't have it in stock, has no intention of stocking it, or perhaps knows it doesn't exist.

Democrats know what voters on the coasts are stocking up on, but what about the rest of the country? Or young people everywhere? Or Latino voters or African American men? The Democrats seem to not know what they are buying or, more cynically, think they know what they *should* be buying. There are a lot of voters not buying what they perceive as the Democrats' elitist offering. And listening to what they want, in a democracy, if they want that at all, works both ways. If voters out there are disconnected from politics, it means that those who traffic in politics, the seemingly hyperconnected, are disconnected from people who are disconnected out there.

I get constant reminders to check my privilege. At a hotel bar in Cincinnati in March 2025, several people were quietly working on laptops. One woman who works for the US Army Corps of Engineers was watching Trump's address to Congress on her phone, her brow furrowed, when a couple walked in and tried to liven the mood.

"Hey, it's not a library, people," he says. He asks us where we're from: Baltimore, Salt Lake, Phoenix, me from Boston. They're from St. Louis. I say, "Nice city." He says, "It sucks." Basic geo-location shared, he asks us, generally, but pointing at me, what city is our favorite to visit. I say, "Domestic or international?" He quickly replies, "Wow. Way to whip your dick out!" Humbled, I attempt to course correct and say, "Pensacola," which is true, among others I have visited on this journey. He nods. He's never been there, but it sounds nice.

And this isn't just true for differences in experiences but in political outlooks. Democratic missionaries spreading the gospel of the sacredness of democracy and infrastructure investment and the soft diplomacy of USAID assistance best check their privilege as they proceed.

This desire to reach out to those who are disconnected is a good first step. Some in the Democratic Party are willing to put sweat equity into the effort. One proposal pops into my inbox in early April 2025. It reads that we should "invite voters to personally inform us about how the government can be relevant to their lives and actually make their lives better."

That would be eye-opening! But my guess is the lesson would be for the person who asks the question, "What can the government do to make your life better?" They might hear "nothing," or to leave them alone, or to stop regulating things, or taxing them to death, or to stop making it harder to start or maintain a business.

This is the level of disconnect. The "haves" know, across the spectrum, left to right, what the government can do, from massive investment on one end of the activist agenda to massive tax cuts and deregulation on the minimalist end. Everyone else is caught in the middle, taking it from both sides. Can the government be relevant to their lives? I'm all for asking the question. But we have to accept the answers, and if they prove unsatisfying, we have to ask different questions, and, maybe more importantly, not judge the answers to whatever questions we ask.

It's a particularly fraught time to reach out to others. People everywhere pine for a simpler time when disagreements weren't so...heated. Some people enjoy a good political argument—but they can be, well, dangerous: to friendships, to family relations, to neighbors. Time tends to soften memories of past confrontations; we grow as individuals, or maybe we just get older.

And then I remember that in May of 1856, South Carolina Congressman Preston Brooks, a pro-slavery Democrat, crossed the Capitol and beat Massachusetts Senator Charles Sumner, an abolitionist, nearly to death with his cane, breaking it as repeated blows rained down, pinning Sumner under his desk, resulting in years of recovery for Senator Sumner, and a hero's welcome back home for Congressman Brooks.

REFLECTION

The political reckoning in this country has been a long time coming, and the reality is that the foundation of our democracy has aged and been neglected. The citizenry's lack of attention to its upkeep—a carelessness encouraged by those in power—has led to this structural crisis. The problem is we live in the political house that rests on this crumbling foundation.

This shrugging apathy alone would be enough to threaten our democracy, but coming at the time of the ever-quickening technology revolution allows information, if not always just the facts, to flow freely on countless media platforms, often spread with malevolent intent, undermining our centuries-old faith in our democratic systems. And faith might have been the last thing holding the crumbling foundation together. The word *democracy* itself has been made toxic, and who wants to salvage a contaminated space, with half our housemates unbearable and hostile? Maybe it's time to move on?

Such faith in secular institutions thus shaken, voters look beyond traditionally accepted political norms for something from those seeking power that will break through their cynicism and give them hope, change, or something new.

As previously discussed, when both a prominent journalist and the First Lady hinted that Franklin Roosevelt may have to assume dictatorial powers to meet the challenges he faced in 1933, Roosevelt held fast to the accepted boundaries of Constitutional authority. He attempted to bend it to his will at times—most famously an ill-fated attempt to pack the Supreme Court to further muscle up the New Deal—but he never risked a break.

But 2024 was not 1932, when one in four people were out of work. The discord is deeper, if more subtle, and speaks to the disconnect of today's voters and nonvoters, and their increasing isolation. If the Great Depression was a fight for survival, today it is about facing the loss, perhaps forever, of the American Dream.

Some I talk to cannot understand how we arrived at the political reality we are in, how the undermining of our political norms and the resulting disconnect could be so profound as to lead to the choices presented to us during the 2024 campaign, let alone the results themselves. It's cliché to say that in politics we need to meet people where they live, but it is the sad reality that we each have very little understanding about the places where people do live, beyond the metaphor of our democratic house, outside our own real neighborhoods but narrow viewpoints.

PART TWO

LOST COMMUNITY

CHAPTER FIVE

STUCK IN PLACE

Tiffany and her daughter's father, Calvin, both in their mid-forties, an age where family generations younger and older can tug at both ends of a person, just want to get away from Rockford, Illinois, where they both grew up. Even Wisconsin, just thirty miles north, would be better because Democrats don't control everything there. One of Calvin's buddies is pushing for Tennessee. But how to afford it? "They just make it so hard," Tiffany says, more than once, leaning wearily against the side of the booth, the lunch hour rush having passed at one of the six Machine Sheds across the Midwest. The regional chain was launched in 1978 with a "five-word Constitution," according to their website: "Dedicated to the American Farmer." The salad bar is a heap of coleslaw, with an equally impressive pile of the creamiest cottage cheese ever curdled. It's April 2024, and the Machine Shed is one institution that appears to have adhered to its constitution.

For Tiffany, the vision, and the lunch shift, aren't cutting it. She does not crave a return to the agrarian lifestyle. Her daughters spend too much time on their phones, she says. But she acknowledges that at the end of a long day, all she wants to do is escape to her Facebook page on her phone, which is lively in a way the counter isn't.

Calvin's on there too. He's launched a construction firm remodeling kitchens and bathrooms, which is getting some traction, and he posts time-lapsed videos of his work. "We'll see where it goes," Tiffany says.

But the deck seems stacked, and she doesn't like the idea that the decisions are made by others, people who haven't had the experiences she's had. She believes in rights and that her exercise of the Second Amendment is under attack by

Democrats from Chicago and beyond, and that people in far-off places should not decide whether she is allowed to buy a gun.

"I feel like the country has really gone to shit for people like me, a fucking lower-class person," she says, and if Trump can ameliorate that trend...well, Tiffany's voting for a president, not a pal. "Fuck it, he doesn't have to be our best friend."

Asked directly whether she thinks democracy might have passed its expiration date, Tiffany, who is open and unbothered about not following the news and had not heard about Trump's nod toward dictatorship, seems a little surprised and doesn't love it, but warms to the subject. A strongman who utilizes the Justice Department to go after citizens he doesn't like? "Everything has gotten so bad that if that's what it takes to get out of it, that's what I want," she says.

She's not particularly boastful about her Trump vote, but she is decidedly more vocal about what's playing out on campuses on the coasts. That day, the protesters occupying Ivy League buildings while demanding sustenance be delivered to them by means of their on-campus meal plans had gone viral. Nor would those protesting on campuses be impressed with statements and videos on Calvin's Facebook page—machine gun videos and fairly broad political proclamations, some of which have been questioned for accuracy by other Facebook commenters. There are no Machine Sheds on the campus of Columbia University, and God knows what they put in their cottage cheese at schools like that.

Keeping an attentive eye on her few remaining lunch customers who might need a to-go box or help getting to the car, Tiffany is curious about how many jobs the protesters have worked and what kind.

Her judgment has little to do with Gaza. Her Facebook page proudly sports a photo of a woman's manicured hand clutching a man's calloused, dirty one, with the message, in part, "You need to understand there will be days where he will most likely be tired and he'll barely have time to take a shower and give you a kiss and head to bed to get some much needed sleep to start it all over again the first thing in the morning. Do not take this kind of man for granted. He might come off a little rough around the edges because of his dirty hands and greased stained shirt, but this man will love you."

Rockford, Illinois, once the home for the leading manufacturer of furniture in the entire country, boasts a dinosaur museum with an impressive mastodon skeleton gracing the entrance. Tiffany can relate, her way of life heading the way of the mastodon—"a fucking lower-class person," she reiterates—because she waits tables and her partner has a job that callouses his hands. Jobs like that used to lead places: upward places or at least to roads out of Rockford.

And it is indeed hard to get ahead, let alone get out, and can they leave when the girls are young and having family nearby is so important? How can they move up, even just a little? Tiffany and Calvin, both of whom work hard and play by the rules in the fashion that reaped all manner of American idylls for generations before them, can't figure how to get out.

Arlie Russell Hochschild writes of this dispiritedness in *Stolen Pride: Loss, Shame, and the Rise of the Right* in her study of economic and cultural loss in Appalachia. "Almost everyone I spoke to in Eastern Kentucky quickly nodded when I asked whether they'd ever been put down for being hillbillies."[1]

Mayor Andrew Scott of Coal Run, Kentucky, told her, "When I travel, I see how a lot of people outside our area see us in eastern Kentucky. It's not just those photos of barefoot kids in ragged clothes and mussed hair that President Lyndon Jonhson showed the world. We know how we're seen, and they barely know us. Then we've got put-downs by liberal comedians and commentators making fun of us for being fat, drugged out, talking funny, being poor and prejudiced. Tell me, should I have to defend myself against outside critics like that?"[2]

A TINY FROG ON THE EDGE OF A MASSIVE POND

The landscape of western Washington State syncs perfectly with what folks hailing from outside the Pacific Northwest would imagine. To drive through Washington's 3rd Congressional District, which hugs the Oregon border on the south, abuts the Yakama Nation reservation to the east, and runs into the Pacific in the west, is like flipping continuously through a View-Master—it is a seemingly never-ending landscape of winding roads, lush coniferous forests, and rugged coastline laced with virid fields that are currently awaiting the wildflowers

---

1   Arlie Russell Hochschild, *Stolen Pride: Loss, Shame, and the Rise of the Right* (The New Press, 2024), 41.

2   Hochschild, *Stolen Pride*, 41.

of spring. This relentless wilderness—dotted with small towns and solitary log cabins as well as roadside eateries and motels that appear to be frozen in time—creates scenery so picturesque and so all-encompassing that it feels a bit like entering a movie set.

Indeed, there is a powerfully nostalgic aura to the place that leaves visitors yearning for summer camp, but with a gnarly cross-breeze and sheets of rain that blur the outlines of the peaks looming in the distance.

Today, South Bend declares itself "The Oyster Capital of the World," but at one time had an even loftier, if less molluscular, appellation. Originally billed as "The Baltimore of the Pacific" in the late 1890s, it had a promising start when the Northern Pacific Railroad identified it as the site for their ocean terminus on the Yakima and Pacific Coast branch line. The Panic of 1893, the nation's worst economic crisis until the Great Depression arrived, changed those plans, and the altered course was apparently irreversible. Today, "The Baltimore of the Pacific" numbers just over 1,500 inhabitants.

The gateway to Willapa Bay, South Bend, and its surrounding villages in Pacific County supply about one in every six American oysters. The bay itself is gorgeous—upon arrival in South Bend, a visitor emerging from a dense section of forest might be greeted by a massive bald eagle that has stretched its wings and swooped just a few feet over the windshield. Signage alerts to the presence of large herds of Roosevelt elk that roam the woods and fields abutting the bay.

At the beginning of February 2023, at the Chester Tavern in South Bend, bartender Tammy, in her late fifties, was happy to talk. She grew up "deep in the woods." Her daddy worked in the logging industry, so that was where they had to be.

The picture she painted felt bleak compared against the amazing vistas and cute markers of a thriving shellfishing culture; the depiction that Tammy provided of daily life for those living in the area was dark as well.

She described a brutally depressed local economy with a growing housing crisis. Back in 2010, Tammy was getting paid between $3 and $6 an hour for jobs and was paying $350 a month in rent for a three-bedroom/two-bath house that she loved. That felt fair enough to her. Today, she guessed that the same house would go for over $2,000 a month. Tammy was proud to have made the decision to buy a place for herself about a decade ago—she reckoned that if she hadn't bought back then, she'd be "sleeping under a bridge" today.

In 2016, Washington State voters passed Initiative 1433, which mandated gradual increases to the minimum wage. In 2023, it was up to $15.74 an hour. Tammy said that, if not for the law, places like the restaurants she often works in would still be paying her five bucks an hour. Nonetheless, she made clear that with rents increasing as quickly as they have and with the price of groceries, even $15.74 leaves people underwater.

The conversation briefly turned political. Tammy discussed the fact that many folks in the area are conservative and that the combination of President Trump and the pandemic brought out the worst in people—including people she has known for years and would never have imagined could be so nasty.

As a bartender during the pandemic, she was forced to navigate controversial masking and social distancing requirements that put customers on edge and made some downright ornery. Add in a few cheap beers and the "loudmouths" would earn the label. Tammy's guess, however, was that the loudest complainers probably didn't even vote. "You can't complain like that if you're not willing to go vote!"

Tammy said that even in the tiny logging community of her childhood, she could recall how big a deal Election Day was. Everyone went to the polls—it wasn't a question of whether you were going to vote. She can't remember if her parents were Democrats or Republicans, and perhaps with good reason. The first president she can recall them being really excited about was John F. Kennedy. After that, though, it was Ronald Reagan who they loved. And after him was Bill Clinton. A fairly broad ideological delta. Nowadays, Tammy feels like that sense of civic duty has melted away. People talk about politics, but there is a bitter tone to the whole ordeal.

Tammy seemed sad as she enumerated all of the challenges her community is facing. Logging and fishing jobs have disappeared, affordable housing is nowhere to be found, and an acerbic political discourse is driving neighbors apart from one another. The list goes on. She mentions crumbling roads, despite conversations about an impending additional forty cents on the state gas tax (a calculation some contest; the Tax Foundation think tank reported Washington had the fourth-highest gas tax of any state in the country, while a January 2025 report by the personal finance website NerdWallet ranked it fifth).[3] Tammy sneered as she described the beautifully kept highways and roads up near the state's capital of Olympia.

Asked how all of these challenges left her feeling, Tammy paused before deciding on her answer: "It makes you feel like a tiny frog just trying to stay afloat on the edge of a massive pond."

ABSOLUTELY NOT SEATTLE

In the tiny pond of Cathlamet, Washington, the barista Michelle stated very bluntly that their town of 532 souls is "absolutely not Seattle." She homeschools her children, and they rarely go to Seattle and Portland unless they have to. "We try to avoid them if we can; it's just not really my thing."

There aren't a lot of visitors from either place in Cathlamet either. Michelle said they'll get an occasional day-tripper from Portland, but other than that, they stay away and she's fine with it. Most of her customers are locals or tourists from farther away. People are also moving into the region and finding their way to her coffee shop, some all the way from California.

Cathlamet, sitting on the Columbia River, less than an hour and a half from Portland, Oregon, is the county seat in Wahkiakum County, but it is also the only town that's even incorporated. The biggest employer, she said, "has to be the school, or maybe the county." It's definitely not big tech like in the big cities. But they are also far away from their fur-trapping past, the business that first put it on the map in the early 1900s.

Christopher, living over the river in Astoria, Oregon, put it bluntly: None of the towns in the area are still working the jobs they were founded for. The oyster capital of South Bend was dealing with changes in logging and fishing, and there's not a lot of fur trapping in Cathlamet.

Astoria is navigating a transition to a tourism economy. At the mouth of the

---

3   Adam Hoffer, Jacob Macumber-Rosen, "Gas Taxes by State, 2024" Tax Foundation, August 6, 2024. Taxfoundation.org.
Taryn Phaneuf, "State Gas Taxes: What They Are And How Much You Pay" Nerdwallet, June 30, 2025. Nerdwallet.com.

Columbia where it meets the Pacific, the port city of 10,000 seems to rest on the edge of the world. Founded in 1811, it was the first permanent American settlement west of the Rockies.

The town has run the full arc of a northwest economy: Trapping, shipping, fishing, logging, and then the dwindling salmon population. In the 1940s, you'd find thirty canneries in the city, but global competition eliminated all of them by 1975. Timber faded with Canadian competition, mechanization, and environmental regulation.

Change is hard, particularly when the economy relies not on tangible things like fish, trees, and furs, but rather on the vagaries of the choices of tourists. "In the summer we get slammed," recounted Sam, a server and aspiring jazz singer. "I'll get to work to open up the restaurant, and there will already be people in line waiting to come in."

People are moving into Astoria from all sorts of places. The jazz singer from California who moved on the advice of a friend was a little shocked to find that, though the community is not "affordable," it was far better than what he was paying back home. Plus, he ended up with a lucky deal on his studio apartment.

Long Beach, Washington, has a similar story, boasting beaches and a fancy summer town aesthetic. "It's changed so much since I was a kid," recalled Kim, who lives just outside of town. "It's so much more built out." She described a video she watched of the main strip from the 1980s. "Only one building on the whole strip is still the same!" The changes are welcome, she says, depending on who you ask.

CONJURING HOUSE

In Burrillville, Rhode Island, I'm told I should visit the Conjuring House, the home that inspired a horror movie franchise, The Conjuring Universe. You could stay there, at least until recently, but they may have lost their occupancy license according to local scuttlebutt. I'm not familiar with the house or the films, but it's amazing the random cultural touchpoints you encounter, town to town, when traveling around the country.

More importantly, Burrillville, population 16,000 or so, is typical of the former mill towns that dot the Blackstone Valley, straddling the line between the non-ocean part of the Ocean State and the non-bay part of the Bay State of Massachusetts. The history of both states is very focused on the sea, but the mills of the mid-nineteenth century in the twenty-five communities that form the Blackstone River Valley National Heritage Corridor tell the compelling story of the arc of the American Industrial Revolution.

These towns have struggled in this century, remote from major highways and therefore the jobs that congregate along them, idle mill buildings that line the drive into the area, a lack of investment, stagnant populations. Until 2016, Burrillville was a marginal blue town. In 1988, Michael Dukakis bested George H. W. Bush 52 percent to 48 percent here, his pledge to take the "Massachusetts miracle" of a booming local economy national resonating with voters in a neighboring state.

But in 1992, Burrillville, while still giving Democrat Bill Clinton the win with 38 percent of the vote, gave independent candidate Ross Perot more votes than President Bush, with 32 percent. Voters in Burrillville took to Perot's candidacy, a nonpolitician promising a populist economic message. He had built a wildly successful business and said common sense things in his Texas plain speaking way that connected with people in Burrillville: "If you see a snake, just kill it—don't appoint a committee on snakes." Or, "When building a team, I always search first for people who love to win. If I can't find any of those, I look for people who hate to lose." And this: "The budget should be balanced, the treasury should be refilled, the public debt should be reduced, and the arrogance of public officials should be controlled." Perot could also deliver a working class-style takedown of those who maybe lived in the towns in Rhode Island that could see the ocean, who perhaps didn't have to work a real job for a living, "Action is greater than writing."[4] By 1996, the bloom on Perot's Texas rose had faded, as second acts of populist candidates often do, and Bill Clinton won the town outright, over both Perot and Kansas Republican Senator Bob Dole.

From 1996 through 2012, the winning percentage of the vote for Democratic nominees slipped from 55 percent to 53 percent, and in 2016 it fell off the cliff, Hillary Clinton losing Burrillville outright with just 35 percent of the vote. In the past three elections, Trump has climbed from 56 percent to 57 percent to 62 percent.

---

4   "Ross Perot Quotes," Quoteswise, accessed May 25, 2025, http://www.quoteswise.com/ross-perot-quotes-3.html.

FORGOTTEN MAIN STREET

"Remember when you could go to your local hamburger stand and get an incredible diner-style burger for a few bucks…?" reads the top of the menu at the Pascoag Cafe on Pascoag Main Street in Burrillville. It's just down the street from the Dunkin's, built on the site of the old lumber mill, where several enthusiastic believers are giving out "free Bibles" at a busy intersection. An occasional supportive horn honk causes them to give out a yell for Jesus. The accompanying lawn signs confirm that Jesus Loves Us.

The cafe menu asks me to "Stop by and try one, at $5.99," with "a generous side of shoestring fries cooked to perfection," and a twelve-ounce Bud or Bud Light draft included. I stop in ten minutes after the opening at noon. Several regulars have beaten me to the counter, one with a can of beer in front of him, but others are sipping Dunkin' iced coffees, and there's a movie I can't identify with Greg Kinnear that is capturing no one's attention on the big screen. I decide on the burger, hoping for truth in advertising, even if there is no mention of a gluten-free bun. Though I might pay later for this, I vow I will enjoy actual bread for the first time in a long time.

An alarm of some kind sounds for a couple of seconds, but no one moves. Again, and then three short bursts. The patron to my left, Bobby, in his early seventies, is hitting the horn on his motorized wheelchair. He gives me a wink, under his ball cap and behind a thick white beard and glasses. There is no one behind the counter to take my order so he's summoning someone from the back. The bartender, having a smoke outside by the front door, comes in, and Bobby apologizes—he didn't know she was on her break.

He comes over from the assisted living facility just up the street. "I can't stare at four blank walls all day long." He had a stroke a year ago and is conscious of the lack of clarity of his speech, but he's a lively conversationalist and clear to me. He's got a little Forrest Gump in him, a wanderer reflective of the times. He returned here to his hometown when his father passed, now some years ago, to care for his mother. But in between, he lived in San Diego, in the '70s, hitchhiking out there with a friend just to see it. On the way back, after the novelty of roller-skating to work wore off, he stopped in Colorado because of the mountains.

He's done maintenance work for a motel, been a cook in a restaurant, hauled potatoes from Maine to Louisiana, and tended a seventy-five-acre farm in

Maine, living with his girlfriend and her parents, chickens, and blueberries. The berry harvest is backbreaking work. The chickens take care of themselves and sometimes give you double yokes. Bobby spent eight bucks yesterday for six eggs. He misses the chickens, and he misses Maine, the farm close to Bar Harbor, the ocean a short distance.

I ask him why he left, on separate occasions, the climate of San Diego and the beauty of Maine without mentioning that both sound more exotic than Burrillville. He missed the four seasons in the former, and he split with his girlfriend in the latter. He's happy here, in that it's home and people know him. I ask him about the political shift over the past several elections from marginally Democratic to solidly Republican.

Bobby was enjoying telling me stories from the past, a stranger providing a blank canvas to paint his landscape of remembrance, and now I've introduced politics. He tells me he hasn't voted for a while, since he was summoned to jury duty up in Maine and didn't want that repeated; the case was too close to home. He knew both parties to the court action, side-by-side restaurants in a dispute that escalated to one party pulling a gun. Bobby thought the action was justified, and no one was shot; the verdict was so rendered. Certainly expecting no *quid pro quo*, he nonetheless ate breakfast *gratis* in a certain establishment for a period of time.

Bobby's not sure how to comment on Burrillville's reaction to the election, but he offers the word "disconnect." I'm not sure exactly the context, but I'm hyper-attuned to that word, which I hear a lot, and the gentleman to his left, who perks up at my question, nods.

Pascoag Cafe has a *Cheers* feel; the people are friendly, and it's OK if conversations are overheard. It's not a place to hide, but a place to relax and catch up. The bartender is as friendly as everyone else I've met here, tattoos running up her neck and spilling over her jaw in lacy spikes.

A middle-aged man tells the bartender that she never makes a burger for him. She says, "I made you one the other day!" He says, "But you wouldn't make me one last night." "It was 11:30! I already scraped off the grill," she says. His comeback falls flat: "But the menu says the kitchen is open till midnight." The patrons are on the bartender's side in this one. Even Norm never asked the *Cheers* staff for food at 11:30 p.m.

In small towns, it's hard to even find people to engage with, particularly in the winter, so I cycle through a few places that I know will bear fruit: coffee shops, bars, barber shops, antique stores, farm stands. My dog Willa is a secret weapon on the few occasions I can travel with her. Having a human companion helps too; it feels less awkward when approaching a stranger. Outside Boston, everyone is friendly but, to my Boston sensibilities, not that curious. Back home, we have to find a connection with every new person we meet. In most of the country, I think people view that as prying, and there is a respect that if you want to share personal details, you are the one who can choose to do so.

I tested this theory during a stop in Ohio. I said in Boston we would ask where you live, what you do, what parish you were born in. The woman thought, and said, "I think we'd ask what high school you went to."

If the Pascoag Cafe is an institution in town, Elayna's, farther down the street, and the brew pub across the street are newish and making a go of it, attracting people back to the town core. Her establishment might be new, but Elayna is a townie. She wants to make clear that she proudly lives in Burrillville, Rhode Island, even if their son, when he rears back in his yard swing, might break the plane of Douglas, Massachusetts. She and her husband are "meh" about their two-bedroom house itself, but do love Wallum Lake, a good-sized body of water close by that also straddles the state line, and being out on their pontoon boat. From October to March, she wonders why they live in their house, then spring arrives, and the lake comes alive.

Her husband delivers propane and is out of the house at 5 a.m. She has worked in restaurants since she was eighteen, behind the bar and in various jobs since. When a building became available on Pascoag Main Street—a bar on the first floor had opened in February 2020 and failed in the pandemic—she saw the opportunity to own her own place.

Two years in, Elayna's is doing fine. The place features an "I wonder if the wine thinks about me too" sign behind the bar and ad hoc food—charcuterie on the weekends, assorted premade sandwiches, or her husband will fire up a Crock-Pot of something. She opens up at four and has reliable staff who work part-time, though it's hard to find people. If there is a gap, she's there, and her husband joins on weekends.

There are positive signs on Pascoag Main Street. For instance, the brew pub has attracted food trucks that park outside. Chum's Electro & Hardware Shop is sadly closing after being open for generations (perhaps inevitably in a Home

Depot world), but the tired building may be redeveloped by George's Pizza and Pub next door.

Elayna shuts down political discussions around the bar quickly if she needs to. She is happy to have discussions and is a political person herself, so she likes a lively back and forth. But things are kind of toxic. A good friend makes comments about the "orange man" (Trump), and that statement sometimes acts like kindling. Elayna asks her friend why she would open with that and tries to promote respectful rules of engagement.

Politics wasn't something one discussed when she was growing up, though participation was encouraged, and she has voted since turning eighteen. She never knew who her parents voted for, just that it was important to do so.

A Trump voter, she posted on Facebook a picture of a boat parade in Narragansett Bay a few years ago, her parents' boat, and others, decked out in American, other patriotic flags, and Trump flags; there were a thousand boats or more. She loved the display and the day out on the water, as people do when we gather with others who feel the same way we do, and didn't post it as a way of shoving it in people's faces. Personally, my Facebook feed was, for a time, full of posts about pro-Harris rallies, the resistance, or Black Lives Matter protests after George Floyd's murder.

The next day, she got an angry direct message from a friend, who is gay, saying she wasn't the person he thought she was. She was stunned and replied that he shouldn't assume who she was because of her vote. She thinks Trump, while bombastic, wants to do right for America, and feels that he earned her vote. She did not vote for him to take away rights from her gay friends.

In the late fall of 2023, she came home one night, and her husband asked if she'd like to adopt a baby. She needed a minute, she told him, to process that question. The hour was late, and she had stayed to clean up the bar. A family friend, who had just had her fifth child, was finalizing a difficult divorce and felt she could not keep the child. Elayna was forty-two, had a nine-year-old son, had just started a business, and had a husband who left at 5 a.m. every day for his job.

They had hoped for a second child, but at forty-two? With a nine-year-old? They felt for their friend but decided their son had to be on board with this if they were going to upend the family dynamic in this way. They explained the situation to him, knowing they would be introducing a six-month-old brother in quick order without the usual nine months to prepare a soon-to-be older sibling. He replied, "He needs us."

She's just finished this story, late sun splashing through the windows, when a second customer, Maureen, comes in for a glass of red wine and a bite to eat. She has an enthusiastic bark in response to the news. Elayna mentions she's doubled the restaurant's space. "Wait! What?" Maureen exclaims as she whips around to take a look. She and her husband moved here—well, technically to neighboring Douglas across the border—from Newton, Massachusetts, where they could get more house, and cheaper, now that her husband has retired. Plus, she could finally get the horse she had dreamed about. A lifelong rider, she would do so when she could, around the South Shore of Massachusetts, but now, any time she wants, she's off on the trails, a dream come true.

She is a property manager for a public housing authority and started off after college working for an investigation firm based in the Charlestown Navy Yard in Boston, a profession better known by private eye, though it was more routine than TV portrayals. But her experience provides interaction with a lot of people, and a lot who struggle with life.

It brings a certain skepticism, which some might feel is a cynical take at times, in people's motivation. She is inclined to question and wonders what the real story is with Signalgate (the *Atlantic* editor added to a "principles call" using the messaging app, Signal, about the US attack on the Houthi, which is dominating the news).

I mention Ross Perot and she says, "I think I voted for him!" but back then, she would have been in Newton, where she would have been in the distinct minority. She moved here for the open space, the trails available for riding, the affordability compared to Newton, and not because of the kindred politics. It's just an added bonus.

NOTHING WITHOUT PROVIDENCE

Democrat Seth Magaziner has represented the Second Congressional District in Rhode Island, which includes Burrillville, since 2023, winning with just over 50 percent of the vote in the more conservative of the two congressional districts in the state, against a popular Republican mayor of the city of Cranston.

Magaziner is "to the manor born" of a fashion; his father, Ira, was the senior advisor for policy under President Clinton and helped to craft the failed precursor to the Affordable Care Act, derided as "Hillarycare," and now focuses on the Bill, Hillary, and Chelsea Clinton Foundation's international initiatives.

The younger Magaziner is a graduate of Milton Academy in Massachusetts, Brown University in Rhode Island, and has a master's in business administration from the Yale School of Management in Connecticut. Before election to Congress, he was the elected Treasurer of Rhode Island, where he established the Rhode Island Infrastructure Bank (RIIB) to finance green infrastructure projects.

When he ran for Congress, he did not live in the district he hoped to win. This is not uncommon, and unlike other offices, there is no requirement that you live in the district that you wish to represent. District lines change every ten years, sometimes wildly, depending on the states, so there isn't a lot of geographic cohesion in most of the country.

But in Rhode Island, with only two districts, each taking a chunk of the hyper-Democratic capital city of Providence, with Gabe Amo in the First District, hugging the wealthy, left-leaning coast district, and Magaziner with the rest of the geography in the smallest state in the union, the contrast is evident. Of the fourteen towns Donald Trump carried in Rhode Island, Magaziner represents ten.

During his first race, he and his wife bought a house in Cranston, the hometown of his Republican opponent, the former mayor, and said they would move there—again, not a requirement, but an important gesture, I suppose, to the people who live where you hope to represent. He listed it as his address on the ballot in 2024.

WPRI-TV in Providence asked him why, though he had purchased the Cranston home in 2023, he and his family had not yet moved into it and to the district he represents, from his home on the east side of Providence, in his colleague's district. In late March 2025, a full two years after buying the home, he gave the following statement: "My wife and I bought a house in Cranston with the intention of renovating it and moving there. But since then, our family circumstances have changed. My wife has a new job that requires her to commute to Cambridge [Massachusetts], we had a new baby, and the house in Cranston needs more work than we anticipated. Therefore, we have decided that the best thing for our family at this time is to stay in our house in Providence."[5]

Unlike a lot of people I talk to, Congressman Magaziner isn't stuck in place solely because of costs, housing primarily, but because of what also affects a lot of people: what works for the family. Additionally, a lot of people don't have the luxury to stay where it works for their family if their job requires them to be elsewhere. Magaziner *does* have this luxury, and where it works for him just doesn't happen to be in the congressional district he represents in Washington.

Rhode Island is small in population and land mass and has an intimate, familiar vibe. A local chef, dubbed the "Calamari Ninja," was the sensation of the 2020 roll call of the states at the Democratic National Convention that nominated Joe Biden. Even pandemic-era conventions have work to do—you have to "meet" to approve a party platform, and you can't leave until you have nominated candidates for president and vice president. But do you accomplish this when thousands gathered in a large arena would be contrary to the party's message on social distancing and might result in the actual illness, hospitalization, or death of the party elite, who skew older—in some cases dramatically so—than the general population?

The virtual call of the states from Alabama to Wyoming featured reports from each, highlighting the best they had to offer. Enter, via video, the Calamari Ninja himself, Executive Chef John Bordieri of Iggy's Boardwalk in Warwick, Rhode Island, clad entirely in black, his salt-and-pepper beard covering a chiseled jaw, framed by the windswept coast of pebbled beach and boundless sea, holding a plate of fried calamari in his black gloved hands. He holds it out, silently and seductively, while Little Rhody's votes in 2020 are cast for the Biden/Harris ticket. The bit goes viral and the Democrats swoon; it's so…real.

Four years later, Bordieri told a reporter from the *Associated Press*, "I'm a Trump supporter, to be honest with you. But I was told to tell everybody that I'm independent."

Michael Dukakis won Rhode Island in 1988, and the state has voted blue since. But looking forward to 2026 and 2028, the Democrats would be smart not to take for granted the voters in the Ocean State, particularly the ones who don't have oceanfront property.

---

5   Eli Sherman, Tim White, "Magaziner won't move into his congressional district after all." WPRI, Providence, RI, March 28, 2025.

CHAPTER SIX

STICKING WITH PLACE

If NAFTA re-sorted the economy on the global and national scales, it upended it in a lot of American communities built around manufacturing and other traditional industries that found themselves in a changed marketplace. While NAFTA grew the overall economy in the United States, Mexico, and Canada, uniting the three nations competing with the European Union and China globally, its sharpest impacts were felt locally in American towns dependent on the policies of the past that had worked for them, even when the powers that be knew that the global economy needed to adjust or fail.

Place is central to who we are. A high percentage of Americans live their lives close to where they grew up and, even if they relocated as adults, that place remains "where we're from." We cannot ignore the impact the transition to the global economy has had on our relationship with "place." As NAFTA's long tail began to wag the increasingly shaggy dog of the American economy, the digital revolution pulled each of us into ourselves, finding community online and not out there. We became disconnected from money-fueled politics that increasingly moved away from person-to-person contact. As a result, in a lot of places I visit, there is a disconnect in the community, where, speaking politically, the connection should be the strongest.

A midsize city mayor once told me his day was all potholes, garbage cans, and shade trees. We get most of our services from the city or town we live in. And in conversations, the strongest awareness of the role of government in people's lives is with the executive: the president, a governor, or mayor. The legislative process at the federal, state, and local level is more of a mystery, often opaquely process-oriented and technical. The focus group back in Massachusetts didn't quite know how to answer a question about the legislature. This has spilled down to the local level, where people feel disconnected from the places where they live or grew up.

In Mt. Vernon, Illinois, south of the capital of Springfield, John, in his late thirties, is the third generation to run his used-car business, but a recent reclassification of a lot of land he owns, from agriculture to commercial, has increased his annual property tax bill from $1,250 to $6,700—up *436 percent*. What strikes me is not his frustration over this but his seeming acceptance. He seems more baffled than angry. His current plan is not to fight city hall but to move his third-generation business to Western Tennessee, he says—greener grass.

Or bluegrass. Driving south from Mt. Vernon and over the Ohio River to Kentucky, I stop at the Chamber of Commerce in Paducah, home to the National Quilt Museum. A woman comes in looking for a welcome packet, having just moved from southern Illinois. She came to escape rising taxes but also out of a desire for her and her husband to live in a growing community with entertainment and dining options. Outside, Paducah's downtown is filling up with quilters for an annual convention, a local pub welcoming them for a bourbon tasting. It's 10:30 a.m.

4,000 PERCENT

Taylor, Texas, prospered in cattle and cotton when the railroad came through 150 years ago. A century later, it voted against allowing the interstate to come through, and Round Rock, to the west, reaped, allowing Interstate 35 to pass close. Tech HQs now dot the landscape there.

Today, Taylor is a quaint town with frontier-era buildings sprung up around a handsome town square with a bus station where young guys on bikes pop wheelies and talk in Spanish with older guys waiting for the bus. Houses fringing the square are decorated meticulously for Halloween 2023. The theater hasn't seen a show for a long time, but an optimist would see potential in the wide main street and empty storefronts.

The clerk in the sporting goods store moved here after thirty years living in Austin and working as a programmer for the US Geological Survey. He's here for the peace and quiet, enjoying his retirement part-time job, and happy to be away from the frustration of living in Austin—the beneficiary and casualty of a massive influx of people and money in the last fifteen years. He says that it's impossible there to get the police to respond to routine traffic accidents, unless one is blocking an intersection, or even for a house break-in. They prefer to have private insurance handle those incidents.

Around the corner, the Ideal Barber shop has a shrine to John Wayne and reruns of *The Virginian* playing on what might be my grandparents' TV. For twenty-five bucks, you can get a straight-edge razor through warm shaving cream in addition to a haircut. "Traffic is getting busy," the barber tells me, and it might be time to "tell the wife that [they] should move farther east." He got caught in traffic the other day, backed up for a high school football game, one light to the next.

The Man Store on Main, next to the sporting goods store, is two years old. The shop has a select feel, unique shirts and shorts, the prices are decent, and it seems geared to a younger demographic.

Ross, the young proprietor, tells me the store is doing well, an investment for his parents, and a good opportunity for him, in his mid-twenties and ready for the responsibility of running it. His dad is still in the oil business. They're back here after stints in Amarillo and Beijing and wanted to have something local to focus on.

I mention my conversation with the owner of the Man Store to the sporting goods clerk when I stop back in to buy a T-shirt promoting the local team, and he nods and says that owner is related to the owner of his business. He says everyone is related. The five members of the City Council have deep roots in town. The mayor is the great-nephew of a famous cowboy who toured with Will Rogers.

Just outside downtown, on the way to Hutto, a flock of cranes works on the first of nine Samsung manufacturing plant buildings that may eventually employ 18,000 people, just more than the current population of Taylor.

The barber isn't a fan of Samsung coming to town. He says that small towns aren't equipped to handle such a massive development. Where will they get the water? He wonders what Taylor will be like in ten years but says he won't be around to see it. He doesn't say if this is contributing to his gaze farther east or a quick calculation of the actuarial tables.

The other barber nods in agreement, but the gentleman in his chair says nothing. After the gentleman leaves, my barber tells me he's "the banker. Several generations." The banker recently took over, after his father, who was in his late seventies "caught COVID" and passed. I take the banker's silence to mean he's less concerned where Samsung might get their water. You have to check your words when someone has a straight-edge razor to your neck.

There is a movement to change the city charter for "more transparency," though not because of the City Council approval of the Samsung development or lack of study of water availability. The move is fueled by the Council's decision to ignore their handpicked compensation consultant's recommendation and instead increase the councilors' own compensation "4,000 percent," from $25. I do the quick math in my head and decide the declaration is hyperbolic, but the main objection seems to be on the process. If there was much debate over development, and the lack of process, no one mentions it.

A pay grab is easy fodder fueling outrage and voter action. The consequences of a water grab, in a place with not a lot of it, is maybe too consequential to galvanize action.

Taylor thrived with the railroad and survived the highway. Ten years from now will tell how it adapts to Samsung. There will be more traffic, no doubt. And the shrine to John Wayne will be gone. Or moved east.

A drift away from the ability or willingness to tap into the vagaries of local government means that we're detaching ourselves from the decisions that can have the most immediate impact on our lives.

DON'T FENCE ME IN

I was told a story that may or may not be true. Several years ago, a town north of Reno was holding a public meeting to approve a casino. Speaker after speaker rose to object. They didn't move here to live next to a casino. Finally, an older man, frustrated by his neighbors, said that he too had moved here to get away from someplace else, long before they did, and he didn't move here to find himself having to live next to any of them either.

Nevada is both wide open and very city-fied, ranking fifth in urban density, just behind Massachusetts. But less than 1 percent of its land is urbanized, a full

85 percent being owned by the federal or state government with a portion being sovereign nation land.

At the Old World Coffee Lab, with a slight hipster vibe, south of the Truckee River in Reno, Nevada, a longtime political operative and native Nevadan talks about the escape, the *raison d'etre* that unites non-natives who make up 75 percent of the state's population. Their aim is to flee traffic or smog or cultural changes, and they're attracted by the open vistas and libertarian spirit—not to mention the good jobs at good wages.

The current governor, Republican Joe Lombardo, rocketed out of the primary when Donald Trump endorsed him in 2022 and beat incumbent Democrat Steve Sisolak, a "good guy" I'm told, but rejected because he embraced Democratic directives "from Washington." Voters wondered if he had been co-opted by them, for higher ambition.

Nevada is a service industry state dependent on non-natives from other states and other countries. Recently, two separate phenomena have combined to influence public opinion. Videos of lines of migrants crossing the border have an impact here, and crime of a specific type, the recent incidents of numbers of people carrying out goods from stores in a coordinated robbery, a variation of the smash-and-grab, gets noticed, I'm told.

In a military memorabilia store (heavy on World War II keepsakes), just off the main street in Carson City, the owner tells me his expertise is in armaments. I'm standing in his cluttered space trapped between the knife display and the World War II uniforms as he tells me his story, moving here from California, where policy changes killed the movie industry in the state. He needed proximity to supply armaments for movies, but when movie shoots became mobile, he could relocate anywhere.

He has a bigger house, more land, property taxes of around $2,500 dollars, and is happy not looking back. Detaching yourself from a company town, the movie capital of the world, while trying to remain in its orbit can be a scary prospect. But the industry is so diffused now, whether California killed it or not, or it just responded to the siren's allure of other states' financial incentives, that he finds this perch to be quite to his liking.

Space is at the center of the issue for the protesters assembling in front of the State Capitol in Carson City, a little more than thirty miles south of Reno. They have been here every Wednesday afternoon for six years. The Wild Horse

Preservation League seeks to end the federal Bureau of Land Management program of "killing wild horses from helicopters to free up the land for cattle grazing."

"We think," one says, "that there is enough land for cattle and horses." I attempt to be neutrally agreeable and say, "There does seem to be a lot of land." When asked, I tell them I'm from Massachusetts, and she declares, "I'm from Longmeadow!" Which prompts another to say, "I'm from Westfield!" The first turns to the second and says, "You're from Massachusetts?" A third chimes in, "Last week it was three Geminis, this week it's three people from Massachusetts." It makes sense to me that three people from Massachusetts would think there is enough wide-open space in Nevada for a lot of things. I can't speak for Geminis.

The Capitol sits on a main north-south route through town, with steady traffic. It's hard to cross for a pedestrian as the traffic is going at a pretty good clip. Some passing drivers honk their horns in support of the "stop killing wild horses" signs. Then a car slows, a window is rolled down and a woman says, "You're only hurting the situation."

The leader, sitting on the stone ledge, six years into this crusade, asks me what she said, as it was delivered in a neutral tone. I tell her, and she says they get one negative comment a day. What are the odds I'd be there at the right time to hear it?

The legislature is not in session and hasn't been in a while, but there they are every Wednesday. I ask if this protest is having any effect with state-elected officials. "They know who we are."

SNAPSHOTS FROM ARIZONA

People come into Arizona from California," I'm told by a couple in Sierra Vista, Arizona, a growing community southeast of Tucson heading toward the border. The husband continues, "They come with their ideas and opinions, and they get to Arizona and want to make it more like California."

"We're conservatives," his wife says, "and don't forget, it's not just California. It's Seattle and Portland. People come here from all of these places with their politics, and then there's us."

They talk about how silly it is, to leave somewhere that you don't like and then come to Arizona wanting to make it the same as where they left. He's semi-retired, after a career as a military officer. She's a fully retired schoolteacher. Of all the places they traveled during his military days, Germany was their favorite, but for semiretirement, they chose Sierra Vista. All four of their kids went to Arizona State University. After college, they moved all over the country but will come back to Arizona soon, they're told. The Grand Canyon State is the place the whole family names when they're asked about "home."

When I stop at a coffee shop in Tucson before heading south, the owner mentions that 20 percent of the proceeds will go toward a women's abuse charity. She moved here from the East Coast and is excited about the idea of more people moving in from the West Coast. "People here are really narrow-minded," she says.

She hoped that the mass migration from California would challenge that narrow-mindedness. "A lot of people think they're progressive, but they really have no idea of the meaning of the word." In the aftermath of George Floyd's death, she says, people didn't know what they were fighting for. "Maybe they just wanted to get on TV."

Further south in Bisbee, Arizona, Seth owns a coffee roasting business and also practices an unusually generous business model. "You can just hang out here and drink coffee for free all day if you'd like." He doesn't sell retail, just mail order. People with new money from California are here. "They sell their homes for millions and come down here to invest." The parking lot across from his shop just sold to an investor planning on putting up a gate to charge people for parking there.

Another had bought a series of units "and was going to start charging rent per square foot at exorbitant rates."

"It's no Aspen," he said. "There's not any skiing, not much hiking, no recreational water spots. Nothing. And people want to do it anyway. It just takes away from the charm." The town is full of charm, with only five thousand or so people living in Bisbee now that the mines have been shut down. The community is tight-knit.

"Everyone knows everyone's first name. Like, there aren't even last names," he said. I ran into another Bisbee local during an excursion to Tombstone—yes, *that* Tombstone. Unprompted, she said the same about Bisbee. After a bit more chitchat, she told me that Seth is a friend. There are no shoot-outs at the O.K. Corral; based on whom I run across, there's just good people.

There was also the bartender, a tourist in Tombstone, originally from Chicago and now living in Mesa, who told me he can't afford rent anymore with the increases he blamed on Californians, his rent having increased from $900 to $1,500 per month.

Back in Sierra Vista, the conservative couple is chatting with a man currently living in California but considering a move, which brings him to town. "He's fine though," the husband assures me. "He's a conservative."

It's a random sample, but most aren't natives. At the Tumacácori National Historical Park in Santa Cruz County, Ranger Rick, I kid you not, greets me in human form, outdoor fit and in his early sixties. He warns against the western fence lizard, a native to Arizona, as they like to sit on fences to get a good vantage point. They are particularly flamboyant this time of year. Rick has a touch of this, speaking through his walrus of a mustache.

He's a native, like the lizard and unlike most humans I encounter, worried about his own set of external forces, and what it might mean for his home and its future.

Rick used to ride horses clear across the desert. He and his high school friends would even ride down and hop over the border into Mexico to swim in the natural pools. "You can't explore like that anymore," he says. And it's not just the fences. You could get shot. By a rancher, perhaps, or anyone else who felt you shouldn't be there. Rick gets it, though. "We've all got to protect what's ours." He's a proud gun owner, too.

Rick's brother works for a security company that transports undocumented immigrants to be deported. He drops them off at the wall. While spending so much time down there, he fell in love with a woman from Mexico's Sonora region. He tried everything he could to bring her into the United States. He offered to pay a bond, whatever it took. But the documentation process was too much. So he paid someone to smuggle her past the wall.

Rick thinks the border wall was such a waste of money. Not only is it ineffective, but it's destructive. The lights along the top of the wall are killing the microorganisms that support the agave plants growing nearby.

Rick is a conservative. He's also a conservationist. Words are funny, and people are complicated.

STICKING WITH MY NEW PLACE

If seemingly everyone, except Rick, is from somewhere else, everyone seems to be really quite pleased to be here. The woman at the rental car check-in counter came here for college and graduated last year. She's going to join the police academy next year, but she failed her polygraph test when they asked her about whether she's smoked weed, so her application is on hold. Someone at the Phoenix Police Department told her that's no problem though. Just wait until it's been two years since she's used it, and they'll take her then. She's happy to wait.

They're desperate for people, she tells me. She's not excited to be a cop, but the $10,000 signing bonus and the promise that they'll pay for law school someday is too enticing. And maybe she'll love the work. Plus, anywhere is better than LA.

The guy sitting alone at the bar in the brewery in Mesa is in head-to-toe Seattle Seahawks gear. He's lived here for decades though. People come to Arizona because wherever they're from is a disaster, he says. That's why he's here. However, he has lots of concerns. The border is a big issue, especially who is coming across it. "I didn't have to deal with that where I'm from," he points out, Canadians not exactly pouring across the border.

He's worried about universities and "what they are pushing on kids." He thinks it's shocking that people in other places, like where he's from in Seattle, don't respect other people's property. He just can't understand that. He bought a new house in 2017 for $350,000 and sold it last year for $750,000. He's downsizing now.

The bartender from the brewery is from Chicago. Arizona changed his life, but he's not sure he can afford it forever. The young man canvassing for a ballot initiative in downtown Tucson is from Massachusetts. "Screw that place, though," he says. "Way too expensive." The cab driver to dinner is from Virginia, and from somewhere else before that. The return cab driver is from Egypt. He says people up in Phoenix don't say hello to you. He wonders if they're too worried about their jobs to notice other people.

The woman who works for the Tucson Recreation Department was born in California but moved here when she was little, so she's basically from here. She feels like she's from here, at least—a "desert rat." She's soliciting feedback from the community on the city's plans for upgrades to a local park, clipboard in hand.

A woman and her husband selling prickly pear cactus art on the side of the road are from Maryland, just outside D.C. They moved here three years ago. They can't stand Maryland, and they *really* can't stand the people there. "It's really the worst," she says. They love it here, though, so they understand why people are coming. But people should really stop trying to change Arizona once they get here. They want to turn it into something else—something that the prickly pair really doesn't like. They came here to get away from that stuff. "Those people should really just go back to wherever they came from," she says.

MONUMENTS

At Cameron's, several blocks southeast off the Courthouse Square in Cleveland, Tennessee, a bottomless cup of coffee is $1.99. I'm asked my order, followed by a pause, and then I'm asked if I want a menu. Outed as not a regular, I can report that the hash browns are just right—crispy and filling the whole plate, the perfect foundation for two eggs sunny side up. They're open on Memorial Day, but the woman behind the counter wasn't happy about it. Last year they made too much money to go back to being closed on holidays.

On the opposite side of the square, a Confederate soldier, in granite with rifle in hand, casually stands sentry on his pedestal looking north, up Ocoee Street, toward the mall. I confess I stopped on my way to Cameron's to see if there was any Memorial Day display adorning the statue, but all was quiet. I have visited family in this town for thirty years and driven by this monument dozens of times, but I never stopped to look at it.

This quiet holiday morning, I inspect it and notice an obelisk just slightly shorter behind, to the memory of three young Cleveland scions who died in an 1889 train wreck in Virginia, east of Roanoke, while on their way to New York and then to Paris to prospect business opportunities. Their ill-fated journey was so momentous—such an exotic odyssey for local young men— that two thousand people came to see them off from the Cleveland station.

William Steed co-owned the local pharmacy with his brother and was travelling with two textile heirs, William Marshall of the Marshall Planing Mill and John Hardwick of the namesake woolen mill downtown, which would become the largest in the world by the time of the Wall Street crash of 1929.

In the early morning of July 2, the railroad embankment at Newman's Fill collapsed, "plunging it into the washout. Survivors remained stranded for hours, while passengers trapped inside died in a fire that ripped through the wreckage," according to the account posted on the Historical Marker database.[1] Steed's was the only body recovered, returned, and buried in Cleveland.

Forty years earlier, the people of Cleveland overwhelmingly voted against secession. As a result, the Confederate Army occupied it through the fall of 1863, as it was on an important rail line. That link to points south and north allowed Cleveland to rebound faster than many other Southern cities at the war's end.

The city looked to the young men, their grand adventure, establishing business connections in New York and Paris, as the town's ticket to further prosperity. One year later, on the anniversary of their deaths, their friends placed the monument at the top of the most prosperous street. Twenty years later, the Daughters of the Confederacy placed the soldier directly in front of it.

At a service I attended in April 2022 at the Faith Family Church in North Canton, Ohio, guest speakers Dave and Ashley Willis took us through an exercise. Dave asked us to notice everything in the sanctuary that was red and then asked us to close our eyes. When they were closed, he asked us to think about everything blue that we could remember.

Sometimes we see what we want to see in a place we live or visit. Sometimes we see what we are meant to see. Visitors to Cleveland, Tennessee, for the past century have seen the Confederate statue while driving past the grand homes on Ocoee Street, placed there well after the war, to be a symbol of the reimagining of the war as one of a noble fight for states' rights, preservation of heritage, and resistance to post-Reconstruction integration.

But the story of Cleveland is better represented by the memorial hidden in plain sight right behind it. Not to the memory of a lost cause, but one to lost promise, standing sentry over a prosperous city, who took up their cause and moved forward, not back, in the face of devastating tragedy.

---

1   "1889 Thaxton Train Wreck Historical Marker," November 2, 2024, https://www.hmdb.org/m.asp?m=84781.

HALL OF FAME CITY

The Pro Football Hall of Fame in Canton, Ohio, is a destination trip for a lot of people, to the point that the shrine's operators get away with charging for parking in addition to the hefty entrance fee, though I can't see a legitimate reason to do so other than that they can.

They don't charge for parking at the William McKinley Presidential Library and Museum, but we still walk to it from our hotel downtown, through a residential neighborhood of bungalows and turn-of-the-century American Foursquares. McKinley's final resting place sits 108 steps up from the curb, and several joggers take advantage of the granite StairMaster to quicken the heart rate in this flat part of the country.

McKinley is one of four men to serve during war, make it home safely, and then be assassinated while commander in chief. His final resting place, behind the locked crypt gate at the top of those stairs, is impressive. His museum is like worthy efforts across the country without adequate budgets: mannequins in period costume, standing next to period artifacts, with small descriptions that tell the story of the McKinleys chronologically.

Donald Trump has fixated on McKinley, his protectionist tariffs but also his expansionist policies, which were egged on by Theodore Roosevelt even before McKinley selected T.R. as his reelection running mate in 1900, replacing the late Garret Hobart, who died while in office. And it is true that the United States was a transformed country after McKinley's presidency. One wonders if Donald Trump channels his inner McKinley in his desire for additional lands: Greenland, the Panama Canal, maybe even Canada. During the Spanish-American War in 1898, the United States seized Guam and Puerto Rico, which it still possesses, as well as Cuba and the Philippines.

The average home price in the Canton area is $139,000. I point this out to the newly engaged young colleague travelling with me from Boston and quickly calculate a monthly mortgage in my head with 10 percent down, well below what it would cost to rent half the square footage back home. He's quick with his response: "But then I'd have to live in Canton."

This is no reflection on the city. Other than the spring cold snap, there is a lot to like about Canton. But there is no job luring him here, no family reason to return here, no climate to entice someone so young. Place is so central to who we are that it cements most people statically, geographically, and often socioeco-nomically, for generations. His job, his family, his life's connections are in a very expensive part of the country, where the prospects of home ownership are more distant than here in Canton. But he would need a more compelling reason than a reasonable monthly mortgage to move. And so it is for most people.

FAMILY TIES

Henry, a sixty-something-year-old government contractor, moved back to Canton to take care of family. His job has him travelling back and forth to far-flung destinations, so home base can be anywhere reasonable. His son served a prison sentence of three years for theft but is now out and doing okay, Henry says. The lad has an apartment and a job, but only because he lied on the applica-tions for both, checking "no" to the question of past convictions.

Henry's here now, neither father nor son in a position to be far away from each other, and it gives Henry a chance to think about his next work chapter. There is no doubt that the work he does, travelling all over to sometimes dan-gerous places where the government needs civilian contract support, has taken a toll on him and on his family. He works in supply chain and has seen both the inefficiencies and the effectiveness of US government overseas operations. He thinks maybe he could apply what he knows at a local government level.

Because he paid $150 a month for the phone charges, Henry was able to keep in touch with his son while he served his time in the nearby for-profit prison. But he couldn't bring in sneakers from outside, instead buying them from the prison-selected vendor. He has thoughts about the government off-loading the housing of prisoners to for-profit companies.

At one of the entrances on the Canton city line, there is a "Heroin Aware-ness" billboard, reporting the year-to-date numbers in the city: 489 overdoses, 135 lost lives, and 704 lives in treatment. It's March 11, 2022. I wonder if the numbers are wrong or haven't been zeroed out from totals from last year.

Henry's son's drug addiction had long been spinning out of control. After his conviction, Henry discovered emails from him talking about robbing a bank. When his son was released, Henry confessed to him that, before leaving for an extended trip to Afghanistan, he tipped off the police to his son's crime. Henry told him he feared if he hadn't, he would have returned to find his son dead of an overdose or from a hail of bullets.

THERE'S NOTHING HERE FOR YOU

In *Hillbilly Elegy*, a book I found important to read when it came out in 2016, then relatively unknown author JD Vance makes the case that successful people who grew up where he did had a thumb on the scale to counter challenges out of their control. His was his grandmother.

At the only home I have ever lived, where all of my ancestors have ever lived, the Commonwealth of Massachusetts, I mention to a member of Congress that the Democrats' message to the residents of all the Cantons across the country seems to be: "You should move. There's nothing here for you."

He replies, "Maybe they should." This isn't meant as cruel, but realistic. It's what someone who has the ability to do so would do. Hillary Clinton wasn't wrong, if perhaps a little off-key on the nettlesome politics, when she said that coal jobs were gone.

If you lose your job in Ohio, let's say in the coal industry, the remedy you might hear from Democrats is that you should be retrained for the new clean economy. And that might lead someone to think: *I'm a fifty-five-year-old who needs three years to get the last child out of the house and another five until I can live off retirement. I don't need to be retrained. Or move to where the jobs are. I need a job, here, where I live.*

Democrats have lost the connection to *place*. Take a look at the last few electoral maps—even in years in which the Democratic candidate triumphed—to witness just how much of the country senses this disorientation emanating from the party that once fashioned itself as the choice of the common folk. The maps are awash in red, with dashes and dots of blue; if we converted from an Electoral College system to measuring votes by landmass, the Democratic Party would cease to exist altogether. As the party grew increasingly disconnected in their rhetoric and at the polls from voters in the South and broad middle of the country, it disengaged from the places where they lived as well.

NAFTA and its successors didn't help. Identity politics don't help. Insulting voters—telling them the dreams on which they were raised and which they have cherished are now in the national dustbin—really doesn't help.

I stop around the corner from Joe Biden's childhood home in Scranton, Pennsylvania, to fill my car up with gas. There was no "I did that" sticker of Biden pointing at the price of gas, spinning fast as the pump dings again and again. But it costs $75 to fill up my car when I'm there, three years into his administration.

His old neighborhood is lovely. I can see why it's such a touchstone for him, and it seems like a great place to grow up. It looks like the one I live in. I believe the people who bought Biden's childhood home from his grandfather Ambrose Finnegan still live there. There is a notice on the curb reading "From This House to the White House." The future president was ten when they moved, his father having lost his job. We are welcome to take photos from the street or sidewalk.

I take a picture and then look the address up on Zillow. It is the same square footage and lot size as the house I live in. But you can buy ten houses on this street for every one on my street in Belmont. This place may ground Joe Biden in his political philosophy, but he is a long way away from living here—or knowing what it's like to live here and buy groceries and gas and keep the lights on, while hoping your job holds on long enough to get that last kid launched or make it to the point at which Social Security kicks in.

In the keynote address at the 1984 Democratic Convention, former New York Governor Mario Cuomo discussed the role of the Democratic Party in this country's history. "Ever since Franklin Roosevelt lifted himself from his wheelchair to lift this nation from its knees—wagon train after wagon train—to new frontiers of education, housing, peace; the whole family aboard, constantly reaching out to extend and enlarge that family; lifting them up into the wagon on the way."[2] Cuomo quoted Roosevelt to remind Democrats in 1984 that it wasn't enough to oppose the policies of Ronald Reagan. The Democrats needed a plan of their own.

Reagan won the 1984 race against former Vice President Walter Mondale in a historic landslide. Mondale perhaps sealed his fate at that same convention when he said, "Mr. Reagan will raise taxes and so will I. He won't tell you. I just

---

2   Michael E. Eidenmuller, "American rhetoric: Mario Cuomo - Keynote Address at the 1984 Democratic National Convention, accessed May 25, 2025, https://www.americanrhetoric. com/speeches/mariocuomo1984dnc.htm.

did."[3] Mondale, of course, wasn't wrong about the need to raise revenue to hedge the ballooning debt, which ballooned under Reagan's second term.

But the voters weren't up for an eat-your-peas, there-is-no-Santa, cold-showers-build-character presidency, and they weren't up for a return to Jimmy Carter in the person of his vice president. And the Democratic core was loath to chase after those lunch-bucket Democrats Mario Cuomo waxed about. They had been gathered and lifted up into the party wagon train, rewarded with well-paying jobs and the American dream, brought to you by the New Deal and the Great Society, and they chose to jump, the ingrates, at the first sign of the charlatan B-movie actor. Good riddance, sneered the Democrats.

And so the Democratic Party, finding its place increasingly in wealthy enclaves, prides itself on what is only a memory of what it once was and whom it once, in both the literal and figurative sense, represented, a touchstone if you will. Joe Biden will always love Scranton, but he doesn't live there anymore. Nostalgia is not a substitute for actual connection to the people in the places they live, especially come election time.

And if it renews a spark in 2026 or 2028, a response to the shame in the electorate for what they did in 2024, is that what Democrats hope to achieve? The consolation prize? The rejection of the incumbent, for disqualification? Haven't Democrats done that once? The Democrats may seek a shiny star of their own, create their own cult of personality. They have done so before.

But Franklin Roosevelt wouldn't have told someone out of a job in Ohio that they should move.

LARRY BIRD AND EUGENE V. DEBS WALK INTO A BAR

Eugene V. Debs ran for president as a Socialist five times, the last while serving a prison term for sedition in 1920. He said, at his sentencing, "Your Honor, years ago I recognized my kinship with all living beings, and I made up my mind that I was not one bit better than the meanest on earth. I said then, and I say now, that

---

3   "AllPolitics - Democratic National Convention," accessed May 25, 2025, https://www.cnn.
     com/ALLPOLITICS/1996/conventions/chicago/facts/famous.speeches/mondale.84.shtml.

while there is a lower class, I am in it, and while there is a criminal element, I am of it, and while there is a soul in prison, I am not free."[4]

Debs was a Democrat when he went to prison but came out of it a Socialist. Vermont Senator Bernie Sanders is an admirer of Debs, and I can hear a bit of Sanders in Debs's declaration. But even as a sitting senator who twice came very close to winning the nomination for president by running on a muscularly progressive platform that rejuvenated the far-left fringe, freeing everyone from jail might not look good in opposition ads.

The Debs home is a museum run by the Eugene V. Debs Foundation on the campus of Indiana State University in Terre Haute. The director, in her mid-twenties, was nice enough to show me around when I popped in, telling me a tour of the three-story home usually takes ninety minutes. She studied Debs at ISU and was offered the job when she graduated.

I tell her I have about thirty minutes, and she says she'll hit the highlights. She has trouble doing this, everything about Debs rating very high, but she seems to fit ninety into thirty without a breath, including long passages from his speeches. She takes great exception to the charge that the vibrant blue tiles around the fireplace in the dining room were "imported from Italy," first levied at Debs during his campaigns. "It's documented they're from Michigan, for God's sake!" she says.

Debs organized the workers of the Pullman Company to strike in response to reduced wages resulting from a loss of orders after the economic panic of 1893. President Grover Cleveland sent in the army to squash it, and Debs did six months in jail. It was a pivotal time for the labor movement. In its aftermath, the Socialist Party of America was founded in Indiana.

Senator Sanders wasted no time after Kamala Harris's defeat to call on the Democrats to refind its purpose. He called the campaign "disastrous" and said "it should come as no great surprise that a Democratic Party which has abandoned working-class people would find that the working class has abandoned them. First, it was the white working class, and now it is Latino and Black workers as well."[5]

The reverence is also real at my second stop of the day, the Larry Bird

<hr>

4   Eugene V. Debs, "Statement to the Court, Upon Being Convicted of Violating the Sedition Act, accessed May 25, 2025, https://www.marxists.org/archive/debs/works/1918/court.htm.

5   Alexander Bolton, "Sanders: Democratic Party 'has abandoned working class people'," The Hill, November 6, 2024.

Museum next to the Terre Haute Convention Center. Debs ran for president five times; Bird made the NBA Finals five times. Bird himself donated a lot of memorabilia, came to the opening, and with Kevin McHale and Robert Parish, raised three Celtics championship banners to the ceiling. As a Celtics fan, I pay my respects and ask the docent for a recommendation for lunch.

I'm directed to the Copper Bar a block down, an institution with walls filled with photos of prominent locals, including Bird. I order "Amy's Salad" of greens topped with grilled chicken, covered in pesto and melted cheese. Ann Connolly tells me that it's a creation of the owner's wife, presumably Amy.

Ann, the bartender, has just moved here in late winter 2025 from Philadelphia. Asked if she's a fan of the Eagles, who won the Super Bowl the month before, she replies "rabid." It's a lot more affordable here, and her son, who is in the engineering program at ISU, suggested she come out and save some money. She's been working at the Copper Bar for a few weeks and likes it.

I ask how she likes Terre Haute. She shrugs slightly, but she's still well in the adjustment window. Philadelphia and Terre Haute are pretty different places, though Philly has museums too.

Her son cautioned her not to walk around downtown at night. She replied, "When did you become the parent?" But downtown empties out at night, and there is a homelessness and opioid-addiction problem.

Terre Haute is like a lot of small and mid-sized cities, struggling to attract business and residents to its downtown core. The mayor, a Democrat, is new, having defeated the Republican incumbent. I tell Ann I Wikipedia'd him on my way here. Brandon Sakbun, twenty-nine years old.

"I know. He comes in here sometimes." Her son's age, she says. "I carded him! I had no idea he was the mayor."

Ann left big-city Philadelphia not because of crime but the cost of housing. She's adjusting to a small city, where problems can be amplified and empty storefronts are hard to fill, but apartments are cheaper.

It's easy to peg crime to big cities, and there is a partisan opening to do so; most cities are led by Democrats. But crime looms larger in smaller cities, which are less equipped to respond to a surge and have less activity downtown, empty storefronts, and little to no housing in their cores. It's hard not to root for Terre Haute and its young mayor. At least the Copper Bar takes its responsibility not to serve minors seriously.

SPEAK SOFTLY AND CARRY A BIG PITCHFORK

Leaving Terre Haute, I drive west across the Illinois line, the fields stretching out, the stands of trees in their final stages of hibernation. My car clock does not adjust for the time change, but I leave it as we're a couple of days away from Daylight Savings Time when it will sync back up. I have the luxury of time to visit the "largest pitchfork," a claim endorsed by an official mention on a state highway sign.

Cities big and small have to adjust to economic factors out of their control. The landscape is littered with hollowed-out downtowns peppered with former-ly hollowed-out towns well past their boom times that have rebounded. Casey, (pronounced KAY-zee) Illinois, has a population of 2,400 or so, and a "down-town" that punches way above its weight.

"A small town with a big heart" is the hometown of David Hanners, a 1989 Pulitzer Prize winner for *The Dallas Morning News* for Explanatory Journalism, noted proudly on the Casey welcome sign.

The barista at the Casey Coffee Co. tells me that she's not sure what big thing came first, the outsized pencil on the curb out front, the ruler, the rocking chair, the barber pole, the mailbox, or the taller-than-the-building Chevy key, with the verse from Matthew 16:19 (NIV): "I will give you the keys of the kingdom of heaven; whatever you bind on earth will be bound in heaven, and whatever you loose on earth will be loosed in heaven."

I find the wind chime and the taco and the birdcage but not the pitchfork, the barista telling me it's not walkable from downtown. I ask if the gimmick attracts visitors. "Yes. Sometimes people drive six hours to come here," she says. And as if to prove this, I encounter a family of four visiting the heartland from Taiwan. They very much like the display but wonder why there isn't a place to get lunch.

KEEP DENTON WEIRD

The LSA Burger Company in Denton, Texas, is the first gourmet burger place to "honor our state's musical legends and trailblazers." The large mural upon entering the first-floor bar depicts them, left and right of Jesus Christ Himself, a hamburger and fries in front of him, a beer at his right hand, though it probably belongs to Janis Joplin, who is taking the Apostle John's seat. The description underneath reads, "From Bethlehem to the Brazos, From Nazareth to Nacogdoches, He's the great composer of forgiveness." The guests at the Last Supper are all Texan musical giants recognizable by first name—Willie, Selena, Waylon, Buddy, Roy—except Jesus, known for other gifts.

The unconsecrated actual burger, enjoyed from the second-floor roof deck overlooking the square, is forgiving, the mustard and mayo spread a perfect mix, and the staff young since this is a college town. College towns have the best energy, no matter what your age. One waiter has a Sam Bankman-Fried 'do, and another could be stunt double for pop culture maven Chuck Klosterman. Denton is happening.

The square's centerpiece is the wedding-cake-like four-story City Hall built in 1896 but closed since January 2024 for renovations that will update its HVAC system.

The bohemian vibe common to college towns—here comprised of students from Texas Woman's University, North Central Texas College, and the University of North Texas who populate the downtown, working and eating and shopping and just hanging out—gives those of us of a certain age nostalgia for what Austin, Texas, used to be famous for. Saying "keep Austin weird" seems a little weird now. Austin is now one of the most affluent cities in the United States, with all of the traffic and inflated prices that come with that honor. A 2024 report pegged it as the nation's 10th wealthiest city, and tops in growth of millionaires with an astonishing 110 percent between 2013 and 2023; in second place was the Bay Area at 82 percent during that same period.[6] But I enjoyed Austin when they kept it weird.

As we cheer economic growth, success, and the enrichment that comes with it, we pine for the days when great cities were small and "authentic" to what made them, or what they became. Denton is right there, maybe at the cusp of something bigger. It may be far enough away from the talons of the vast geography of Dallas/Fort Worth/Plano to maintain their cloistered success.

And cloistered spaces protect.

––––––––

6   "Wealthiest Cities | USA Wealth Report 2024," Henley & Partners, n.d., https://www. henleyglobal.com/publications/usa-wealth-report-2024/americas-wealthiest-cities.

I always try to get my haircut on these trips because the person wielding the scissors has to talk with me. Denton has options, including side-by-side establishments. The door to the one on the left is locked, but I am welcomed to the right. Libby is happy to cut my hair, and though finished with their apprenticeship, they tell me they've never cut a man's hair before.

But they would like to learn how, and the more traditional barber shop next door is locked, and I still need a haircut. In Maine, a barber who had set up in the little town of Oakland, about 20 miles north of the state capital of Augusta, was making a go of it and told me that learning to cut hair during the pandemic was hampered by the lack of real heads to practice on. They relied on wigs perched on Styrofoam heads.

Libby tells me they didn't grow up with men in the house—no brothers and their father was never around. I'm in, and I take my seat. Eli, who has worked at the shop for two years, supervises. Libby starts out tentatively, with cautious strokes, and I can feel Eli's more practiced hand pressing Libby's on the back of my head. Cutting hair is for the bold.

They tell me this is a queer-run salon, all the employees fall on the queer spectrum, and 75 to 80 percent of their clients do as well. Both are native Texans, Libby moving from a small town, but not so small that it didn't have a Walmart, "so people from even smaller towns" would visit. Eli moved to Boulder, Colorado, but is back. He and his husband are raising two children, fourteen and thirteen.

The Tried and True salon is a safe space, and clients are comfortable there. Cutting hair is an intimate exercise, not just for the LGBT community and not just in Texas.

Marian Ryan, the district attorney of Middlesex County in Massachusetts, started a program called "Cut it Out" to train stylists on how to recognize signs of domestic violence, hair being a target of choice when an abuser wants to gain physical control of a victim. Hair stylists and barbers get to know their customers pretty well, and there has always been an element of therapist to the job.[7]

Sitting down in a chair in a salon—any salon—is loaded with chances of being misgendered for those in the queer community. You might present as a woman

---

7   More about this innovative, and impactful, program can be found on the Middlesex District Attorney's website: https://www.middlesexda.com/sites/g/files/vyhlif11841/f/uploads/middlesex_cut_it_out_2015.pdf.

to the stylist, ask for a short haircut and get a pixie instead of what you hoped for, Eli says. Tried and True never genders and always uses they/them until a client shares their pronouns. When making an appointment, they always ask for pronouns, which didn't sit well with one woman, whose husband posted a scathing Google review.

"The vibe of the salon has changed" since Trump was reelected, Eli says. Their social media used to be outspoken about being a queer space. Now they're more careful not to use social media tags that would identify their clients. Eli watched Target pull pride items because of threats against their employees. Libby mentioned a pleasant surprise when HomeGoods, a happy place for them, had a display when they were last in.

Eli continues, "I get why people are afraid because Texas is a pretty harsh state to live in as a member of this community." He is a gay trans man and is used to being very open about this but is quieter now because it's hard not to feel like a target. Community is important in less volatile times, especially for those whose families are not supportive, but particularly so now.

In Boulder, Colorado, where Eli lived for a time, there is only one gay bar that he's aware of, and on his last trip there, he found it a sleepy affair, with just a few patrons at the bar waiting for trivia night to start. Eli makes the point that in Boulder, which is a very welcoming city, there is less need for a dedicated, and safe, space. Every place is pretty safe and welcoming.

Eli runs a queer hiking group that meets monthly, a community that doesn't have to be in a bar, where they can meet face to face. It feels like it's happening "slowly but all at once" to Eli, that Trump is establishing this rhetoric of "Christian values" and "traditional marriage, and it's having an outsized impact here in Texas. "The most powerful man in the world, his words trickle down and affirm feelings of people who already feel this way. It happens sneakily," Eli says.

Eli continues, "Nobody was thinking or caring about trans people ten years ago, but Trump's using it as a touchpoint for hate and division, for fear mongering." Transitioning just four years ago, when thirty-one, Eli took his cue on bathroom choice from women. When he got a dirty look while about to walk into the women's bathroom, he knew he was at that point in his transition, the start of a beard on his face, that he would not do that again. "I'd prefer never to use a men's bathroom. They're disgusting." But he had crossed the Rubicon.

This assault on the queer community has exposed class distinctions within it, Eli thinks. He presents as a man, tattoos up the arms and exposed across his torso under his tank top, with a full, if patchy beard. He sees and now benefits from the privileges of the "patriarchy." Trans women are the ones facing the most oppression because of this inherent and now further politicized exposure. Gay Black women feel it differently than gay white men. As do the gay men in Texas versus those in Colorado. The Trump assault hits differently. "No one cares about trans men competing in sports," Eli says.

Eli's older daughter can vote in the next presidential election, something she is looking forward to doing. Eli says she told him, "Trump won't be on the ballot, and I can be part of a movement of change."

GRAYBEARD

Inside the Hickory Street Lounge, they lament Denton's apparent paucity of supermarket options. These guys are experts; one works in the industry, a profession that evidently permits a little daytime recreating. Hot and sunny outside, it's cool and dark inside the lounge, and the jukebox is playing the blues. Everything sounds like Stevie Ray Vaughan, memorialized on the LSA Burger mural a few blocks away, but in reality is the work of more minor musical figures like Tab Benoit and Joe Bonamassa, a New Yorker for crying out loud.

The bartender is sipping water from a thermos whose size draws comments from the regulars. "Hydrate or diedrate, bro," she responds in between complaints about how aggressively the government taxes the cannabis industry, in which she has a fiduciary interest.

The graybeard at the bar is, in fact, the younger of the two regulars, both of them connoisseurs of the supermarket game. "That one's the MILF Kroger," says Graybeard. When his counterpart mentions another venue, he replies, "That's the swinger Kroger. That's the upside-down pineapple Kroger," an inverted pineapple being the emblem of adventurous couples.

Both are jealous of communities lucky enough to boast an H-E-B, evidently the gold standard of Texan supermarkets. "I call us the red-headed stepchild," bemoans Graybeard. Interestingly, H-E-B was formerly known as the Howard E. Butts Grocery, until Mr. Butts realized that H-E-B might be more marketable to housewives back in his day.

"I grew up in South Texas, so I grew up around H-E-Bs," the older gentleman says, with a little pride. "We'll go out of our way to go to Frisco to go to an H-E-B." Frisco is a little more than a half hour away but doesn't meet his every need.

"If I have to buy meat, which I normally don't because I slaughter my own, I go to Sam's Club," he says. His daughter and her husband live in Gonzales, near San Antonio, and his father is in assisted living in Corpus Christi, so he'll load up the travel trailer when he visits. "When you can watch 'em make fresh tortillas right off the machine—" he enthuses before Graybeard cuts in: "That's epic right there—"

"Now it's time for fajitas, and I want to throw some fajitas on the grill."

THE DISTRICT

Back in Pensacola, I'm talking with Mike, forty-nine, who has run a successful business going on twelve years with a loyal clientele drawn to the "District," a collection of bars, restaurants, and music venues. He was one of the first bars to shut during the pandemic. I ask how he survived. "Savings" and borrowing from his mother back in Kentucky. His mother wondered how liquor stores could remain open as essential, while he had to shut the doors.

He thought, "I have liquor. I have toilet paper." He opened the front window and offered his stock for sale. The local authorities came by to see what he was up to, but they left him alone.

After Hurricane Sally hit in 2020, half the city lost power. His remained on. After a while, the city advised those without power to dispose of their perishable food within seventy-two hours. Realizing those without electricity would lose their food stock, he organized the kitchens on his side of the street and offered to cook the food of those on the other side.

While we're chatting, other patrons chime in, echoing what those who live through extreme weather events know: We're all in this together. One moved down with his now ex-wife from Chicago. He stayed. She stayed. Another came down from Ohio and builds massive dock structures.

Despite family still in Louisville, Kentucky, Mike would not move back. The city isn't the same; he cites homelessness. Here, he can walk to a minor league ballgame, a live music performance, or a show on its way to or from Broadway.

Traffic is reasonable. He came for the climate. He stayed through the pandemic and the hurricane. He's here for the long haul.

ALL POLITICS CAN BE LOCAL AGAIN

The reality is that though we love stories of escape, most of us are where we are for the long haul. We're less mobile than we once were as a country, and housing costs stick us in place.[8] The widening wealth gap contributes to this. An aging population finds those in the middle tending to aging parents while raising children.

Given this, it makes sense that public policy would follow this reality, that it would address conditions on the ground, where people live. The Biden initiative on infrastructure investment was a big, bold federal initiative that was policy implemented top-down. The local impacts were real, but the implementation skipped the translation for voters on the ground in the cities and towns that benefited from the program. This works across the board. Federal education funding comes with strings attached. Locally, people see strings.

If you ask people what their local challenges are, and how the federal government could be helpful, most will scratch their heads. In the spring of 2025, voters think Donald Trump is attempting to answer this question while the Democrats regroup.

8　James Pethokoukis, "Why are Americans less mobile than ever before?" American Enterprise Institute, March 11, 2020, https://www.aei.org/economics/why-are-americans-less-mobile-than-ever-before/.

CHAPTER SEVEN

IS IT THE ECONOMY, STUPID?

The North American Free Trade Agreement, signed by President Bill Clinton in December 1993 but first championed by Ronald Reagan during the 1980 campaign, took down trade barriers in Mexico, the United States, and Canada, and remade the economy of each. Clinton at the time said, "NAFTA means jobs, and good-paying American jobs."[1]

The more level playing field allowed competition, which led to shifts in markets and job growth more than job loss, but that loss would be concentrated in certain geographic areas. NAFTA did create good-paying jobs in the US, but not for those who lost theirs to Mexico or Canada.

Cotton was once king in Arkansas, but globalization and competition from synthetics caused diversification in crops to rice, soybeans, and wheat. There is a museum dedicated to this economic revolution in Little Rock.

The design of the William J. Clinton Library and Museum, I'm told by the reverential docent, was inspired by the President's desire to enshrine his vision of an administration that would build a bridge to the twenty-first century. I have always felt we should leave building design to trained architects. But Clinton did alter Reagan's original NAFTA vision and the bilateral agreement with Canada signed by George H. W. Bush to his own construct, and he's allowed to do whatever he wants with his own Presidential library.

---

1   National Archives and Records Administration, September 14, 1993, https://clintonwhitehouse6.archives.gov/1993/09/1993-09-14-remarks-by-clinton-and-former-presidents-on-nafta.html.

I would have also advised that the building as a metaphor needed some work. The building ends before it "bridges" the Arkansas River. The actual bridge that does cross is a hulking mess with an overlaid trail path. Two decades after NAFTA, the realities of its impact, particularly on smaller cities and towns, combined with the effects of his program of welfare reform and the war on drugs have a lot here thinking about Clinton's promise of a new economy. Would Fleetwood Mac's "Don't Stop Thinking About Tomorrow," the campaign anthem played triumphantly during his inaugural festivities, have the same hopeful impact on voters today?

Arkansan Wilbur Mills bridged the New Deal through the Great Society. A powerful chairman of the House Ways and Means Committee from 1958 to 1974, he was instrumental in the creation of the Interstate Highway System—so critical to the economy of the state, rail and river development, Medicaid and Medicare, and the protection of Social Security. He knew the importance of keeping voting senior citizens out of poverty. Generations of Democratic voters could link federal action with family financial security.

A Democrat himself, Mills would be an anachronism in today's Arkansas, but the Clinton-era economic policies that provided both the answer to the Bush-era recession and the fulfillment of the cry, "It's the economy, stupid," have also grown dated. President Biden thought Build Back Better and strong economic indicators in a bounce back from the COVID slowdown would persuade voters, and you can follow the thread of his philosophy of government back through Clinton to Mills to the New Deal.

But voters in Arkansas and in other places I have visited don't make that connection. In Georgia in January 2022, I talked to business owners about how they coped through the pandemic. None mentioned federal funding as a lifeline or credited either Trump or Biden. Federal emergency assistance, so critical to businesses making it through the crisis, left no enduring imprint in the minds of its beneficiaries.

Repairing roads is a tangible thing. In rural Maine, people daily find themselves stuck at a temporary light while roadwork reduces travel to one lane. I hear about roadwork all the time in places I travel, like from the receptionist at my dentist's office in Watertown, Massachusetts, who talks about how it makes it much harder to get to work. No one ever mentions how it creates jobs.

Clinton promised that "bridge to the twenty-first century" in his 1996

Democratic National Convention address, en route to a convincing reelection over superannuated war hero Senator Bob Dole. Thanks largely to the economic policies embraced as well by policymakers from both parties who adhered to the neoliberal worldview, that bridge's yield, a quarter into the twenty-first century, remains debatable among Americans—particularly those who most benefited from safe passage through the protectionist policies in place pre-NAFTA.

Standing on the banks of the Arkansas River in December 2023, I see a rusted old bridge that's not carrying anyone across.

I'M YOUR NATIVE SON

Posey is an unincorporated town, small enough to be omitted from most maps of southern Illinois. The town amounts to the intersection of two county roads in the center of Clinton County, which sits just to the west of Marion County, the birthplace of Williams Jennings Bryan, the prairie populist who achieved fame as a thirty-six-year-old Nebraska congressman by taking the Democratic convention in 1896 by storm, leaving it as the party's nominee for president.

Behind the grain elevator are the railroad tracks that connect Posey to the City of New Orleans line, the daily train from Chicago to New Orleans, immortalized in the lyrics of Steve Goodman and famously sung by Arlo Guthrie.

"Farmers are extremely intelligent," Joe, in his sixties, who grew up in Clinton County but moved to attend college, says. "They have to be. Their living depends on macroeconomics, physics, chemistry, mathematics, and biology. One wrong calculation, and a whole harvest can go haywire. That's a year's income," he adds.

He describes Posey and the surrounding towns as a tight-knit German farming community, with the distinguishing factor between people in town being the split between Lutherans and Catholics. In Clinton County, he said, they all managed to get along just fine.

I asked whether anyone actually spoke German during his childhood. He said it was common enough that the kids would pick some up here and there. He laughed as he remembered one phrase in particular that he and his brother had a good handle on by the time they were teenagers: *"Wenn ich bin achtzehn, ich bin so raus hier."* He translated: "When I'm eighteen, I'm so out of here!"

The family farm is a nostalgic foundational block in this country, with each one a small business, sometimes bigger, and critical to the economy, everyone would agree. But there are 141,000 fewer family farms today than just seven years ago, and 20 million fewer acres, according to the American Farm Bureau Federation (AFBF).[2] Younger farmers are popping up, but the number of farmers over sixty-five far outpaces those coming up.

In February 2024, AFBF President Zippy Duvall said, "The latest census numbers put in black and white the warnings our members have been expressing for years. Increased regulations, rising supply costs, lack of available labor, and weather disasters have all squeezed farmers to the point that many of them find it impossible to remain economically sustainable."[3]

EASY MONEY

William Jennings Bryan won his party's nomination in 1896 by taking on the "Bourbon Democrats" of his own party and his party's president, Grover Cleveland, who, despite the economic panic and lingering recession of 1893, clung to the gold standard preferred by the monied interests. In his "Cross of Gold" speech at the convention in Chicago, Bryan spoke for the farmer:

> The farmer who goes forth in the morning and toils all day,
> who begins in spring and toils all summer, and who by the
> application of brain and muscle to the natural resources of
> the country creates wealth, is as much a business man as
> the man who goes upon the Board of Trade and bets upon
> the price of grain.[4]

Bryan's championing of the family farm, and his promotion of free silver to

---

2   News Release, "New Census Shows Alarming Loss of Family Farms," American Farm Bureau Federation, February 13, 2024.

3   News Release, "New Census."

4   Michael E. Eidenmuller, "William Jennings Bryan: Democratic National Convention Address - 'A Cross of Gold,'" American Rhetoric, accessed May 25, 2025, https://www.americanrhetoric.com/speeches/williamjenningsbryan1896dnc.htm.

ease money supply, won him support in farm states but not the presidency three times. Today, few I speak with in those states think the Democratic Party is fighting for family farms or even understands the business side of things.

The food insecurity rate is between 9 percent and 19 percent of the population by state, North Dakota with the lowest number and Mississippi with the highest, according to Feeding America.[5] That amounts to 66,000 North Dakotans and more than half a million Mississippians. Representatives Tracey Mann, a Republican from Kansas, and Jim McGovern, a Democrat from Massachusetts, head the House Hunger Caucus. McGovern has said, "Food is something that unites all of us—something that brings everyone to the table. Ending hunger and improving nutrition are bipartisan issues—something everyone should be able to get behind because they just make sense."[6]

Ending hunger *should* be a bipartisan issue, and while there are people who are hungry in every state, the Democrats are disconnected from farm states, where one has to understand farming as a business as well as a food producer. Most Democratic members of Congress are ignorant of the business end of farming, with some exceptions—like McGovern, from Worcester, Massachusetts, the second-largest city in New England, but who has taken it upon himself to serve on the Agriculture Committee. There has been a concerted effort to recruit military veterans to run for office as Democrats, and it's good to have that experience in Congress, but it could also use more farmers.

TRACTOR SEAT TO BARBER CHAIR

In February 2024, I'm told by Annette, the owner of a barbershop in downtown Mobile, Alabama, that the city has improved over the three decades she has owned the shop. Of course, business has not returned to pre-pandemic times—people are in the office less, and there are barber options in the burbs. But she

---

5　Child food insecurity, accessed May 25, 2025, https://www.feedingamerica.org/sites/default/files/2019-05/2017-map-the-meal-gap-child-food-insecurity_0.pdf.

6　"Representatives Jim McGovern, Tracey Mann Announce Relaunch of Bipartisan House Hunger Caucus," US Representative Jim McGovern, February 9, 2023, https://mcgovern.house.gov/news/documentsingle.aspx?DocumentID=398957.

has a loyal clientele. She credits the Republican mayor on the improvements, a theme we hear repeated, regardless of party affiliation. Mayors get credit.

Sandy Stimpson moved from a forty-year career in his family lumber manufacturing business to the mayor's office, defeating two-term Democrat Sam Jones, the first African American to serve in the office. Stimpson, who is white, was rewarded with a higher percentage of the vote in his reelection.

Downtown Mobile is putting on its Bourbon Street best, bar after bar mixed with vacant storefronts all decked out in purple for Mardi Gras, which Annette proudly tells me was started here and not in New Orleans. The barricades are up in anticipation of the parade, a full day away, and at 10 a.m., the streets are pretty deserted. The gentleman walking his schnauzer on the grounds of the Basilica of the Immaculate Conception in Cathedral Square urges me to go inside and take the circular stairs down to see the crypts of the Cardinals.

The Convention Center is hosting the Gulf States Horticultural Association, but Mobile has long been associated with shipbuilding. Austal USA remains contracted by the Navy and Coast Guard and is Mobile's largest employer with 4,500 workers.

With such a critical industry dependent on government contracts, it helps to have a member of Congress on the Appropriations Committee, and Mobile has one in sophomore Jerry Carl. As a result of redistricting, Carl finds himself pitted against fellow Republican Barry Moore.

Carl, who, according to the Cook Political Report is a "wealthy real estate businessman, an appropriator [occupying a coveted seat on the House Appropriations Committee]and the latest in a long line of Republicans focused on securing federal dollars from Mobile's defense and shipbuilding industry."[7] Moore also has a claim to fame. He voted against certifying the 2020 election. The day after January 6, he joined the minority in voting to overturn the election, and he cosponsored a bill to name the AR-15 rifle the National Gun of the United States.

In the primary in March 2024, Moore defeated Carl and went on to win the district outright in November. Before the Republicans regained control of the

---

7   "Alabama's New Congressional Map Triggers Competitive Primaries," Cook Political Report, February 23, 2024, https://www.cookpolitical.com/analysis/house/alabama-house/alabamas-new-congressional-map-triggers-competitive-primaries.

House of Representatives in 2010, "bringing home the bacon" in the form of earmarks, funds congressionally directed to a specific project or use, was a way to show the voters back home that you were working for them, where it mattered, returning tax dollars to the district. It was a tangible thing, and serving on the Appropriations Committee was so coveted, subcommittee chairs were called "Cardinals."

Without that personal connection, it's harder for voters to make it, and candidates connect more on noneconomic messages—in this case, guns and election denialism—and the ordained, Pope-blessed Cardinals remain in the basement of the basilica.

CENTERING OURSELVES

The town of Bushton is the geographic center of Kansas and the state itself the geographic center of the lower forty-eight, an honor Kansans would lose if Canada becomes the fifty-first state, a prospect Trump dangled early in his second term. As I move west, the grass growing in the fields awaiting seeding in early April 2023 is thinner and less lush than I've noticed in previous days.

As it turns out, more than a third of Kansas is in Exceptional Drought (the highest level) and the rest of the state is considered Abnormally Dry to Extreme Drought by the National Weather Service. Turning south on Highway 156 to Great Bend, there seems to be more smoke on the horizon, but it turns out to be blown dust I learn while talking to the receptionist at the Cheyenne Bottoms Wildlife Area.

One of the education specialists there tells me about the drought happening in Kansas and at the wildlife refuge, which is severely affected, as well as farming and cattle ranching. The refuge is a critical rest stop for 750,000 to one million migratory birds annually. They stop in Kansas wetlands that are normally teeming with small worms and other invertebrates, food shorebirds need, and seeds that some of the waterfowl feed on. It is the largest interior wetlands in the United States, and right now it is bone dry, hence the dust.

The birds are currently not stopping because there is nothing to stop for. Long-distance birds depend on stops to rest and fuel up because they can only store so much fat, especially the small ones. They may not make it to the next available source of water, and if they do, the sites may be overcrowded, making them more susceptible to predators.

The economic effects for the area are felt beyond the wildlife impacts, in a region where agriculture is the predominant industry and cattle raising an important source of income. Dry and hot weather has led to mass deaths of livestock and other animals. An employee at the wildlife center tells me the wheat crop is just about bust for the year because of the drought. It's not yet clear how severe the economic impact will be on the farmers, but it's not looking good.

GINI COEFFICIENT

Corrado Gini, an Italian statistician born in 1884, came up with a way to measure income inequality. The Gini coefficient shows that the gap between rich and poor is widening in high-income economies like the United States and Canada, according to a study by the Peterson Institute for International Economics (PIIE), a think tank based in Washington, DC.[8]

South African-born Elon Musk makes an easy target for Democrats as the poster child for greedy oligarchs. *He's not even from here!* While it's perhaps a good political tactic as well as good public policy to focus on the obscene and ever-increasing wealth of those at the very pinnacle of the economic ladder, Gini's scale paints a picture of how the growing divide affects what voters do when they go into the voting booth and how Democratic rhetoric may miss the mark.

Stop focusing on the pinnacle and look at the pits. While "the United States remains the most unequal high-income economy in the world, the disparity reflects a surge in incomes for the richest population segments, along with sluggish or even falling incomes for the poorest."[9] And as the poles of Gini's graph move further apart, the middle class drops and shrinks. In 1970, 61 percent of Americans lived in the middle class. In 2019, it was 51 percent and dropping.[10]

There is good news when you widen your gaze beyond the United States.

---

8   Peterson, "How to Fix Economic Inequality?", PIIE, November 17, 2020, https://www.piie.com/microsites/how-fix-economic-inequality.

9   Peterson, "How to Fix Economic Inequality?"

10   Peterson, "How to Fix Economic Inequality?"

"Inequality between the poorest and richest people in the world has noticeably declined in recent decades. Trade has been a critical driver of this, cutting the number living in extreme poverty by half since 1990. Total trade as a share of GDP in developing countries has doubled since 1985," the PIIE study points out.[11]

It continues, "The richest Americans have been able to save more of their money and grow their wealth faster than the average American since the late 1980s." According to a Pew Research Center study, "only upper-income families in the United States grew wealth between 2001 and 2016, gaining 33% at the median. Middle-income families experienced a 20% loss in median net worth while lower-income families lost 45%."[12]

This may contribute to the decline in people moving. According to Census data, after World War II as much as 40 percent of the population made a move, a figure now down to around 10 percent. The postwar economic expansion, the GI Bill, the boom in babies, and the Interstate Highway System allowed people to unstick themselves from where previous generations had been planted. But that part of the American Dream—hitting the open road in pursuit of infinite possibilities—isn't an option for most people today. Of the 10 percent today, just under half did so for housing-related reasons, and a good percentage for family reasons. Only 20 percent did so for a job opportunity.

DWIGHT D. EISENHOWER NATIONAL SYSTEM OF INTERSTATE AND DEFENSE HIGHWAYS

I've had some kicks driving on Route 66, one of the original numbered highways; I've taken parts of it in Missouri and Oklahoma. The song that made it famous was written in 1946 by Bobby Troup, who initially conceived it about

---

11   Peterson, "How to Fix Economic Inequality?"

12   Juliana Menasce Horowitz, Ruth Igielnik, Rakesh Kochhar, "Most Americans Say There is too Much Economic Inequality in the US but Fewer Than Half Call it a Top Priority; Chapter 1," PEW Research Center, January 9, 2020.

Route 40, where he and his wife started cross-country from Pennsylvania, but she persuaded him that "Get your kicks on Route 66" was catchier. Troup went on to '70s fame starring in the hospital drama *Emergency!* with his second wife, Julie London, which I watched every week because it also starred my younger sister Linda's teen crush, Randy Mantooth, which was his actual name, and not a show business moniker. In the '70s, the strongest advocate picked the program, and the rest could watch or not.

But if Route 66 got us on the road, the Interstate Highway System transformed the postwar country. On January 30, 2024, in an article posted on *Medium*, economist Harish Ganesh lays it out: "The United States GDP has grown 340% since the development of the Interstates in 1956, from $3 trillion to $19 trillion. According to the United States's Federal Highway Authority, 25% of the nation's productivity increase from 1950 to 1989 can be attributed to the Interstate system."[13]

The national network of highways brought us closer together, tamping down obvious regional differences, presenting, if you don't venture off the major byways, a uniform American makeup—an application of interchangeability at exits across the map—fast food, chain hotels, gas station choices. The internet further flattens things, allowing us to check our personal social media offerings anywhere we may be traveling.

This mask of uniformity hides differences, but they peek out if you're looking for them. Some are obvious, and I wonder from time to time if the Massachusetts turnpike could sustain a Buc-ee's, but they're fun to visit in Texas! Driving from Memphis over the Missouri River and leaving the iconic pyramid headquarters of the Bass Pro Shops behind, it's hard not to notice you're in mostly truck traffic heading to Little Rock, even during the day. In some places you share the road with American brands; in others the percentage of Teslas goes way up. The northeast is more apt to wear its political beliefs on bumpers, and "I bought this before he went crazy" stickers pop up after Elon Musk's appointment to head up DOGE.

---

13   Harish Ganesh, "Paving a Road to Prosperity: Assessing the Economic Impacts of the U.S. Interstate System," *Medium*, January 31, 2024, https://medium.com/boston-economist-publication/paving-a-road-to-prosperity-assessing-the-economic-impacts-of-the-u-s-interstate-system-cbfc6415f1a5.

BIG THINK

Edward Bernays was called "The Father of Spin" several decades before Donald Trump was born, and author Larry Tye's excellent book on Bernays was written almost twenty years before Trump ran for president.

In the early part of the twentieth century, at the birth of modern public relations, Bernays came up with what Tye coined the "Big Think" and Bernays thought of as "appeals of indirection." It was "lateral thinking—mapping out a solution based on a client's standing in the wider economy and society rather than on narrow, vertical considerations."[14] Early in his career, Bernays was hired to sell more cigarettes for the brand Lucky Strike. You can think about how you capture a bigger slice of the market, or you could expand the market. Bernays, at the beginning of the last century, viewed women as a huge untapped market for cigarettes and made smoking a matter of equality.[15]

When Mack Truck hired Bernays in the 1940s because they were losing shipping to rail, which had a countrywide network, he thought long. You can fight over market share, or you can solve a bigger problem that no one thought of. The "Paving America" campaign would make it easier to ship goods.

Bernays assembled the coalition by banding together anyone who would have an economic interest in more vehicles on the road. Add in a national security issue, like the potential need to move weapons or large numbers of people quickly if the Cold War turned hot, and Congress responded in 1950 with millions of dollars for the system of interstate and defense highways that transformed America.

I don't know if Donald Trump studied Bernays. I doubt it. But he is a master of lateral thinking. Voters ranked the economy as an important issue when entering the voting booth, but some voters considered trans athletes an important enough issue to consider. Tariffs have historically been left to economic and foreign policy bureaucrats to negotiate and rarely rise to front-page news, but Trump has discovered that focusing on them can replace attention to traditional indicators that determine economic health. Threaten 50% tariffs, or 75% or higher, and when a trading partner capitulates, declare economic victory.

---

14   Larry Tye, *The Father of Spin: Edward L. Bernays and the Birth of Public Relations* (Holt, 1998), 52.

15   Tye, *Father of Spin*, 23.

CHAPTER EIGHT

NOBODY LIKES THAT SHIT

The 3rd Congressional District in Washington State is a massive and wild land area that stretches from the ragged Pacific coast and scenic Long Beach Peninsula far inland to the foothills of Mt. Adams and Mt. Rainier and the western edges of the Yakama Indian Reservation. In between is the heart of timber country—vast forests and tiny lumber towns dot the drive. The largest city is Vancouver, a suburb of Portland, Oregon, across the Columbia River, with just under 200,000 residents.

The 3rd is represented by Marie Gluesenkamp Perez, thirty-six, who flipped the seat from red to blue in 2022. Political observers love "nontraditional" candidates who come out of nowhere, are given no chance, speak truth to power, and defy all odds to storm Washington, Mr. Smith-style. She and her husband own a car repair shop and live in a house they built themselves. *Politico* welcomed her to Washington in January 2023 with a story titled, "She fixes cars. Can she fix Congress' elitism problem?"[1] and followed it up in July of 2024 with "She's a Blue-Collar, Bible-Quoting, Israel-Supporting, Pro-Choice, Millennial Latina. Is She the Future of Democratic Progressivism?"[2]

Democrats will point to her as an example of how they're the party more in touch with the working class. She even fixed a car radio for North Carolina

---

1 Natalie Fertig, "She Fixes Cars. Can She Fix Congress' Elitism Problem?" *Politico*, January 19, 2023.

2 Natalie Fertig, "She's a Blue Collar, Bible Quoting, Israel Supporting, Pro-Choice, Millennial Latina. Is She the Future of Democratic Progressivism?" *Politico*, July 1, 2024.

Representative Virginia Foxx, a MAGA Baby Boomer! Crossing aisles and fixing dials.

Politics elevates unique personalities, but the secret to Gluesenkamp Perez's success is less her singular resume and more her understanding of exactly who she works for while serving in Congress. Established strategic wisdom may have recommended in 2022 that she tack toward the middle and run a by-the-book campaign of broad Democratic pronouncements in the hope of presenting herself as the noncontroversial alternative to the fringe politics of her opponent, who beat the more mainstream Republican incumbent who had voted to Impeach Donald Trump in 2020.

She wasn't particularly interested in taking advice from traditional Democratic strategists. In fact, her penchant for railing against the Democrats' rural strategy became a staple of her campaign. She spoke honestly, kept her integrity, and unleashed an effective ground game, her team knocking on over 40,000 doors—no small feat in a rural district where houses aren't exactly right on top of each other.

She ran a staunchly pro-choice campaign, as a populist, and opposed monopolies on economic issues like right-to-repair, allowing repair shops access to car data controlled by manufacturers. "DIY is in our DNA," she says. She opposed a ban on assault rifles but supports raising the age of eligibility for purchasing a gun to twenty-one.

She sums up the Democrats' connection problem with rural voters specifically, and a lot of voters generally, this way: "I think that a lot of these traditional Democrats, the MO is to go into a community and start explaining shit. Nobody likes that."[3]

"It's not rocket science. It's about listening to your district."[4]

POWER

Gluesenkamp Perez's district includes Longview, which celebrated its centennial in 2023. *The Columbia River Reader* published a 12-part expansion of its

---

3   Fertig, "She Fixes Cars."
4   Fertig, "She Fixes Cars."

"People + Place" monthly feature to highlight changes in ways of life along the lower Columbia. In it, journalist Hal Calbom neatly lays out the hundred-year history of hydroelectric power and its impact on the economy of southwest Washington. He writes that it's a story of "extraction"—a regional journey to find the balance between the exploitation of a powerful wilderness rich with resources, and the preservation of an iconic ecosystem and sustainable, independent way of life.

"The ability of their abundant water to create power, first through water wheels or heated to power steam engines, was never lost on the pioneers. Nor was the politicalization of power, whose generation and distribution was mainly in the hands of private parties and monopolies," he writes. He continues, "Here the contradictory character of the Pacific Northwesterner emerged dramatically; disenchanted by an ineffectual government and a prolonged depression, people began to call for collective action. But collective action required planning, administration, and regulation, and that's what 'governments' did. And in the politically charged 1930s, 'government' threatened that dread disease—socialism."[5]

Calbom goes on to describe the process by which voters ventured into the public power movement with the creation of a Public Utility District (PUD) in 1936. The timing was ideal for it, as the first federally funded hydroelectric dam (Bonneville) had recently come online. It was the people seizing "power" in more ways than one. The structure of the PUD, and the abundant power, allowed it to cut rates twice in its first year of operation.

Today, this industry, which helped put food on the tables of Washington families for generations, is facing intense scrutiny and increased regulation in the wake of newfound evidence regarding the price that we pay for extraction. Whether it's mining, logging, or fishing, we know now that the costs of manipulating our land and water are greater than we could have ever imagined. This problem is not unique to Washington State, of course, and it's multifaceted and complex. A few coal miners in Pennsylvania, West Virginia, and Kentucky would also like a word with the powers that be about the economic whiplash that comes with greater government oversight.

Dams were originally considered by many to be the first "clean" power, but

---

5   Hal Calbom, *Empire of Trees: America's Planned City and the Last Frontier* (Columbia River Reader Press, 2023), 159.

research conducted in recent decades has begun to quantify the massive damage that they've caused to nearby communities as well as to river ecosystems and surrounding wildlife that relies on the river. We also now know that hydroelectric reservoirs produce massive amounts of greenhouse gasses.

Politicians in the state, including the clean-energy-championing Governor Jay Inslee, grapple with how to replace the benefits provided by the dams before eventually moving to remove them altogether.

The same tensions that Calbom lays out as having shaped the identity of early Northwesterners is at the heart of much of what I have been hearing from folks on the road—individual liberty versus collective accountability, personal freedom versus organized action. Here in the state of Washington, much of this centers on the concept of power—electrical, political, economic, collective, and individual power.

PLEASE REMOVE YOUR BELT

In the breakfast room of the Country Inn & Suites by Radisson in Charleston, South Carolina, the sparsely bearded TSA agent says the system is broken. "It's different everywhere. I've never seen the government do anything that makes sense," he says, and he's addressing the issue at hand. No TSA line is the same, there's no uniformity even among those in uniforms. Sometimes the hats and necklaces have to come off, sometimes they don't; the laptop sometimes has to go in its own tray, and concealed carry privilege is occasionally permitted. The rules shift, always, and that means that—even for those who work hard and follow the rules—it's hard to find an edge and make things move faster.

Emma's doing just fine, though unlike the TSA agent, she isn't a federal worker, so she doesn't have that perspective of the sensibility of the government. Nearing retirement age, she's cleaning up ketchup and coffee spills. "People are just sloppy in the morning, but I don't mind." Her granddaughter's coming back from London, and her son-in-law is going to get her tickets to a Dallas Cowboys game, one of two items left on her bucket list: visiting Paris and attending a Cowboys game. She's working part-time now after retiring from a retail job at a high-end place where they needed to close to the public when certain people came in. "I met Elizabeth Taylor!"

Charleston and the whole region have been growing, Emma says, people coming from cold parts of the country like the Northeast, "where it snows after the first of April," to places like Summerville, South Carolina, where she grew up. It's been growing by leaps and bounds. Charleston is getting more and more tourists from all over.

Breakfast at the Radisson is populated by people fueling up for work, but work's not guaranteed in Charleston when it rains. It's not for Max, sporting Miami Hurricanes shorts and a ski cap. "Boss man texted me. No work today. You want to work, but no work. You don't want to work, then that's when there's no text, and you work," says Max, sounding every bit the post-COVID millennial, though he's older than that. The precipitation starts lightly but comes later in force, almost sideways, the beautiful palms listing with the wind. It rains so hard, the TV rebroadcast of a tennis tournament from the night before pixelates mid-serve. You don't hop on a ladder and start weatherproofing when the palm trees are doing the lambada. So Max lingers.

He holds court, familiar with some of the other members of the breakfast club, some of whom have been here for a while and like him. The breakfast room's TV is set to a local news channel beamed in, oddly, not from a South Carolina station but from Connecticut. Among the lead stories is that Larry Lucchino, former president of the Boston Red Sox and mentee of the famed attorney and sports team owner Edward Bennett Williams, has died. Max has a blue remark for the success of the Sox during the early part of the twenty-first century but doesn't notice my worn cap with a red B.

Politics comes up, though no one seems eager to engage. The problem is not necessarily with Biden but with the system, Max says, and that's why Trump will probably win. Definitely in his—Max's and Trump's—home state of Florida.

"They just can't fix it," Max says, shortly before pouring himself a final coffee before heading back up to his room. "And it'll keep going back and forth, back and forth, 'til somebody can. Or find something else."

GUNS

Grapevine, Texas, is a truth-in-advertising town. Along Main Street, you can stroll from Landon Winery to Grape Vine Springs Winery, past Sloan &

Williams Winery to Messina Hof Winery, just past Kilwins Grapevine across the street. If that's not your cup of tea, half a mile away, over Route 114, just before you hit the sprawling city that is Dallas-Fort Worth Airport, you can spend all day, I imagine, at the Texas Gun Experience.

To me, it's massive, a sprawling complex of sales floor, twenty-five- and fifty-yard gun range, and event space. They emphasize safety and employ a Range Safety Officer. It is well-staffed, and when I stop in, everyone is engaged in catering to a clientele of men and women, and the front desk is checking in groups for the range.

They're happy to host your corporate event there, or perhaps you might be interested in the "Last Shot" bachelor or bachelorette party package. On their website, which requires you to verify you are over twenty-one years old, one review reads, "Our event was OVER THE TOP for our group of thirteen ladies." They have sub guns, rifles, belt-fed guns, and specialty ones, like a Colt 1877 "Bulldog Gatlin Gun" and a Thompson submachine gun. One package accommodates up to forty on their patio, where "a guest of honor [can] fire the impressive M134, with a two-hundred-and-fifty-round belt."

Meanwhile, in a liberal enclave near the coast, Kamala Harris wanted everyone to know that she owned a handgun and, if you broke into her house, she would shoot you. Tim Walz was, and is, a hunter. In his flannel shirt and flyaway fringe of hair, you could almost sense the fresh kill hanging to drain. Harris won two of the states where you are allowed to "permitless carry" a firearm, New Hampshire and Vermont.

New York City-born and -raised Trump has embraced the gun culture of his adopted state, Florida. While there is no evidence he has ever claimed ownership of a handgun, or threatened to shoot anyone who breaks into his home, his position is clear to voters. This speaks to a certain detachment in politics. Guns and God, both embraced by Trump despite his personal distance from both, don't matter to his voters.

Poolside at the Aloft Miami Doral in Florida, close to where people try to shoot birdies on Donald Trump's golf course, dusk descending on this January 2025 evening, a canvas for the blinking lights of planes making their final approach to Miami International Airport, I'm chatting with four men, immigrants all, who work for a Chicago-based logistics company. I ask the owner, originally from England and living in Indiana, what that means exactly. He tells me it deals in "the movement of cargo in the most economical method." Thus, they are meeting in Miami, where they move a lot of cargo.

In addition to England, the others were from Ecuador, Colombia, and Iraq. I poll the four on whom they voted for. Three Trump votes, though the young man from Colombia is careful to tell me he is in the process of becoming a citizen, and did not vote, and supports Trump mainly on social issues, which are important in his Catholic faith. His wife chose to live in Doral for the quality schools. "You need limits—rules—you can't let everyone do what they want to do. Abortion, drugs," he tells me. There must be someone in charge of regulating things. He thinks the Biden Administration signals people who are looking to come into the country, and people come here illegally for an opportunity because they think that was going to be allowed by Biden.

The gentleman from Ecuador, who might be the oldest but certainly has the most experience in the industry, always votes Democratic. He worked for the Chilean airline LATAM before making the move. He hoped Clinton would win in 2016: "She was qualified." He thinks Biden should have made it clear early that he would be a one-term president.

And their colleague's journey from Baghdad to Doral is a wild one. His mother was Greek and his father was Jewish. At the start of the Iraq war, when he was fourteen, they went, fled really, first to Greece, then to Sicily by boat, then to Brooklyn through the UN resettlement program, and finally to Chicago, where family had established themselves. He graduated from Truman College in Chicago, joined the Army, and returned to his birthplace for two tours with the 82nd Airborne. Back home, he worked for Lufthansa Cargo and then moved to his present job, which he likes very much.

He supports Trump mainly on the issue of guns. I wonder about the Democratic ticket's embrace of the issue, talking about their personal ownership and if that made any difference for him. "No," he says. Regulation of guns is too embedded in the Democratic platform for Harris's and Walz's pronouncements to matter or sway his vote. "They're taking guns from good people."

FREEDOM

You can stroll the streets of Kennesaw—a northwestern Atlanta suburb and the starting point for the Civil War's Great Locomotive Chase, in which Union raiders commandeered a Confederate train—without carrying a firearm or even owning a firearm, despite the municipal ordinance that requires every head of household in the city of some 33,500 people to own both a gun and ammunition. The law was passed in 1982, a retaliatory statute to Morton Grove, Illinois, which had passed a ban on handguns. It was exotic legislation back then. In similarly vindictive fashion, though perhaps a bit more puckishly, Kennesaw's neighboring town of Acworth passed its own ordinance requiring citizens to own a rake. The rake mandate was stripped from the books in 2009, point having been made, I suppose.

The Kennesaw ordinance is more about the message sent, the idea that criminals might think twice about breaking in when they know the homeowner is, by law, strapped. "It's a deterrent," says James Rabun of the Deercreek Gun Shop downtown, who told me the anecdote about "poli-tics." An elderly gentleman, likely the shop's founder, snoozes in a wheelchair by the front window, sporting a faded yellow T-shirt with the word "FREEDOM" emblazoned on it.

Across Main Street stands "The General," the original locomotive involved in the famous 1862 chase when, according to a nearby plaque, "it was stolen by the Northern raiders who tried unsuccessfully to wreck the Confederate supply line between Atlanta, Georgia, and Chattanooga, Tennessee, and recovered by the Southern crew after an 86-mile chase that has been the subject of books and motion pictures."

Back in the gun shop, Rabun says that he's buying more guns than he's selling, a function of estate sales and folks needing some extra cash. He doesn't know the precise figures but contends that Kennesaw is a relatively safe city, and the numbers back him up. According to city-data.com, the violent crime rate in Kennesaw was a little more than half the national average in 2022, and the property crime rate less than half.[6]

---

6   "Crime Rate in Kennesaw, GA," City-Data.com, February 20, 2025, https://www.city-data.com/crime/crime-Kennesaw-Georgia.html#google_vignette.

THE WAY LIFE SHOULD BE

In New England, along with New Hampshire and Vermont, Maine is a permitless carry state, and Harris did win the state, minus the second congressional district, including its one electoral vote.

When you cross the Piscataqua River on Route 95 from New Hampshire to Maine, you are welcomed with a greeting I find hard to argue with: "Maine. The way life should be."

I was on a trip to Texas in November 2023 when a troubled trained sharpshooter killed eighteen in a bowling alley in Lewiston, Maine. The news of the shooting played on the screen in the breakfast room in the motel in Austin, but no one seemed to take notice. Social media seemed confused about Maine, thinking it was like Massachusetts, gun-free. Some from Maine wondered, since "everyone" carries, why fire wasn't returned. Of course, Massachusetts is not "gun-free," and not everyone is carrying in Maine as far as I can tell. And Massachusetts's strict gun laws do not guarantee that what happened in Maine will not happen there.

I was in Tennessee when twenty-one children and teachers were killed at the Robb Elementary School in Uvalde, Texas. The reaction then was more robust than I anticipated. A plaintive billboard appeared in a rural town center; there was discussion on a local talk radio show on what could be done to prevent such a thing from happening again. Everyone seemed to be talking about it, at least for a few days. But like the waves battering the coast of Maine, all gets washed away with time. Until the next time.

Lewiston's centrist Democratic congressman, Jared Golden, forty-three, a Marine Corps veteran with a 100 percent rating from the National Rifle Association, came out for a ban on assault rifles after the shooting. His district, one of two in Maine, is the largest by area east of the Mississippi River. In most of it, one could fire an assault rifle, blindfolded, and never come near hitting a human being. The Range Safety Officer at the Texas Gun Experience would be horrified, I'm guessing.

In Tennessee, Congressman Andy Ogles from Nashville sent a Christmas card in 2021 with his family positioned in front of a decorated tree, all toting assault rifles. Less than a year-and-a-half later, when a gunman killed six at the Covenant School in his district, he said he was "devastated." Asked to reconcile his literal familial embrace of weaponry with his apparent devastation he said, "Ultimately I think what this does is highlight some of the mental health issues, the mental health crisis we have in this country that needs to be the real conversation we're having right now."[7]

Gun safety advocates don't like to take the focus off the gun, repeating the truism that mental health issues exist in other countries but we're the only country where this happens with regularity. But since 1982, depending on your definition, there have been over 150 mass shootings, and the vast majority were committed by a shooter who identified as male.

Congressman Ogles might not be your cup of tea, but I don't remember any of his colleagues across the aisle taking him up on his offer to "look at the mental health issues" or join him in a conversation about "the mental health crisis."

The Harris/Walz ticket shifted on the issue of guns from the standard Democratic playbook, but it did not move the needle much on voter behavior. Polls showing that voters favor, by healthy margins, "common sense" regulation on assault rifles and background checks. But this doesn't change the reality on the ground. There are 120 guns for every 100 people in this country.

But I'm left with this thought: If we just banned men from owning assault rifles, there would have been very few mass shootings in the past forty years. I mention this to be provocative, and it's not something the Constitution would allow, of course. But it is a fact, it's statistically irrefutable, and it tentacles into many other elements of society.

Maybe the debate over this nation's "gun problem" could start by absolving half the population from the discussion. Women with guns don't seem to be the issue. Perhaps then there could be a focus on what makes an exceedingly small number, relative to the population, of men commit mass murder. Congressman Ogles might not see it this way, but he may be on to something.

---

7   Rose Horowitch, "Rep. Andy Ogles, whose district includes Nashville, is criticized over a gun filled Christmas photo," NBC, March 28, 2023.

REFLECTION

If people everywhere in my travels feel disconnected, they very much bear the consequences of broken federal policy. Every school shooting sees the same response: ephemerally heated debate in Washington, and cynical appeals for money to fight either side of the cause legislatively, while the local community is left to grieve and move on, not just in red or blue states and not just in communities with a certain economic demographic, but everywhere.

Regulation of our natural resources are debated far away from the source, and the changing reality on the ground results in broad-brushed policy talking points in a system of checks and balances that are no longer nimble or responsive to real conditions and competing interests.

The middle class drops in real income and shrinks as a percentage of the population, and there is no bipartisan "big think" to propel the next generation across an economic bridge to the twenty-second century. Tech professionals, cognizant that the artificial intelligence horizon that once seemed so distant is now upon us, are encouraging their children to go into skilled trades and creative fields, presumably more resistant to AI, *The Wall Street Journal* reported in March 2025.[1] And the thinking presented in the Heritage Foundation's "Project 2025" document, embraced by the Trump Administration tariff strategy, is to force everyone backward over Bill Clinton's twenty-first century bridge to the twentieth, when America was great in their eyes.

The Democrats beckon, certain that they serve the country with the best of intentions, for those who feel stuck in place and those who have sought refuge

---

1   Callum Borchers, "Parents in Tech Want Their Kids to Go Into the Arts Instead," *Wall Street Journal*, March 5, 2025.

in places that seem to fit better, but the certainty cannot in any way repair the severed connection.

Back at the beginning, the Founders set the number of federal representatives at sixty-five. Congress being the branch of government closest to the people and the House of Representatives being the body directly elected by (some of) the people, each member represented slightly over 57,000 people, the population of a good-sized small city in America today.[2] I talk to a lot of people in cities this size who know their mayor and what she or he does.

Today, each of the 435 members of the House represents roughly 747,000 people, an impossible number to get to know, or even have your name known by.[3] This anonymity cuts both ways, insulating members at a time when polls show disapproval of Congress as a body, but feeding the disconnect, your representative being so distant.

I ask everyone I can who their member of Congress is. Most have no clue. Almost everyone can name a member of Congress, but it's usually someone with a high profile and it's usually not theirs. A small business owner in Corona, California, knows who his congressman is, Ken Calvert, but then adds, "I wouldn't know him if he walked through that door."

If Congressman Calvert did walk through the door, the proprietor might ask him why it seems members of Congress come out richer than they go in, or could anything be done about housing? A member of Congress today might thank their circumstances that they don't have to interact the way a small-city mayor might.

And the distance widens.

---

2   Drew Desilver, "House of Representatives is same size as in Taft era," Pew Research Center, May 31, 2018.

3   "Crime Rate in Kennesaw, GA."

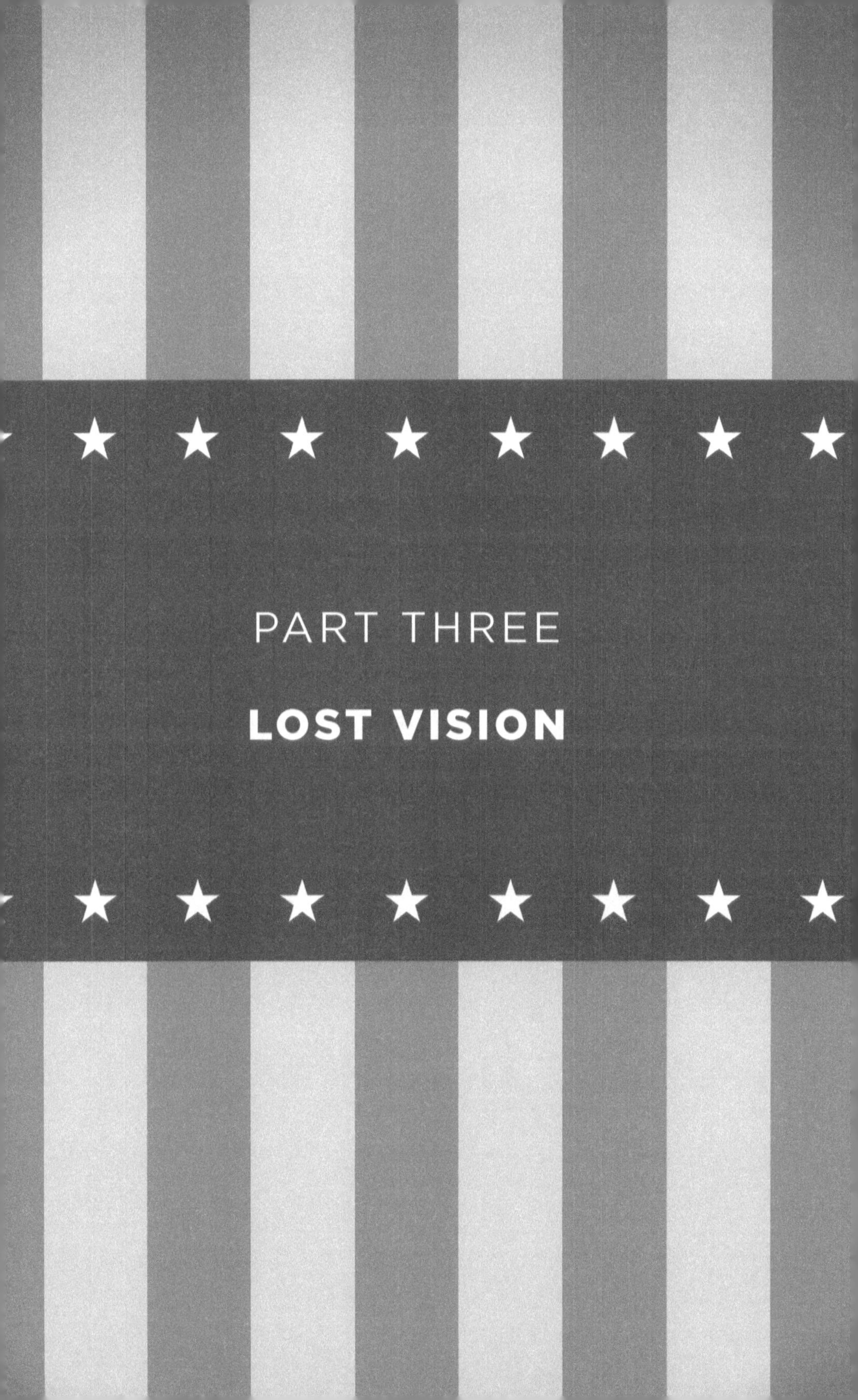
PART THREE

LOST VISION

CHAPTER NINE

GREED

If you had the inherent qualities, desires, and skill set needed to position you to grow up to be a robber baron, the 1830s was a great decade to be born. While the antislavery movement began to pick up steam, Chicago was incorporated as a city, and Arkansas and Michigan admitted states, some babies who would one day become quite wealthy were born. It was one perfect time in the history of the United States for those with an innovative mind and an understanding of financial markets.

The nation had coalesced, four decades into its democratic experiment, into a stew of the right ingredients: industrialization encouraged by the Founders, promotion of experimentation, physical expansion of the country racing toward the West Coast, and the revolution of the steam engine—all spiced with the blessing of immigration to power the barons' boundless ambition. The 1830s produced men who learned to sup from the intoxicating mix to astounding financial success.

Marshall Field, Andrew Carnegie, James Fisk, Jay Gould, James J. Hill, J.P. Morgan, Frederick Weyerhauser, James Fair, and John D. Rockefeller would be worth a combined $1.3 trillion in today's dollars, higher than the GDP of all but nineteen countries in 2024. If you live in a time that knows no bounds, what bounds tie you to the average human experience?

The Gilded Age (1865–1902), opulent in its economic expansion and opportunity for those newly reaching our shores, yet ugly in its exploitation of the same, made America an economic juggernaut as it stepped onto the world stage. The world had witnessed the revolution of the steam engine, and it would never be the same.

At noon on a blistering cold January day in 2025, the modern-day robber barons, coming of age in the technology revolution, assembled in the rotunda of the Capitol building in Washington, DC. They bore witness to the promise of the unraveling of a century-plus of regulation and rules that the modern-day oligarchs, the ones Joe Biden warned us about in his last remarks as president, believe hinder innovation. Elon Musk, Mark Zuckerberg, Shou Zi Chew, Miriam Adelson, Mukesh Ambani, Bernard Arnault, and Sergey Brin are worth a combined $1.3 trillion today, and it begs the question once again: If you live in a time that knows no bounds, what ties you to the average human experience?

If the Gilded Age helped the United States become a world power, this one, we're promised, will rocket us to galactic superiority. Not "for all mankind," as in the quaint NASA days, but for America, from the Gulf to the fifty-first state of Canada, a post-apocalyptic future for the free world.

"I want to warn the country of some things that give me great concern. And this is a dangerous concern. And that's the dangerous concentration of power in the hands of a very few ultra-wealthy people," Joe Biden said on his way out the door. "Today, an oligarchy is taking shape in America of extreme wealth, power, and influence that literally threatens our entire democracy, our basic rights and freedoms, and a fair shot for everyone to get ahead," he added.[1]

People agree that greed for wealth, or wealth and power, depending on with whom I'm speaking, is what fuels politics at the federal level. Greed, which Merriam-Webster defines as "a selfish and excessive desire for more of something (such as money) than is needed."[2]

And there is broad agreement that such greed causes a lot of individuals' personal struggles with housing choices, affordability of goods and services, inflexibility in work options, health care costs and availability, and well, just the ability to get ahead and get back to the promise of the American dream.

But there is a sharp divide, depending on who I'm talking to, on who is to blame. In wealthy towns that voted for Harris, it tends to be pinned on the billionaires who are "not paying their fair share" and corporate monopolies that pay no taxes. When Brian Thompson, CEO of UnitedHealthcare, was assassinated on an early December 2024 morning in Midtown Manhattan, my Bluesky feed,

---

1   David Remnick, "An Oligarchy is Taking Shape," The Lede, *New Yorker*, January 16, 2025.

2   Merriam-Webster Dictionary, s.v. "greed," accessed online May 6, 2025.

touted as a safe space for thoughtful discourse, was anything but, with calls to donate to his accused killer's defense fund.

When voters vote against their economic interest, they might do so out of the civic responsibility they have for living and thriving in this country. It can also come with an entitled sense that others should behave in the same way, particularly those who make fantastic amounts of money, and the civic minded don't know how those who have so much can be so selfish. But if the rich don't "pay their fair share," have no sense of obligation, or shame, they must be compelled legislatively to fully participate, some on the progressive end believe.

The late author Kurt Vonnegut wrote in the *New Yorker* in 2005 about an exchange he had with fellow late writer Joseph Heller while at a hedge fund manager's house on Shelter Island, New York. Vonnegut teased Heller that their host made more money that day than Heller ever would from his book *Catch-22*, widely regarded as one of the great American novels. Heller replied that he had something the hedge fund manager could never have. Vonnegut, not exactly considered a hack himself, asked what that might be, and Heller said, "The knowledge that I've got enough."[3] This message resonates with wealthy but not filthy-rich voters, and it's not surprising that Democratic senators and representatives in wealthy districts say things like this. It works well back home and has the added benefit if it's a policy they truly believe in.

In conversations in less wealthy places, the government isn't seen as the one solving any of the problems listed above. In fact, innovation and the private sector might help, I'm told. And folks in these communities see an apparent hypocrisy in Democratic elected officials cozying up to their own band of millionaires and billionaires as well as a lopsided majority of the beautiful people—all of them wealthy—raising money from them, listening to them, vacationing with them. And it makes them ask questions, very prominently among them: *How did Hunter Biden get rich?*

I have taught a course on elections at a small private Catholic college, Stonehill, in Easton, Massachusetts, for twelve years. A lot of my students are the first in their families to attend a four-year college. I ask them privately to define "the

---

3   Narendra Goidani, "'But I Have Something He Will Never Have—ENOUGH,'" *Medium*, March 5, 2019, https://narendragoidani.medium.com/but-i-have-something-he-will-never-have-enough-8036d03d089b.

middle class" by income range, which some analysts peg as two-thirds to double the median household income or roughly $56,000 to $170,000 dollars.

The students' guesses every year range from $20,000 to sometimes $500,000 dollars. That usually leads to a healthy discussion of how politicians portray the "middle class," how they want all or most of us to see ourselves there, and how one or the other might be a champion for us. If you find yourself thinking you are in the middle, at $50,000 or $500,000, it's easier to talk about the economic assault from above and below your station. A Gallup poll released in May 2024 found that 54 percent of Americans consider themselves part of the middle class.[4]

And if you see yourself in the middle, you may be thinking about those on welfare or not pulling their weight on one side, and greedy rich people who do not pay their fair share on the other, are all fair game for attack. Of course they don't mean "us." We're pulling our weight, and we certainly aren't greedy.

The divide among voters is less Trump/Harris and more that socioeconomic sides have picked their candidates. Those I talk to in wealthier communities think Trump and Musk are gaming the system for their financial advantage; those billionaires don't "pay their fair share." When politicians tie middle-class tax relief with higher taxes on billionaires and greedy corporations, it resonates.

In less wealthy communities, people wonder why tax relief for them is tied to punishment for Elon Musk, and it makes them question what the motivation is, the agenda behind the call. What would they use Elon Musk's money for, exactly? Big government needs money to feed added programs, each perhaps worthy when taken individually. But coming in a rush, as happened during COVID under both the Trump and Biden Administrations, seems like a lot, and who wants bigger government? Democrats.

Capitalism is a perverted system when you think about it. When you can least afford it, things cost more: credit, insurance, food. Amanda in Cleveland, Tennessee, who is quick to offer someone in need her basement apartment, which has a kitchen, mentioned to someone staying there for a couple of months that they would be doing a toilet paper run during the pandemic and asked if she wanted any. "No," she replied; her weekly budget allowed the purchase of one roll.

---

4   Megan Brenan, "Steady 54% of Americans Identify as Middle Class," *Gallup.com*, May 23, 2024, https://news.gallup.com/poll/645281/steady-americans-identify-middle-class.aspx.

I know Amanda, and she would not let you run out of toilet paper, but that's not the point, is it?

LET'S GO BRANDON!

The bar at the Twin Peaks restaurant in Independence, Missouri, is full at game time on a Sunday. It's a bye week for the Chiefs, so there's some rooting for Dallas or Pittsburgh, depending on playoff calculus or hometown affection, though it seems both teams are renowned for national fandoms. The man perched in the corner in the bright orange hat orders four shots of Fireball, shouts out several names of regulars, and the bartender obliges.

A woman to my right says, "To the Steelers," and someone replies, "Fight Cancer," but I assume the two are unrelated. There is running commentary on the games and discussion of the Chiefs, who would go on to compete in the Super Bowl in three months. I agree with the gentleman next to me, rooting for Dallas, that the hate directed at Patrick Mahomes is undeserved.

Political ads fill the screens during breaks, though the sound is muted. Kansas City does not sit in a swing state—though Obama made it close in 2008—and the patrons at Twin Peaks have had it with the ads. "They're on constantly," the man to my left casually says to no one in particular. The man in the orange hat is sparring with the wife of a couple to his right. The bartender teases, "No politics. I'm not breaking up a bar fight."

I strike up a conversation with the woman who sat down next to me, originally from Dallas; she and her electrician husband retired here where it's more affordable. Her son is a newish police officer, college not having worked out. She is showing me pictures of his wedding when the shot glasses arrive for us both.

The couple working out their political differences has bought a round for a wider circle, and we're included, in addition to the orange hat. I say, "Thank you," clink glasses with the woman from Dallas, who seems a little skeptical, and notice the wife's "Let's Go Brandon" shirt. Her husband asks what brings me here. In the football banter, I had mentioned I'm regionally bound to support the New England Patriots.

I say I'm researching a book on the state of voter disconnect from our national politics. He asks me why I think that is. "I'm here to find out. You tell me," I say.

After a pause he says, "I think it's greed."

I pause and reply, "I hear that a lot."

He expands, "They're all greedy. The government. They all get rich, they make too much money, the lobbyists."

The woman from Dallas, a little flushed, says she wishes we had better choices. I play moderator and ask generally if they could pick anyone to be the next president, anyone, who would it be. "Anyone?" I'm asked. Someone says Ron DeSantis, and there are a few nods. Someone says, "Obama gave great speeches." They debate for a bit about federal interference, generally, and leaving everything to the states, the greed of Washington dipping into their pockets, and they all agree on term limits.

No one mentions Harry Truman. We're in his hometown, the place he spent his entire life, save his stint in Washington and service in Europe during the First World War. I wouldn't expect to hear his name; Independence is a big city, and Truman left the presidency seventy years ago. Earlier in the day, when I opened the door to the Harry S. Truman National Historic Site Visitor Center on North Main Street, the Park Service employee seemed surprised to see me on this sleepy Sunday afternoon. She handed me a ticket for the 2 p.m. tour of the Truman house, no charge, and invited me to watch the movie, which was starting in a minute. She closed the door behind her, and I had a private showing of *The Trumans at Home*.

Harry married Bess Wallace in 1919, and they resided in the house her mother owned and lived in from that time until she passed away at the end of Truman's presidency in 1953. Talk about diplomacy! Putting Europe back together after WWII must have seemed a cakewalk.

The house itself is large, befitting the Wallaces' station in town, but unremarkable otherwise. Harry and Bess, free to do what they wanted with it after her mother's passing, added a big screened porch on the back. Except for two dinner-sized plates in the china cabinet, one with the presidential seal and one with Harry's image, there is nothing to indicate an occupant of the White House lived there. It is a suburban Victorian of an elderly couple from the 1950s. My millennial tour mate, who skipped the movie to join up at the front door of the house, was fascinated with the TV cabinet and the floor heat grates.

The image of the thirty-third president was carefully curated: A simple hardworking man who loved his family and rose to the occasion when thrust into power. And having done his duty, he returned home to live off his Army pension, walking a couple of brisk 120-paces-a-minute miles every morning.

Truman did not just live off his Army pension. I know this. Presidents retire with lots of friends—some rich ones—who want to help. It's a reality every former president faces, some embracing it more than others, others capitalizing on his former position enough to live comfortably for the rest of his life without crossing the greed line. Each has done so to varied degrees of success or failure. While in office, presidents tell us they fight for the "little guy." But no one would consider anyone who has held the office to be a regular person. And once you're in, like regular old Harry Truman, you hobnob with the rich and famous, who are all around.

And it's unsurprising that family members of a president would seek opportunities to capitalize on the unique relationship, or that others would seek them out. Jimmy Carter's brother, Billy, even put his name on a line of beer, his signature on each can of "Billy Beer" over the quote, "I had this beer brewed up just for me. I think it's the best I ever tasted. And I've tasted a lot. I think you'll like it, too."

Joe Biden warned of oligarchs, and my sense is that people scratch their heads. The implied message is that those who voted for Trump have made the wrong decision in this regard. But they also don't see any evidence that the Biden Administration, at the conclusion of four years, did anything to break up the "monopolies," to fight the oligarchs. Democratic administrations also draw heavily from Wall Street to serve, for advice, for contributions, and often for policy inspiration. When they leave office, many take jobs funded by Wall Street.

President Obama said on Election Night 2008 that "change has come to America,"[5] but he held fast to traditional financial custom, appointing Tim Geithner, a former President of the Federal Reserve Bank of New York, to be his first Secretary of the Treasury.

And in April 2014, Obama hosted a "Next Generation" summit in the White House, which gathered one hundred heirs to billionaire fortunes, to make the pitch of philanthropic leadership. Think about this: An invitation to the White House by Barack Obama only because you will inherit control of enormous wealth.

---

5   NPR, "Transcript of Barack Obama's Victory Speech," *NPR*, November 5, 2008, https:// www.npr.org/2008/11/05/96624326/transcript-of-barack-obamas-victory-speech.

I'M SORRY, YOUR CLAIM HAS BEEN DENIED

Insurance companies presenting themselves as health-care companies while they deny claims for medical procedures administered by people who are actually providing health care is greed at work, people think. Members of Congress who leave richer than when they arrived is greed at work. Luigi Mangione, charged with the second-degree murder of UnitedHealthcare CEO Brian Thompson, plays the cult hero from his perch at the Metropolitan Detention Center in Brooklyn, New York.

But we each get to pick our face of greed. Sometimes it's corporate, sometimes it's those who "feed off the government handout," sometimes it's a government handout of another variety; often it's the government itself.

Hunter Biden seemingly enriching himself off of his father's public position is greed at work, I hear. Arguments to the contrary, or Hunter defenders pointing out that the Trump children are much worse, miss the mark.

In Marietta, Steve Fischer asks why CNN hates Donald Trump so much. I venture that CNN is a business, and the relentless coverage of Trump is good for business. He thinks it's more than that. He doesn't question corporate profits; he's happy to work at a very profitable construction company, and he wouldn't want anyone questioning why he makes what he makes. Elon Musk, too. He is a billionaire, not from greed but from genius in the eyes of many. Maybe it's the government that's greedy by wanting to reach further into his pocket?

While the Gilded Age of over a century ago propelled America to a global superpower, today Donald Trump talks of American economic exceptionalism, and it's appealing to voters. The cost then, and inevitably now, will be borne by those who find that the promise of trickling down wealth may whet their appetite for riches but never wets their plot of economic soil. The counter to Gilded Age greed helped lift those left behind and birthed the labor movement, but while there are singular voices today, there is no such answer in today's Democratic Party.

Fighting the oligarchy and a call that "the billionaires and millionaires" don't pay their fair share in taxes falls flat with a lot of voters I talk to. If you want to lower middle-class taxes, just lower them, they would argue. Not everyone understands the political war on those who are wildly successful. Shouldn't we be encouraging geniuses to innovate and invest? And those who don't answer the call to fight the oligarchs think that those who think we should tend to be pretty wealthy themselves. And isn't Bernie Sanders rich?

Should people pay their fair share? Sure, voters say. But when politicians start talking about people paying their fair share, it's hard not to see themselves in the firing line. After all, the "middle class" has historically been left out of the tax loophole class, so they think the rich will always figure out a way, and it's hard for them to imagine that the politicians who make the call wouldn't figure out the loopholes too. A politician might make good on their fight for the middle class, but very few voters believe those politicians belong to it, or even understand it, even if they hug their middle- or working-class roots on the campaign trail.

CHAPTER TEN

HOUSE UNCERTAIN

The year 1968 was explosive in every layer of American society, its impact rippling through the following years to the end of the Vietnam War; it altered the political landscape for more than a generation.

In 1970, the President's Commission on Campus Unrest concluded that the killing of four unarmed students and the wounding of several more during a protest of the US involvement in Vietnam on the campus of Kent State on May 4, 1970, was "unwarranted, inexcusable and unnecessary."[1] They also felt it was the most divisive time in America since the Civil War.

The memorial on the campus is covered in snow in March 2022, but it will soon will be covered in daffodils with the onset of spring. Fifty years ago, public opinion blamed the protesters. Today that has flipped, particularly among those younger than sixty.

On my way to the campus, I stop at an estate sale. The couple who puts them on in Ohio is part of a national company one can hire to handle the disposition of an estate of any kind. Brown furniture doesn't sell. Mid-century lamps do. Pottery, yes. Hummel figurines, no. Things that were collectible at one time are not presently things anyone wants to collect today. Farm and yard equipment sell. The culturally inappropriate china figurines were in the 50-percent-off-from-marked category.

---

1   "Special Report: The Kent State Tragedy, by the President's Commission on Campus Unrest · Kent State University Libraries. Special Collections and Archives," accessed May 25, 2025, https://omeka.library.kent.edu/special-collections/items/show/3419.

This couple handles thirty or so a year. Some big, some small. Sometimes the small ones make the year for them. This was a mid-century split entry, and the mid-century's families' lives seem frozen in time walking from room to room, as if they had left for a family vacation in 1970 and never returned: paper dolls and paper doll clothes, Hot Wheels speed track, house dresses in the closets, a record player and Bing Crosby records, glass Christmas ornaments in their original boxes and strings of Christmas tree lights (the kind that got hot and burned your little kid fingers if you touched them), the good silver plate, ornamental dishes, portraits of grandma and grandpa.

As I wander, childhood memories within each room, all green shag carpet and brown linoleum, past the pink bathroom to the paneled family room with the faux-brick fireplace in the lower level, I think of the generation of Baby Boomers who would be at home here. My parents paid $14,000 in 1964 for one not as grand as this. My dad recounted that he was terrified, and that if it had been $14,500, they couldn't have afforded it.

A report by the Joint Center for Housing Studies at Harvard points out the change in domestic living, and how elusive the house holding the estate sale I visited in Canton or the place I grew up in in Burlington, Massachusetts, is today. "In 2022, the median sale price for a single-family home in the US was 5.6 times higher than the median household income, higher than at any point on record dating back to the early 1970s," and it was accelerated by the pandemic.[2]

The volatile times we live in may be the most divisive since the Commission on Campus Unrest released its 1970 report on the state of the country after the turbulent decade of the '60s. But today, housing has become destabilized everywhere I go. The volatility of the '60s—sending American kids halfway around the globe to fight and die in a senseless war—led to the end of a presidency ("Hey, hey, LBJ, how many kids did you kill today?"), not an overthrow of the country. In the late 1960s, the American Dream lived, if you did.

It's easier to weather a national storm if you have stable shelter, literally, and in much of this country today, unless you are one of the lucky few who can afford it, that storm rocks everything in your world. And when you add existential crisis,

---

2   Alexander Hermann et al., "Home Price-to-Income Ratio Reaches Record High," Joint Center for Housing Studies, January 22, 2024, https://www.jchs.harvard.edu/blog/home-price-income-ratio-reaches-record-high-0.

climate, a declining standard of living, and assaults on the norms of democracy, it's harder to weather divisive times.

DO YOU REALLY WANT TO KNOW?

The clerk in the convenience store in Cartersville, Georgia, says, "Do you really want to know?" when I ask him how his day is going. I stopped my futile search for seltzer water, which I have determined exists in abundance only in certain parts of New England. I say I do. I caught him just at the time he had received another rejected application for an apartment. Months ago, his wife had a health emergency, which took priority over the rent, ultimately leading to them losing their apartment. They've been lodged in the motel next to the store for weeks, living on state housing vouchers.

Each application for a new apartment costs a nonrefundable $100, and he is now out $1,000. Each attempt takes him further away from stability. He moved his family down here from West Virginia to get away from "the drugs." But he's thinking of going back.

The next morning, outside my room at the Quality Inn on the outskirts of town, I see a school bus idling. The older kids stop in the lobby to get a donut before walking to the high school, and the younger kids file onto the bus. Checking the map on the back of my motel door, the one required to show emergency exits, though every room door here leads directly outside, I see no suites, no kitchenettes. Every room with just a bed, a desk, a dresser, and enough of them filled with families to require a school bus stop.

Cartersville Mayor Matt Santini, in his second term, tells me he's proud of the revival of the downtown, as he should be, and that there is very little unemployment in town. The economic success exacerbated a housing shortage. The families housed in the hotels and motels in town work for a living.

And if you are nicely housed in Cartersville, you might be stuck as well. Glenn is a chef who trained at the Culinary Institute of America and moved here to get out of "Hurricane Alley" in Florida when his kids were younger. He has a blended family: several children of his own, those of his current wife, and the grandchildren that are all local. He's pretty young for such a blessing, and it's anchoring him in place, in a house that is too big for his empty nest.

He and his wife would like to move to New Orleans. This I understand, given his training and profession, and I don't mention his past concern for hurricanes. But how can he, with family so close? He doesn't see a lot of options locally. They're settled where they are, and he adds, "Who could afford to buy my place?" I understand what he's saying. For those of a certain age, who purchased at a certain price point, the current value of their property seems out of reach. Who could possibly have that much money? When buyers outbid each other or pay in cash, sellers want to, and do, take it, knowingly complicit in a seemingly unsustainable Ponzi scheme.

Out in Nevada, evictions are up. A *Las Vegas Weekly* story by Shannon Miller from August 2023 reports that, even before the pandemic, Nevada's supply of affordable housing fell way below demand. But since, "Records from North Las Vegas Justice Court show that since the pandemic, eviction filings increased from 3,931 cases in fiscal year 2019 to 5,328 in fiscal year 2022—or by about 35% in three years."[3]

In addition, "compared to other states, Nevada has the highest percentage of extremely low-income renters that are severely cost-burdened, meaning the renter pays more than 50% of income on rent and housing expenses."

Congressman Steven Horsford (D-NV), whose district includes part of Las Vegas, counties to the north, and counties running west to the California border, told Miller, "Tenants...unfortunately are running out of options to stay housed. Landlords, some of whom are trying to do the right thing...also can't afford to keep people in their units without getting paid. And the system isn't working."[4]

Where there are great challenges, great opportunities sometimes exist. Enter the Siegel Group. On the way back from walking along the Truckee River in Reno, Nevada, I passed The Virginian. A Siegel property, it advertises "flexible stay apartments." It has choices, furnished or not, long-term or not, pet and kid friendly, and presumably "flexible" in looking at credit history.

Founded in 2001 by Steven Siegel (not the actor; that's "Seagal") and headquartered in Paradise, Nevada, the company has leaned into the acquisition of aging or abandoned properties and converting them to housing units in Nevada,

---

3   Shannon Miller, "Tenant Turmoil: Evictions Pile Up As Nevada's Stark Affordable Housing Landscape Worsens," *Las Vegas Weekly*, August 17, 2023.

4   Miller, "Tenant Turmoil."

Arizona, and California, which has the second lowest rate of home ownership in the country. Nevada does slightly better.

I pause to watch the comings and goings for a bit: coming in ones and twos, from work I assume at that hour, going out with dogs on leashes. There is a steady stream of goings and comings. In the opportunity-from-a-challenge department, Siegel is a winner.

Being housed is a crushing burden for people who do not have easy choices. Siegel has stepped into this breach in a practical, concrete way that the government cannot. Siegel's company can buy, convert, and rent. Governments cannot do any of those things easily.

Of course, this is a business that has profited from hardship. The road in Illinois from Springfield to Cairo is dotted with micro-towns of 1,000 or fewer residents, each with a dollar store, and it seemed to me driving through that the only thing worse than a town with a dollar store would be one without.

It might be easy to look at a dollar store or Siegel as exploiters of vulnerable populations, turning a profit from those least able to pay for essential services like housing or food. But on the ground, both do provide essential services. One might die waiting for a Trader Joe's to roll into town or for that available apartment to present itself.

Mike Nicholson, the thirty-year-old mayor of Gardner, Massachusetts, a first-time homebuyer, bid on thirty-eight houses—including one he waited six months for, a bid accepted but contingent on the homeowner's finding a place to buy, only to lose it when the homeowner couldn't find one. Nicholson finally closed on the thirty-ninth bid. The American Dream includes the fairytale of finding a dream home, but when the win comes just before the fortieth try, that probably seems like a dream finally answered. If it wasn't the city he was elected to lead, he might have given up, one suspects. Lack of housing choice is an issue everywhere I go, not just in the ranked high-cost metropolitan areas we read about each year.

BRICKTOWN

Take Oklahoma City, Oklahoma. The neighborhood of Bricktown attracts tourists to the Chickasaw Ballpark, home of the Triple-A affiliate of the Los

Angeles Dodgers, or to those willing to spend a certain price point, Mickey Mantle's Steakhouse across the street, where you can smoke cigars in the bar.

The temporary "penny" sales tax in the city, renewed several times, funds improvements, parks, trail construction, and it helped attract the NBA's Oklahoma City Thunder to town. "We've had a series of good mayors who served several terms," says Dan, who I meet in March 2025 at the memorial to the Alfred P. Murrah Federal Building bombing victims, one month shy of the thirtieth anniversary of the deadliest domestic terror attack in US history.

I mention that it's a great city except for one thing that stands out to me: a lack of people living and working downtown. Outside of the Bricktown tourists, you can safely walk across the boulevard-wide streets on a Sunday morning, against the light, with your eyes closed, and live to tell the tale.

"It's better than it was thirty years ago," Dan continues, "but no one lives downtown." I say there seems to be a lot of new condo or apartment construction in Bricktown, and he affirms. He always tries to live near where he works, saying a shorter commute is on the plus side of work-life balance. He owns a home in the city and the yard that comes with it, not far from work. But though house prices are better here than a lot of places, rents are going up, and even though there's a lot of construction, it's pricing people out.

At The Mick's steak house, I opt not for the $70 steak, though I'm sure it's locally sourced, and order the seafood salad, which is excellent, but by geographical reality not locally sourced. My server, Matt, like Dan, is a native who has returned after living a number of years in Colorado Springs. He loved it there, but the rent increased each year, enough that after several years it tipped the scales for him. He was working to pay for his rent, and scrambling to live, so he came back home.

During the 2024 campaign, Donald Trump proposed to eliminate federal taxes on tips, and when in office, he signed an executive order to do so. I ask Matt if it helps, and he likes the idea. He only makes $3 an hour but does well on tips at the steak house. He thinks, though, it will be a wash for him. There is a cap on what isn't taxed, and he thinks it keeps him in the same tax bracket. Housing is cheaper in OKC than "the Springs," but costs keep going up.

Kamala Harris proposed a first-time homebuyer stipend of $25,000. As spring blooms across the country in 2025, Democrats are hyper-focused on "the resistance," and the housing stipend is not widely mentioned. Most people I talk with discuss the lack of housing options, either finding affordable places to live or stuck in a situation that is not ideal or no longer works (too much or too little house, long commute times, etc.).

Campaigns focus on hot-button issues, flames fanned by partisan media, but across the country, almost everyone I talk to mentions the price of housing. It may be a button to focus on that's not as warm, but I suspect it would get people's attention.

CHAPTER ELEVEN

THE BORDER GIVETH AND THE BORDER TAKETH AWAY

You approach a lot of US towns off an interstate. To get downtown, once off the highway, you typically pass the usual sentries of suburbia: fast food, gas stations, hotels. I've seen my share of Speedways and Holiday Inns.

Of course, in a lot of particularly older cities, the approach is through less economically advantaged—what we used to call "poor"—neighborhoods where the jobs used to be: the factories, odiferous things those living in the big houses closer to downtown didn't want to be near.

I approach Springfield, Ohio, in this way and make my way into a downtown that I can tell is working hard to move past a postindustrial slump. It's easy to find a parking space in the early afternoon, even in front of City Hall. A sound truck, a speaker mounted on the roof, circles, again and again. Bob Avakian, chairman of the Revolutionary Communist Party, has sent his people.

Trump and Harris are the same, Avakian argues in his public statements, though Bob himself held his Communist nose in 2020 and urged people to reject Trump's reelection. We don't, I'm told by the not-quite-middle-aged follower of Avakian holding a stack of fliers, "have an immigration problem. We have a capitalism-imperialism problem." Their position on immigration, if not capitalism, is echoed here, from the Republican mayor to the business owners who benefit from the Haitian community's labor to the longtime residents lining up to speak during the public comment period at the evening's County Commission meeting.

Bruce, a retired American Baptist minister, comes to every meeting to support his elected officials generally, but specifically to be there for them in this particularly challenging time. I ask if he was taken aback when Donald Trump called out their city of 60,000 during the recent presidential debate, alleging that Haitian immigrants were eating the city's cats and dogs. He regrets the circus atmosphere. When I ask him to elaborate, he points to me, an outsider wearing a Red Sox cap, and then broadly around the plaza, small groups milling in the afternoon sun, a camera crew or two, the Communists.

With little more than a month to go before Election Day, Bruce thinks JD Vance will take a hit here, their home-state senator throwing shade at Springfield and causing such disruption and cost. Vance may have won his election as senator in a fairly tight race statewide, but he carried it two-to-one here. Same as Trump in 2020. But when Election Day arrived a few weeks hence, Vance did not take a political hit, the ticket winning the county comfortably in 2024, punching his ticket out of Ohio and into residency in the Naval Observatory in Washington, DC.

Springfield was named after an industrial city in western Massachusetts, but since the turn of this century, this namesake, like its sister city, which suffered its own economic decline decades before, has lost a significant chunk of the manufacturing that built it, 30 percent of the population that made it thrive, and a corresponding percentage in median income that hollowed out the downtown retail. In 2011, long before Vance helped spread the pet-devouring rumors, Gallup judged Springfield in Ohio the "unhappiest city" in America.

City leaders did not take that dubious distinction lying down. They fashioned a leaseback deal to save manufacturing jobs from decamping offshore. They celebrate the American headquarters of Finnish company Konecranes, which bought R&M Materials Handling in the 1980s. And in 2014, the city began a "Welcome Springfield" campaign to attract new residents. As had been the case throughout American history, an immigrant community grew here and stanched the decline. If jobs went unfilled, the manufacturing dominoes would have continued to fall, but companies like Topre, Silfex, and McGregor Metal—not household names, but local lifelines—remain.

The Communists acknowledge they are here deliberately, though. It seems their presence is more about taking advantage of the attention Springfield is getting and less about being supportive of the Haitian community or the city.

I ask the not-quite-middle-aged man where he's from if not from here. "We're all from somewhere," he replies. I ask if the Revolutionary Communist Party is headquartered somewhere. He's evasive. He shows me Avakian's book, protected in a plastic bag like crime scene evidence, Bob's "Constitution," to replace the hallowed parchment document Trump has casually mentioned maybe should be suspended.

To speak at that night's County Commission meeting, one must be a Clark County resident and present an ID before putting their name on the list. The mayor explains the importance of all residents' input. I ask the gentleman next to me—in a black, maybe suede, "Trump country" cowboy hat—if he is from Springfield. He is, but he's here just to watch, not to speak. I listen to the first few who do. It's clear that services are strained, and further so from the bomb threats called into the local schools as well as Wittenberg University in the past two weeks. One person asks if the federal money and the state law enforcement presence couldn't be redirected to hire more local police. Springfield is getting national attention, but the speakers are raising local concerns and not playing to the cameras, at least inside City Hall.

Teri has never seen anything like the media frenzy resulting from Trump's comments. She's mixing martinis behind the bar at the Courtyard Marriott for three trainers from the elevator engineering division of KONE who are tucked into the corner while also keeping an eye on the other tables in the restaurant. She tells me later that the trainers ordered multiple glasses each, which is time-consuming when she's the only one on duty. The large group of locals at the nearby table usually call ahead, but they didn't today.

Teri is a native, the middle of seven kids raised by a single dad, Mom having walked out shortly after the seventh. Teri takes the hysteria, the bomb threats, the politicization of Springfield's immigrant-welcoming policy playing out at the Commission meeting across the street, in stride. But she's never seen anything like it. "I don't watch the news now. At all. Especially now."

Springfield, Ohio, is a place you can drive through and not notice, or perhaps you take note of some of the residential architecture, grand homes from a bygone era, or the empty storefronts if you were looking for a place to stop for lunch. But even after just a day here, you notice the people, the lovely college campus, the effort put into creating community, the friendliness of what Ohio native Warren Harding called "normalcy." Coined during his race for the White

House in 1920, for Harding the word included anti-immigrant isolationism. Today in Springfield, normalcy seems to include welcoming immigrants.

Across the street from the college, the local Lutheran church has its own message. "Feed your faith, not your fear."

THEY'RE TAKING THE TURTLES

A seafood snob from New England might snub their nose at oysters in Cincinnati, but I'm feeling reckless and ask the waiter where the oysters are from. "Wellfleet." I say that will do. Ice, planes, health codes—all reassuring factors in ordering seafood in the Midwest, at least for me. The restaurant is attached to a downtown hotel; he asks where I'm in from, and I tell him I was just in Springfield. He shakes his head, which I take to mean he's familiar with the controversy. He's from Guatemala. He came here when he was twelve, so he's been here half his life. He has an almost-one-year-old daughter.

I ask if he came over land. He did. I say he couldn't have come alone. He says no. He came with his six-year-old brother. His mother had come the year before—Cincinnati has a good-sized Guatemalan community—and other family members have since followed. I ask if he has a date for his asylum hearing. He shakes his head no.

In the meantime, potentially life-altering limbo time, he works, keeps his head down, and doesn't travel or do anything that might jeopardize his status. He tells me that his family tried to start businesses back home, first a toy store, then one to sell tamales. The controlling gang in the neighborhood collected protection money each time. When his family missed a payment, he remembers once when he was six, they took his pet turtle until payment was made.

I don't ask what he makes of the charge that Haitian immigrants were eating the dogs and cats in Springfield, and I guess he wouldn't venture commenting on politics. I also don't ask if he is concerned about the threats of mass deportation. What would he say? What *could* he say? His daughter is an American citizen, and his fate is out of his hands.

One year later, the deportations have started, and I wonder about him, if he still works there, and if it's enough for him to keep his head down. His daughter is, I suppose in the new administration's view, half or perhaps more a "birthright" citizen, her mother born in Cincinnati. At the time, I didn't ask him if he was concerned about a potential Trump Administration making good on its call for mass deportations. I wouldn't need to ask him today.

A PLAN AND A THREAT

I meet a lot of people in my travels, in every region of the country but mostly in southern and western states, who are not citizens. And while securing the border is the top concern going into the election, along with the economy, immigration is mentioned less so.

When Donald Trump says that Haitians in Springfield, Ohio, are eating the cats and dogs, it is taken by some to be straight-up racist, while others hear him speak of the need to secure the border. I haven't encountered anyone who espoused the "great replacement" theory, which, according to the immigrant advocacy group National Immigration Forum, "states that welcoming immigration policies—particularly those impacting nonwhite immigrants—are part of a plot designed to undermine or 'replace' the political power and culture of white people living in Western countries."[1]

The white population in the country continues to decline, and more white people die each year than are born. The percentage of the population that is African American has remained steady for decades. The Asian population has shown growth in the past decade, and the Latino population, including citizens who vote, has spiked. There are a number of states with a majority-minority population, and the entire country is on track to follow suit in the coming decades.

In individual conversations, voter focus across the board is very much on border control: who comes across, where they go when they're here, and how they will be sent back if they shouldn't be here. No one, with or without mentioning the "great replacement" theory, talks to me about putting a quota on a certain population. There is frustration with Congress for not coming up with a coherent immigration policy, but that seems secondary with the "crisis at the border."

---

1   Axios, "The 'Great Replacement' Theory, Explained," 2021, https://immigrationforum. org/wp-content/uploads/2021/12/Replacement-Theory-Explainer-1122.pdf.

And I find this frustrating. If Congress—and short of that, Democrats in Congress—tied an immigration policy to economic growth, made the case that a reasonable approach to allowing people into the country would fill the need most see every day, not only in the high-tech world annually supplied by the 65,000 H-1B visas, but to address the "Help Wanted" signs we all see everywhere, I believe it would make sense to voters. Maybe not at first—it's so out of hand, so toxic, but I think people would be receptive or could be persuaded. We shouldn't let the "great replacement" theory gain any more oxygen.

"A path to citizenship" can mean something different to people, and to first-generation immigrants who have trod different paths and who vote, the phrase is supercharged. They toiled down that path. There should be no shortcuts, in the eyes of many of them. I don't find anyone who argues we don't need more workers to fill the jobs advertised in most places I visit. I had lunch in McAllen, Texas, a few years back, right on the border. They didn't lack for workers in the restaurant. A reasonable plan allowing people into the country to work, a distinct step before a jump to a path to citizenship, seems something a majority could agree on.

But something has changed in the stories I hear since Donald Trump assumed office and started deporting people without due process. It's played out in the media every day: people shackled hand and foot, shaved heads, on a plane to El Salvador, or detained at the Canadian border and sent to a detention facility in Louisiana, or prevented from coming back to the country from Germany and held without access to needed medication.

I'm told by a woman who was born in Costa Rica, came here with her parents when she was an infant, and is a citizen, now in her forties, that her boyfriend will "tease" her if they are having an argument that he will turn her in to ICE.

A young father from Chicago tells me that his ten-year-old son is concerned with all the reports of deportations, despite assurances from him and his wife. They are American citizens, born here, as was their older son. But their second son was born in Mexico City, where they lived for a time, and it says so on his passport.

Recently, a landlord in Tennessee was shocked when, one night, he answered a loud knock on his duplex door to find his tenant's boyfriend, who told him that he, the landlord, was "harboring an illegal," meaning the complainant's girlfriend. Daylight brought reconciliation to the couple; the woman who rents is a quiet neighbor; she works and pays the rent on time. But the incident left the landlord shaken, concerned for his tenant, and offered a grim glimpse into how the policy now matching the rhetoric of the Trump campaign can be weaponized.

BORDER WORK

Migrant workers are essential to the economy of many of the states I've visited. Whether that be in Nevada or Arkansas or as I drive along the border in Texas from McAllen to Brownsville. I see them in the fields, congregating around trucks. Porta potties are trucked in as the workers gather to harvest the local crop. On the road into or out of town, I pass by a nondescript industrial building, and people are hanging out in the early morning, waiting for the day's assignment.

I haven't spoken with anyone who has told me they are in favor of an open southern—or I suppose, northern—border. Emma Lazarus in "The New Colossus" wrote: "Give me your tired, your poor, your huddled masses yearning to breathe free, The wretched refuse of your teeming shore. Send these, the homeless, tempest-tost to me, I lift my lamp beside the golden door!"[2] These words, added to the Statue of Liberty in 1903, almost thirty years after the gift from France was placed in New York harbor, were not true then, and they're not true now.

The Chinese Exclusion Act of 1882 barred immigrants from becoming citizens. From the Anarchist Exclusion Act of 1903 to the Naturalization Act of 1906 to the Quota Law of 1921—which put numerical limits on specific countries and set an overall annual cap of 350,000—to today, the country has been strengthened by the immigrants to its shores, but since "Liberty Enlightening the World" was placed on her pedestal in 1886, the country has never had an open border.

Of course, during the Biden Administration, the border was not "open" as Donald Trump charges. And the border has not been closed since Trump's

---

2   Emma Lazarus, "The New Colossus," Poetry Foundation, 1883, accessed September 29, 2025, https://www.poetryfoundation.org/poems/46550/the-new-colossus.

second inauguration on January 20, 2025. People in border states, and in those states that border those states, and in every state that is addressing the influx of migrants—a 2024 Republican US Senate candidate running in Massachusetts declared it "now a border state"—would appreciate a coherent policy on immigration from Democrats. And it has to be something better than, "Donald Trump killed the bipartisan border bill."

WHEN IS A RIVER JUST A RIVER?

In the book *Kings of Texas* about the famed King Ranch, which is larger than Luxembourg,[3] author Don Graham writes this about the Rio Grande Valley at the time of the war with Mexico:

> The point is emphatically this: the river was a river, not a boundary. What was being created here in this arid region was a civilization Spanish and Mexican in its articulations and institutions, and the people felt themselves separate from both interior Mexico and the rest of what eventually became Coahuila y Texas....
>
> The...Rio Grande thus became a political and divisive boundary separating families in Matamoros, for example, from their kin on the other side of the river: two riverbanks, two countries. Such division seemed unnatural and wholly against the grain of a century of relative stability based on the ancient patterns of stock raising and farming, trade and religion, and a common language. The boundary seemed completely arbitrary to one nation and completely justified in another.[4]

---

3   Texas State Historical Association, "The History and Legacy of King Ranch: A Texas Icon," Texas State Historical Association, accessed August 2, 2025, https://www.tshaonline.org/handbook/entries/king-ranch.

4   Don Graham, *Kings of Texas* (Trade Paper Press, 2004), 26.

Standing at the Brownsville side of the border to Matamoros, Mexico, I watch a steady flow of cars and people on foot crossing the international border from Mexico in a familiar Saturday shopping way, pulling carts behind them past the vegetable stands and specialty markets with purchases from Brownsville's bustling downtown. It's almost exclusively Latino shoppers and sellers, and mostly Spanish is spoken. There are two riverbanks, two countries, but one people here at the border.

It's cliché to say you need to physically see a place, or a situation, to fully appreciate it, particularly a complicated one involving an issue of national importance. Members of Congress routinely make trips to the battle zones and our military outposts across the globe, as they should. And here, there are high-profile visits to the border wall, elected officials meeting with those who protect it. And those not living anywhere near the border see it through the lens of these visits and the debates about the wall construction. But to know this place, you have to take a step back from the wall itself and look at the region and its people—on both sides of the border.

Do Democratic members of Congress, the vast majority not representing a border, conflate border security with immigration policy? And more importantly, do their constituents do so, inflamed by the racist overtones of MAGA rhetoric?

Borders need to be managed. One of the coping jokes from 2016 among Democrats was wondering how Canada would manage the northward panicked migration triggered by a Trump win. And that was before the tariffs of 2025. And before Trump made menacing overtures of turning Canada into the fifty-first state.

Despite the political rhetoric, there has been a general consistency in this management from administration to administration. When President Obama was criticized for his border policies, his backers cited statistics indicating that he deported at a greater clip than his predecessor, a Texas Republican. But the border has been weaponized through political rhetoric. The Obama Administration did not pound the table over enforcement actions, and the Trump Administration pounds the table harder over, at least in the first term, the same enforcement actions.

The new sections of wall don't impede the people who live here in their daily lives. I'm told this by a woman who crossed into Mexico for a medical appointment but got delayed coming back because the crossing was temporarily closed, which happens from time to time. "They may be looking for someone." She keeps a car on the Mexico side, which is essential.

Border patrols seem more active on the highways an hour or so north, and I encounter one between Brownsville and Corpus Christi. I'm waved through, right behind a pickup with a "Don't California my Texas" bumper sticker. The real enforcement activity happens, in my observation, between Brownsville and the secondary border checkpoint farther north. Every so often, a patrol car is perched watching traffic or you see blue lights flashing up ahead to find a truck pulled over on the side of the road. Border security is regional as well.

If we follow Graham's historic thinking that Mexico looks at the wall as arbitrary and the US looks at it as justified, then on this side, the focus is on the physical. Do we build a wall? Do we not? How many border officers, planes, cars, and drones are needed to secure it? Is the border a military line, to be held and strengthened?

And on the Mexico side, they would look at it as a river valley with families on both sides, and they might think that it's not about managing the river crossing but about the management of the migration of human beings. Many native-born Americans feel the same, it should be noted. Separating the stateside crisis of migration and the underlying causes that take root in countries south of Mexico, from the daily business of immigrating into this country, a story just about all of our families share, seems to be the atmosphere here.

At its heart are language, heritage, custom, family, and also faith. This is a very Catholic part of the country. If we relieve the pressure on the border, the crisis, we have "a civilization Spanish and Mexican in its articulations and institutions,"[5] according to Graham, and that is what it feels like here.

The Rio Grande itself twists and turns and doubles back and swings wildly from Hidalgo to Brownsville, and thusly the border barriers do, too. Driving along an industrial corridor in a very straight line, the wall sneaks up on you, fades back, disappears, then comes up screaming right beside you. Topography dictates the wall placement: Section, gap. Section, gap.

I see a neighborhood up ahead that looks like it backs into the border. It's a newish subdivision, right up against a Trump section of border wall, the Rio Grande just beyond. A homeowner has run his dog fence off the border wall.

---

5   Graham, *Kings of Texas*, 26.

CHAPTER TWELVE

LISTENING FOR GOD

John F. Kennedy finished his inaugural address in January 1961 by asking for "His blessing and His help, but knowing that here on earth God's work must truly be our own."[1] The first Catholic elected to the office, he was careful to state his intentions, to counter voices that were sure the Pope, at the time Pope John XXIII, would be running things from the Vatican. In his remarks to the Greater Houston Ministerial Association in September 1960, designed to address the suspicions of papal puppeteering of American affairs, he said:

"It was Virginia's harassment of Baptist preachers, for example, that led to Jefferson's statute of religious freedom. Today, I may be the victim, but tomorrow it may be you—until the whole fabric of our harmonious society is ripped apart at a time of great national peril."[2]

The Ole Sawmill Cafe, just south of the cloverleaf interchange of I-40 and AR-1, is nestled among Forrest City, Arkansas's wealth of fast-food franchises. This is decidedly not a chain restaurant.

But all is not well, even during the December 2023 holiday season. Pat notices "a lot of anger and a lot of drama" here, though she notes it's not restricted to the aromatic confines of her place of employ. She was attacked by a coworker,

---

1   "John F. Kennedy's Inaugural Address, 1961," The Gilder Lehrman Institute of American History, accessed September 29, 2025, https://www.gilderlehrman.org/history-resources/spotlight-primary-source/john-f-kennedys-inaugural-address-1961.

2   "John F. Kennedy, speech to the Greater Houston Ministerial Association-September 12, 1960," accessed May 25, 2025, http://www.presidentialrhetoric.com/historicspeeches/kennedy/houstonministerial.html.

she says, resulting in a concussion and ensuing migraines. When she called the cops, one talked with her inside while the other yukked it up outside with her assailant, who was younger, prettier.

"There's corruption, everywhere," Pat says. "The police station, the courthouse. I told him, I've never seen anything like y'all's corruption."

The anger, the drama. Even a seventy-seven-year-old coworker always brings the drama, she says.

Her customer agrees that it's like that all over, and that some blame Biden, some blame Trump. Pat agrees but thinks it goes deeper. There's not a lot going on in Forrest City. The indistinguishable hotels, clustered around the cloverleaf, appear in surfeit for a city of 13,000 people.

But anger does not seem a newcomer to a city that is, indeed, named for Nathan Bedford Forrest, he of Confederate generalship and Ku Klux Klan fame. In 1889, a riot kicked off in the afternoon and bled, literally, into the next day over Black residents' efforts to make political inroads in the county elections, resulting in several deaths, including that of a Black man named, poignantly, "Americus." Blacks fled the city, and by 1900, all white Democrats ran unopposed across the county.

The town did not hold its first racially integrated prom until 1988. Why not in the 1960s, when integration was court ordered? Because social clubs and families simply organized private, racially segregated dances instead. Forty-one years after Jackie Robinson integrated Major League baseball, Black kids and white kids finally went to the same high school dance.

Today, Forrest City seems possessed of a certain malaise. Pat, for her part, only has a few more payments to make before she pays off her place, and then she's getting out. She's sick of the corruption, the drama, the anger.

And she's not particularly rosy about the future, doesn't see anyone offering the type of solutions she'd like to see. "I think there's only one who can fix it, and that's God," says Pat. "And He's coming soon. And He's not going to be too happy."

If asked, Pat would probably conclude that the country had flunked JFK's inaugural assignment.

"CARRY ON WAYWARD SON"

I'm sitting in the sanctuary of the Faith Family Church in North Canton, Ohio, on a Saturday night. With 3,788 seats in a 298,000-square-foot building, this is not a bantamweight house of worship. The usher is very welcoming and invites us to sit where we like. As I do in large auditoriums, I climb up high to take things in.

The parking lot is suburban mall-sized and staffed like Gillette Stadium, home of the Patriots football team, where I'm always trying to remember where I parked. They have police details directing traffic. Couples, groups of teens, ones and twos holding Bibles or small pads to take notes, greet each other across the aisles. By the start, there are several hundred here with plenty of room for more.

We're here early enough to watch the place fill up. A chance, as we say in my church, to center ourselves in the quiet of the moment. And I do take things in, the wide expanse of it, unadorned by religious symbols, the stage set for musical performance.

Soon the house lights dim, and a rock drumbeat underscores praise to Jesus. The band is young, the guitar is strong, and the vocals are good. The congregation is uplifted, and it's hard not to be uplifted along with them. The band sings with conviction.

God plays a big role in elections. A study by Pew Research tells us that white Americans who regularly attend church services voted for Donald Trump over Joe Biden in 2020 roughly 60/40. Those numbers flipped for those who attend church services only occasionally.[3]

Politics was not discussed at Faith Family. The homily was given by Dave and Ashley Willis, a Georgia husband and wife who counsel couples, families, and individuals, and the sermon focused on how to have a healthy marriage and family life. They were honest and hopeful for the success of relationships, didn't sugarcoat rocky times, and were clear about the faith that sustains them.

Dave quoted: "'The Earth is the Lord's and everything in it. The world and all its people belong to him.' It starts with Him, it ends with Him."[4]

---

3   Justin Nortey, "Most White Americans who regularly attend worship services voted for Trump in 2020," PEW Research Center, August 30, 2021.

4   Psalm 24:1, NLT.

The lyrics to the Christian rock songs performed were simple, and I could understand how they would provide comfort and strength to those who believe. The rock band Kansas is a favorite of mine. It took a friend to point out the Christian influence in their later music, but it was also present in the early songs I loved without judgment in high school.

In the sanctuary of Faith Family, Jesus is front and center. The life lessons the Willises talk about, seamlessly, one picking up just as the other one pauses in a well-choreographed presentation, will benefit those there willing to receive the lesson.

As I sit high up above the stage in April 2022, we've just come through a pandemic that has claimed over 1 million lives in the United States. A small-town barber who cut my hair in southern Illinois told me he lost fifteen customers to COVID.

"It starts with Him and it ends with Him."

Benjamin Franklin wrote to his wife in July 1757 after avoiding a shipwreck off the rocky coast of France. "Were I a Roman Catholic, perhaps I should on this occasion vow to build a chapel to some saint, but as I am not, if I were to vow at all, it should be to build a light-house."[5]

Personally, I'm in the lighthouse camp. As much as I understand the words Dave Willis says, it is not my faith language. But if you run a business, you need to understand how to read numbers at a certain level, even if they confound, and to understand the electorate you need to understand the role that religion plays in some voters' decisions. Democrats can continue to exasperate themselves over the separation of church and state, or they can ask how "true" Christians could possibly support a candidate who does not behave like one.

Joe Biden is a deeply religious man. His faith has sustained him through unspeakable loss. During his lengthy political career, he spoke of it in personal terms, respecting that it is so for everyone. I suspect it would seem crass to him to talk about it as Donald Trump does, while holding a Bible upside down. Maybe you've been at a gathering when a boor enters and dominates the space, to the point that you can no longer stand it, and the only reasonable move is to remove yourself.

---

5   Adrienne Bernhard, "The Invention That Saved a Million Ships," BBC, June 21, 2019.

It wasn't that long ago that Democrats talked about making inroads with evangelicals. After all, you can make a good case that their core values align better with the corporal works of mercy: Feed the hungry, give drink to the thirsty, clothe the naked, shelter the homeless, visit the sick. But Donald Trump dominated the space Joe Biden held in reverence, and in doing so, broke through to those who thirsted for a public official to proclaim praise to Jesus. I might not understand evangelicals, but I hold fast to no false gods.

And the Kansas lyrics from their biggest hit fill my head, and I hear them with a renewed appreciation of the meaning that went into Kerry Livgren's writing of the song, informed by the poem "Pilgrim's Progress." Music has a special power to reach listeners in different ways, and as we age, to rehear for greater understanding.

THEY KNOW NOT

Like a lot of American cities, Cincinnati is undergoing noticeable change.

A mix of old and new architecture, the Carew Tower at forty-nine stories was the city's tallest building and is undergoing its own conversion. Off the impressive art deco lobby on the first floor, Bill Masterson, the longtime barber in a space considerably warmer than the cavernous concourse, reports that everything around him seems to be transforming into apartments and condos.

On Plum Street, the Romanesque-style City Hall, completed in 1893 at a time when Cincinnati was known as "the Paris of America," resembles a church. It sits next to an actual church, the Cathedral Basilica of St. Peter in Chains, that paradoxically looks more like a government building than its neighbor.

According to the Reverend Jan Schmidt, the basilica's rector, its downplayed religiosity was no accident. When then-Bishop John Baptist Purcell was planning the new diocesan seat, the Know Nothings, an anti-immigrant and anti-Catholic movement standing candidates for office, were on the loose, and antagonizing them did not seem prudent, according to Father Jan, whose own father was a member of the parish.

The cornerstone was laid in 1841 in a neighborhood of Irish immigrants at the time, and the parish swelled with newly arrived Germans. Their descendants added grace notes more than a century later: transepts, a rectory, and a haunting mosaic behind the altar of Venetian glass of Christ seated on a throne, handing a set of keys to St. Peter. Flanking him are two other depictions of St. Peter, one as he is released from a Jerusalem prison, the other of St. Paul visiting him in a Roman prison. In Latin, the inscription from Acts reads: "And Peter was kept in prison bound in chains." It is Ash Wednesday 2025.

The Cincinnati Enquirer, which also traces back to 1841, prints a story about neo-Nazis and the Ku Klux Klan peacocking around a northern suburb that was founded pre-Depression expressly as an enclave for African Americans shut out of other communities. Lincoln Heights remains heavily Black today. *The Washington Post* covered the story the week before: "For weeks, men carrying rifles have guarded the roads around Lincoln Heights, Ohio, stopping and questioning those who approach." Residents wore "masks and body armor...They say they're protecting their own. And they're on edge."[6]

A truckful of neo-Nazis had posted themselves on an overpass on the edge of town, toting their own rifles and red swastika flags. "Pop-up Klans use KKK flyers for attention," blares the *Enquirer's* headline, along with a photo of the racist material depicting Uncle Sam and the words "Leave now...Self-deport."[7] As First Family in North Canton and St. Peter in Chains in Cincinnati demonstrated, houses of worship are sometimes subtle, sometimes not from the outside. Hatred seldom is.

IN GOD WE TRUST

On a Saturday drive in April 2025 from Springfield, Missouri, to Tulsa, Oklahoma, I flip around the dial and catch *Wait Wait...Don't Tell Me* on the local NPR affiliate, stroll through a couple of country stations with a little bit of God mixed in. Sampled, to use musical parlance. After a stop at the Will Rogers Memorial Museum in the town of Claremore, Oklahoma, I'm back on the final stretch and

---

6   Daniel Wu, "Neo-Nazi's targeted a majority-Black town, locals launched an armed watch," *Washington Post*, February 27, 2025.

7   Cameron Knight, "'Quite a Few of Us Out Tonight': 'Pop-Up' Klans use KKK Flyers for Attention," *The Enquirer*, March 4, 2025, updated March 6, 2025, https://www.cincinnati.com/story/news/2025/03/04/kkk-flyers-in-lincoln-heights-man-said-he-targeted-16-towns-on-1-75/80837043007/.

catch the beginning of *The Truth and Liberty Show* with Alex McFarland and his guest Jenna Ellis. I'm not familiar with McFarland, but ten years ago, Ellis wrote a guide for "Christians to Understand America's Constitutional Crisis."[8]

She later, notably, worked in the first Trump Administration, and spent her last month or so working to overturn the results in several states, eventually leading her to take a plea deal in the Georgia case.

McFarland asks about the Left's embrace of "democracy." The reality, Ellis argues, is that the United States is, instead, a constitutional republic. Ellis explains that our rights come not from nature or the nature of mankind, but from God, and it is the government's responsibility to carry out His will. Joe Biden leaned into the secular definition of democracy, and when Donald Trump said he was the only path to the preservation of democracy, it made secular adherents shake their heads.

Donald Trump had it both ways. He talked about his rescue of democracy but leaned into the God lingo and this belief that our Constitution lays out the rules required to serve God's will.

And it seems to me that the argument is that God requires the absolute minimum from our government, not wanting too much interference, and under the Biden Administration there was a lot of interference, in mandates and loan forgiveness at the college level and "woke" regulation in K–12, as well as DEI and investment in lots of things that the government has no business getting in the middle of.

The voices calling for the United States to embrace the notion of being a God-stamped Christian nation are emboldened by the second coming of Donald Trump. And Trump makes clear in his March 2025 address to Congress and through other remarks, dating back to the attempt on his life in July 2024, that God saved him for a higher purpose.

The dueling positions at the intersection of faith and government are stark at present. The separation of church and state, long the foundation of a secular government, are pitted against the "free speech" of the truth proclaiming this a Christian nation, while pointing to both Jefferson's declaration, "endowed by

---

8   "Episode 152-God and Government with Guest Jenna Ellis," Apple Podcasts, March 11, 2025, https://podcasts.apple.com/ng/podcast/episode-152-god-and-government-with-guest-jenna-ellis/id1621982821?i=1000698684282.

their Creator with certain inalienable rights" of life and liberty, and the owner's manual of our republic, the Constitution, written "in order to form a more perfect union."

The nativist Know Nothings, formally the American Party, which instructed its members to reply that they knew nothing if asked about their intent, peaked in strength in the mid-nineteenth century. Operating in the shadows, their real impact is reflected in the architecture of the Cathedral Basilica of St. Peter in Chains, built to impress the faithful but not rile the Know Nothings, in the hopes of worshiping in peace.

HERE'S THE STEEPLE

In 2000, the Church of Jesus Christ of Latter-day Saints approved the construction of a temple in Belmont, just west of Boston, to be located at the highest point, the drumlin rolls that circle the flat of the city on Route 2 going west. Unlike the local congregation's meeting house on a lower point of the church property, a temple, which is reserved for the most devout of Mormons, is meant to be seen, and it is a proselytizing faith.

Some residential neighbors sued. In Massachusetts, the Dover Amendment to the state constitution exempts religious, educational, and agricultural construction from an array of zoning regulations. In Belmont, the height of the temple's steeple, which had been approved by the local zoning board and appealed in court by the neighbors, was the only aspect that potentially could not have been covered by the Dover Amendment. The case made its way through the courts to the state's Supreme Judicial Court, which allowed the steeple.

I was hired to help with the media relations and messaging. The hardest part of the job was one of language. Two years before Mitt Romney's run for governor, Mormons, in a heavily Catholic state—and, more importantly, a heavily Catholic political culture—were deemed somewhat exotic. They baptize their deceased ancestors, for instance. A local lay bishop corrected me, kindly, once for saying "baptism of the dead, instead of for the dead." "Scott, we don't baptize dead bodies." The ritual allows church members to include the relative who had not been baptized in life with the blessings of the sacrament and is the main reason the Mormons have the best genealogical records.

If the church language was unfamiliar, church steeples in Boston are not. In fact, one is quite famous, and we seized on it to make the case for understanding and support, even when the Belmont temple steeple would be topped with a statue of the Angel Moroni, blowing his trumpet, in a full-page ad in the local town paper.

The ad quoted Henry Wadsworth Longfellow's poem of that famous, centuries-old steeple in Boston's North End:

> "Then he climbed the tower of the Old North Church,
> By the wooden stairs, with stealthy tread,
> To the belfry-chamber overhead,
> And startled the pigeons from their perch
> On the sombre rafters, that round him made
> Masses and moving shapes of shade, —
> By the trembling ladder, steep and tall,
> To the highest window in the wall,
> Where he paused to listen and look down
> A moment on the roofs of the town,
> And the moonlight flowing over all.[9]

The two lamps that were hung there in the Old North Church, alerting Paul Revere that the British were coming by sea, led to the spark that blazed through Lexington and Concord two-and-a-half centuries ago. A church steeple aided—indeed, enabled—the creation of a nation.

God plays a big part in voters' minds in a good chunk of this country. Some wonder how Christians can support Donald Trump, for a host of personal issues and policy positions. But Trump has figured out the linguistics that continue to baffle Democratic politicians. He speaks people's language. Trump is a salesman. The key to sales is not to focus on what one is selling, but to focus on what one is buying. Churchgoing voters were buying what Trump was selling because he listened to them and to what they were looking for, while the Democrats offered what they thought Christians should buy, if, in fact, they were good Christians.

---

9   Henry Wadsworth Longfellow, "Paul Revere's Ride" in *The Complete Poetical Words of Henry Wadsworth Longfellow* (Houghton, Mifflin and Company, 1893), 208.

SMALL CRACKS

Sitting near the tabletop shuffleboard next to the open bank of windows on a warm but blustery day at the Moxy Hotel bar off the square in Springfield, Missouri, Jacob is helping me understand the role religion plays in politics. "I was raised in church, but there are cracks, a moment, subtle, sometimes seismic—when you realize that the faith you were raised with and the faith being sold to you are not the same thing," he tells me.

The small cracks. "A Bible study that focuses more on culture wars than Christ, or a sermon that equates righteousness with power instead of humility, or a youth group lesson that speaks of enemies instead of neighbors," he says. "For many of us who grew up in the shadow of the so-called Moral Majority, these moments stacked up over the years until they became impossible to ignore. We were raised on messages of love, kindness, and selflessness—only to watch those same pulpits become platforms for anger, exclusion, and fear."

I ask about his thoughts on evangelical church leaders and influence in politics. "This shift didn't happen overnight. Decades ago, churches started subtly shifting their focus—toward influence, control, and political power." While a lot of attention is paid to the disappearing line between church and state, Jacob sees a disillusionment below the surface, three months after Trump's reelection. "Many of the young people who walk away from church aren't rejecting Christ. They're rejecting the version of Him they were handed, one that looks nothing like the one in Scripture. Jesus preached about lifting the poor, welcoming the stranger. But in certain church circles, the message has been warped. It's about authority and identity. Instead of focusing on personal faith and individual acts of kindness, it's become about proving allegiance to a movement."

And he tells me what effect it's having on a younger demographic. "This is how an entire generation has been pushed away—not by atheism or rebellion, as our elders warned would happen, but by a fundamental disconnect between what we were taught and what we were shown."

The numbers reflect this. According to a study by the Pew Research Center, while 78 percent of Americans over 65 identify as "Christian," the numbers tank with younger groups: 72 percent of ages 50–64; 54 percent of ages 30–49; 45 percent of ages 18–29.[10]

Of those, 27 percent of people fifty years of age or older identify as Evangelical and 23 percent as Catholic. Only 17 percent of those eighteen to twenty-nine identify as Evangelical and 14 percent as Catholic. A full 27 percent identify as "nothing in particular." The numbers may be shifting with an aging evangelical demographic, but Donald Trump won roughly eight in ten votes of those who so identify.

"And here's where I struggle—I have never wavered in my faith," says Jacob, glancing at a group of four who have checked into the hotel and come into the lounge to exchange their "welcome chip" for a complimentary gin and tonic. "I have always believed in God. I have always believed in prayer. I have always believed in grace. Yet, of all the people in my life, it's never been my atheist friends who have judged me for being a Christian. It's been my Christian friends who have judged me for any number of things, including church attendance and pointing out discrepancies between teachings of the church and the teachings of Christ."

Abraham Lincoln, in his second inaugural address, spoke about how both the north and the south felt their cause was righteous: "Both read the same Bible and pray to the same God, and each invokes His aid against the other. It may seem strange that any men should dare to ask a just God's assistance in wringing their bread from the sweat of other men's faces but let us judge not that we be not judged. The prayers of both could not be answered—that of neither has been answered fully. The Almighty has His own purposes."[11]

---

10 Reem Nadeem, "1. How U.S. Religious Composition Has Changed in Recent Decades," Pew Research Center, September 13, 2022, https://www.pewresearch.org/religion/2022/09/13/how-u-s-religious-composition-has-changed-in-recent-decades/.

11 A Spotlight on a Primary Source by Abraham Lincoln, "President Lincoln's Second Inaugural Address, 1865," President Lincoln's Second Inaugural Address, 1865 | Gilder Lehrman Institute of American History, accessed May 25, 2025, https://www.gilderlehrman.org/history-resources/spotlight-primary-source/president-lincolns-second-inaugural-address-1865.

CHAPTER THIRTEEN

THE VERY ONLINE

"It's a case of flyover country versus us in our own echo chamber," Joe Trippi tells me. Trippi and I both worked on Dick Gephardt's 1988 presidential campaign, in that he helped run it at the highest level and produced the ad that won Gephardt the Iowa caucus on a prairie populist's trade and agriculture policy message, and I knocked on doors in southwest Iowa.

Twenty-five years later, our paths crossed again, helping Seth Moulton, a Marine veteran who had never run for office, unseat an eighteen-year incumbent of his own party on the North Shore of Massachusetts. Trippi likes a challenge of the anti-establishment variety, and together we were facing one in that race. Our own poll showed that Seth was trailing, five months before the primary, by fifty-six points, fairly safely outside the margin of error. Our pollster was confident in his advice: There was no credible path to victory and Seth should get out.

Seth did not get out, and the result was a rare intraparty upset in deeply blue Massachusetts. The ad Trippi created for the campaign was, in my opinion, the main reason Seth beat John Tierney by ten points, a sixty-six-point swing from the early campaign poll. The ad informed the voters that Tierney had only passed one bill in his nine terms—which overlapped the presidencies of Clinton, Bush II, and Obama—and voters concluded maybe someone new might do better.

Back in Iowa in 1988, Joe Trippi literally read the room where Dick Gephardt was making his pitch on tariffs on imports of South Korean cars. His "Hyundai" ad moved Gephardt from 3 percent in the polls to the pole position and a win. I mentioned, when we reconnected at the beginning of 2025, that he correctly stated who paid tariffs way back then. Now Trump would argue that South

Korea—and China, and Canada, and Mexico, *ad nauseam*—would pay.

"Yeah, well, we have a standard of living higher than anywhere else on the planet. It's not sustainable—we won't collapse, but we are declining as other players in the global space improve their standing," he tells me.

"When Trump says we're becoming a Third World country, it resonates with people who are feeling this slide. It hasn't reached the echo chamber, where it's a racist take," he continues. "Trump's telling the truth about this, and the Democrats' response was not to explain America's path forward but to say it isn't true, that the stock market is up. We say the economy is great."

"Hillary Clinton told the truth, your jobs are gone, but we should own that it's a result of her husband's policies, while Trump explains to voters how it happened: Socialist Democratic pedophiles who talk about how 50 percent of all jobs will be gone because of AI are to blame. Democrats think we can knock on people's doors every two years, but by the time you knock, you're a space alien that's taking their job with AI. This overlaid real resentments, the lost job, the closed factory."

He thinks that Bush, McCain, and Romney pushed boundaries of acceptable campaign tactics, but Trump was the first to cross the line. And he cites the most glaring example, the claim that "Obama was born in Kenya. It seemed so ridiculous it didn't merit pushback from Democrats, until it did, and the President had to show his birth certificate, which Trump then claimed was a fake." The line crossed, the Democrats, ten years on, still haven't entirely figured out how to counter it. And now that it's been crossed, it is almost impossible to pull back, and it is unclear how the Democrats might counter that.

Between the Gephardt and Moulton campaigns, Trippi revolutionized presidential politics working for Vermont Governor Howard Dean in 2004,[1] creating an online platform, Dean TV, before YouTube. The campaign's "Blog for America" spoke directly to people, and "Dean for America" raised record amounts in small dollars.

That campaign, he tells me, proved two things: how to build an army by directly talking to people, and how to raise money the same way. Trippi has

---

1   This is, to borrow a recent former president's phrase, no malarkey, folks. The Dean campaign shoved presidential politics into a new era of technology, and books were accordingly written chronicling how Trippi and team did it.

thought, since then, and increasingly every cycle, the Democrats were blinded by the latter and ignored the former. In fact, Democratic leaders blundered into a deliberate decision to focus on a handful of congressional districts with virtually no investment in direct communication with people, despite the model laid out by Trippi and his team through innovations like Dean TV.

Conservative voices embraced this innovation and, today, conglomerates like Sinclair Broadcasting control a huge percentage of the media landscape. Trump dominated first Biden and then Harris in modern media outlets like podcasts. "While the Democrats were concentrating on narrow real estate, Republicans were building media platforms to talk directly to people, to counter the Main Street media. Sound bites are down to nine seconds. X [formerly Twitter] and Bluesky have word limits. Republicans have been in people's houses long before you knock on their door." He makes the case that Democrats spend the huge money they raise on ads on media platforms controlled by the enemy.

"We're not explaining to young people why democracy is the best way to address climate change," he continues, or frankly any of the existential threats. When so much is taken away from a generation so early, and Gen Z being the first generation in American history to reach adulthood living their entire life during wartime, with a pandemic chaser, members of that generation become disconnected, deeply skeptical of information that seems spoon-fed to them, and search for their own answers. Further, they are aging into adulthood in a world adjusting fitfully to the technology revolution that is erasing the ethical boundaries that have proved guardrails, even porous ones, to the ever-more-congested information distribution highway.

The landscape proves volatile for young voters navigating the political reality.

DOGE WHISTLE

Patrick Bet-David's *All In* **podcast** is a favorite of David Sullivan, a thirty-year-old wealth manager from Boston, Massachusetts. David is a voracious consumer of information, both for his job and to satisfy his personal curiosity, before work, while at work, at the gym, on the subway. *The Wall Street Journal* first, followed by *Barron's*, *The Washington Post*, the *Financial Times*, and then, seeking outlets outside "legacy media," podcasters James Lindsay, Jay Bhattacharya, Calley and

Casey Means, Michael Shellenberger, Bret Weinstein, Douglas Murray, Tom Bily-eu, Gad Saad, The Diary of a CEO, and Shawn Ryan. He follows conservative political thinkers Victor Davis Hanson and Gerard Baker. His mother bristles at his media choices, but "she listens to NPR, which is state-sponsored radio."

He knows what Dogecoin is. I had no idea until Trippi told me: "Eighteen-to twenty-nine-year-old males are deep into crypto." People of both parties running for office at the federal level need to be versed in crypto to talk to donors, I heard repeatedly from those who work in political fundraising. Big donors want to talk about two things: the Middle East and cryptocurrency. It's not hard to imagine young people listening to their superannuated federal representatives, many of them two decades older than I, and rolling their eyes at what surely must sound like uninformed, behind-the-times pandering.

When launched in 2013, the first "meme" coin, sporting the face of a Shiba Inu shelter dog named Kabosu, Dogecoin was simultaneously an apparent joke, a currency with a market capitalization of $85 billion, an online community, and now the namesake of a government agency.

David, who spends his day managing an older generation's wealth, stays away from crypto and from Dogecoin, which took a hop in price from its steady trading at twelve cents when Trump, at Elon Musk's suggestion, named an agency after it. The mention of Musk triggers a physical reaction in David, almost a spark of energy that you can sense across the plastic table at the local Dunkin', his intense blue eyes widening. A Trump voter in Massachusetts, he's particularly excited about Musk, JD Vance, and Vivek Ramaswamy—briefly in harness with Musk atop the Department of Government Efficiency (DOGE) before departing on Inauguration Day, a little more than four months prior to Musk's own announcement that he would leave his role as a "Special Government Employee."[2] David sees the new deciders in Washington as changemakers who "are articulate and have lived the American Dream, anti-war, pro-free speech," a pushback on '90s liberal values.

He views the Trump coterie as clear-eyed, business focused. He thinks the things they will do may cause short-term pain: "Inflation's gonna come back." But

---

2   Niha Masih, Trisha Thadani, "Elon Musk Leaves Trump Administration After Contentious Tenure," *Washington Post*, May 29, 2025, https://www.washingtonpost.com/politics/2025/05/28/elon-musk-leaves-trump-government-doge/.

he is excited about the pushback against the "holier-than-thou, sanctimonious, rules for thee, virtue-signaling" progressives. "The people with Black Lives Matter signs in their windows" who live in essentially all-white communities (like the one David grew up in) "who think they know better than everyone."

Much ridicule was directed Ramaswamy's way over his call to eliminate every government employee with a Social Security Number ending in an odd number, or an even number, not that it would matter, except to the half of the federal workforce with an unlucky digit. Dave likes the out-of-the-box thinking. "Everyone says they're going to curb government, and they don't, but at least this is a plan." It gives him hope that the second Trump Administration will succeed where they didn't in the first and will finally drain the swamp and stop the revolving door at the FDA, for instance. He cheers Kash Patel, Trump's FBI director, taking on the deep state.

David doesn't understand how Joe Biden can call Trump "a Nazi," say he's a threat to democracy, and then welcome him to the White House like everything is back to normal. "They weaponize everything." Tulsi Gabbard and Robert Kennedy Jr. possess worldviews in friction with acceptable Democratic talking points, and their party "ostracized them."

And this goes for climate change, which David does think is real—but first things first. "Billions of people need cheap energy. The elites, like John Kerry, fly on private jets to push climate policy at places like the World Economic Forum. Let's encourage cheap coal, get people who don't have it electricity first."

The Nobel Prize-winning Soviet and Russian anti-Kremlin author Aleksandr Solzhenitsyn opened David's eyes to the theory that the natural human state is to live in tyranny. "*The Gulag Archipelago* was the most powerful book written in the twentieth century," David tells me. "I believe what he believed—that tyranny doesn't just arrive from a guy who rules with an iron fist. Most humans are essentially sheep and prefer safety and predictability over taking on responsibility, and that the majority of tyrannies are not caused by those who rule with iron fists, but from people lying one hundred percent of the time to themselves and each other."

He applies this to COVID. "How many experts knew masks didn't work and the vaccine didn't stop the spread but kept their mouth shut and kept lying? It's in our nature to be part of the herd and never step out of it, so people prefer to follow and not speak up."

Trippi tells me that Trump's naming an agency looking at government efficiency after a crypto meme, an inside joke with a dog rocketing into space as a logo, means something to young men.

I ask, "Sort of a DOGE whistle?"

"They're deep into crypto; meanwhile Biden's doing press releases on how he's going to regulate it. It would never dawn on Biden to attend a WWE match, something that is also big with young men. We actively push them away," Trippi concludes.

In mid-March 2025, in a podcast with Ezra Klein of *The New York Times*, David Shor, a former Obama campaign staffer who now heads Data Science at Blue Rose Research, says eighteen-year-old male voters went for Donald Trump by 23 percent higher than female voters in the same age group. Historically, he points out that the gap in preference between the genders was pretty steady, and it remains that way for those older than thirty today.[3]

One of the reasons for this, Klein and Shor discuss, is the ability to be "in highly gendered media worlds"—essentially, the Digital Age echo of the John Gray 1992 book *Men Are from Mars, Women Are from Venus*, the best-selling nonfiction book of the 1990s. And among young voters overall, while Joe Biden was banning TikTok, the percentage of young voters who got their news from it quadrupled during his administration, from 9 percent to 39 percent.

AND THE SURVEY SAYS

Lila Guzkowski and Connor Murphy, the two college students who conducted the rolling focus group through 2024 with voters eighteen to thirty, heard about social issues, more from women than men. But the culture war issues—choice, critical race theory, anti-trans rhetoric—couldn't crowd out economic concerns heard across the board. Young voters felt the squeeze two different ways at the same time. Things cost more, plus they faced the prospect that they would inherit a world less prosperous than the one their parents enjoy.

And the politics of "joy" that Tim Walz talked about misses its intended

---

3   "Democrats Need to Face Why Trump Won," Apple Podcasts, March 18, 2025, https:// podcasts.apple.com/us/podcast/democrats-need-to-face-why-trump-won/.

mark with them in their post-pandemic anger over what they had lost, maybe permanently, in an economy that they felt "wasn't working for them."

They felt the Kamala HQ TikTok account "was trivializing the election." Some were "offended by the memes. They felt superficial." One Trump voter thought Harris was "a government robot for diversity points" and that she wouldn't have made it through the primaries if Biden had done what he should have and not lurched at reelection.

"I fell victim to the narrative that young voters were super progressive," said one Harris voter. Trump was viewed by some as targeted by the state, and that he conveyed an "overwhelming sense of strength in his economic messaging." Robert F. Kennedy Jr. reinforced this, because some thought "he's into fitness and health."

And generally, there was a consensus about "how little it all mattered." And if the election didn't matter, it led some to think the "hysteria over the threat to democracy is an elitist take."

SOUTHERN STRATEGY

In 2023, the 500 members of the State Executive Committee, or "SEC," of the North Carolina Democratic Party elected twenty-five-year-old Anderson Clayton as their chair. Young to be sure, but a veteran of grassroots organizing, she is clear that the path to solid blue status in her state begins on college campuses.

Clayton and I are discussing this one spring afternoon in 2024, at the UMass Club on the thirty-second floor of One Beacon Street in Boston, overlooking the golden dome originally gilded by Paul Revere of the new state house, dedicated in 1799. Looking down at several college campuses from our perch, I express that Gaza is the dominant issue in Boston, and there is real anger against the Biden Administration. Clayton is here to raise some of the significant money she will need to rejuvenate her state party's structure. Money is flowing from national organizations (the Democratic Congressional Campaign Committee, the Democratic National Committee, the Democratic Governors Association) into North Carolina, which Biden lost by just over 1 percent in 2020, but the funds are going into the coffers of federal, statewide, and judicial candidates. Big money, shortsightedly, isn't generally interested in little things like grassroots organizing or state parties.

With Democrats, this has been true for a while. Nationally, the party lost sixty-three seats in the 2010 midterm election, and control of state legislatures flipped from blue to red. Barack Obama never really invested, either financially or emotionally, in the party building that might have inoculated members of Congress from the backlash of their Affordable Care Act vote. Obama was not unique in this way; most presidents don't make these investments. Grassroots building is hamstrung in a utilitarian sense by the understanding that investment now realizes payoff well beyond the two-term limit afforded presidents. And once you win the presidency, you are laser focused on a repeat, and once achieved, you review plans for your Presidential library and the legacy celebrated therein to varying degrees of veracity. Big money takes its direction from big players, and there is very little interest in paying for grass seed.

Enter Clayton. She does not give a fuck, a word she liberally sprinkles in her conversation, even in the rarified air of a Boston club. It's April 2024, some 200 days into the Israel-Hamas war, and I tell her of those young voters, mad at Joe Biden for his stance on Israel and Gaza, who may boycott the election, or worse. They are disaffected now but voted overwhelmingly for Biden in 2020. Disillusioned by his foreign policy, focused on the need for bold action on climate change, and not inclined to reward him at the ballot box solely for his partial forgiveness of their student loans, they hang out there like a storm cloud that threatens to burst and drown the re-elect.

Clayton is focused on rebuilding the party in her state but understands the urgency of moving very quickly. They are one *fucking* state Supreme Court seat away from losing everything in a heavily gerrymandered legislative map, and college campuses are energized. If she had the money, she would tap the seemingly bottomless pool of college students who want to work on campaigns, and for the party, to fight back on the assault on their individual rights. For college students in Massachusetts, a state that moved quickly to codify *Roe* when the Supreme Court struck it down, the focus is on Gaza. In North Carolina, it is not.

REFLECTION

The notion of public service has been seemingly upended in these turbulent political times. The steady drumbeat of progress in the United States through the years has had its cadence thrown off by all of the factors we have explored in my travels around the country. Whether people supported Donald Trump or Kamala Harris in 2024, this has disrupted our political equilibrium, and few of us can say what to expect—continued uncertainty or a gradual settling into a new normal.

The Greatest Generation that came to power after World War II, winning it after weathering the Great Depression, led the United States to its position as one of two world superpowers, and then to stand alone for a time, and to the brink of what seems like the dawn of a new world order. In 1973, 81 percent of members of Congress were military veterans. Today it stands at 18 percent.[1]

This generational shift in leadership, this profound alteration in experience and worldview, will have a profound effect on our country's place in the world, particularly at a time when the youngest voters, who reached the age of majority having lived their entire lives while the United States was at war in the Middle East, assess priorities, both domestic and international.

---

1 Drew DeSilver, "New Congress Will Have a Few More Veterans, But the Share of Lawmakers Is Still Near a Record Low," PEW Research Center, December 7, 2022.

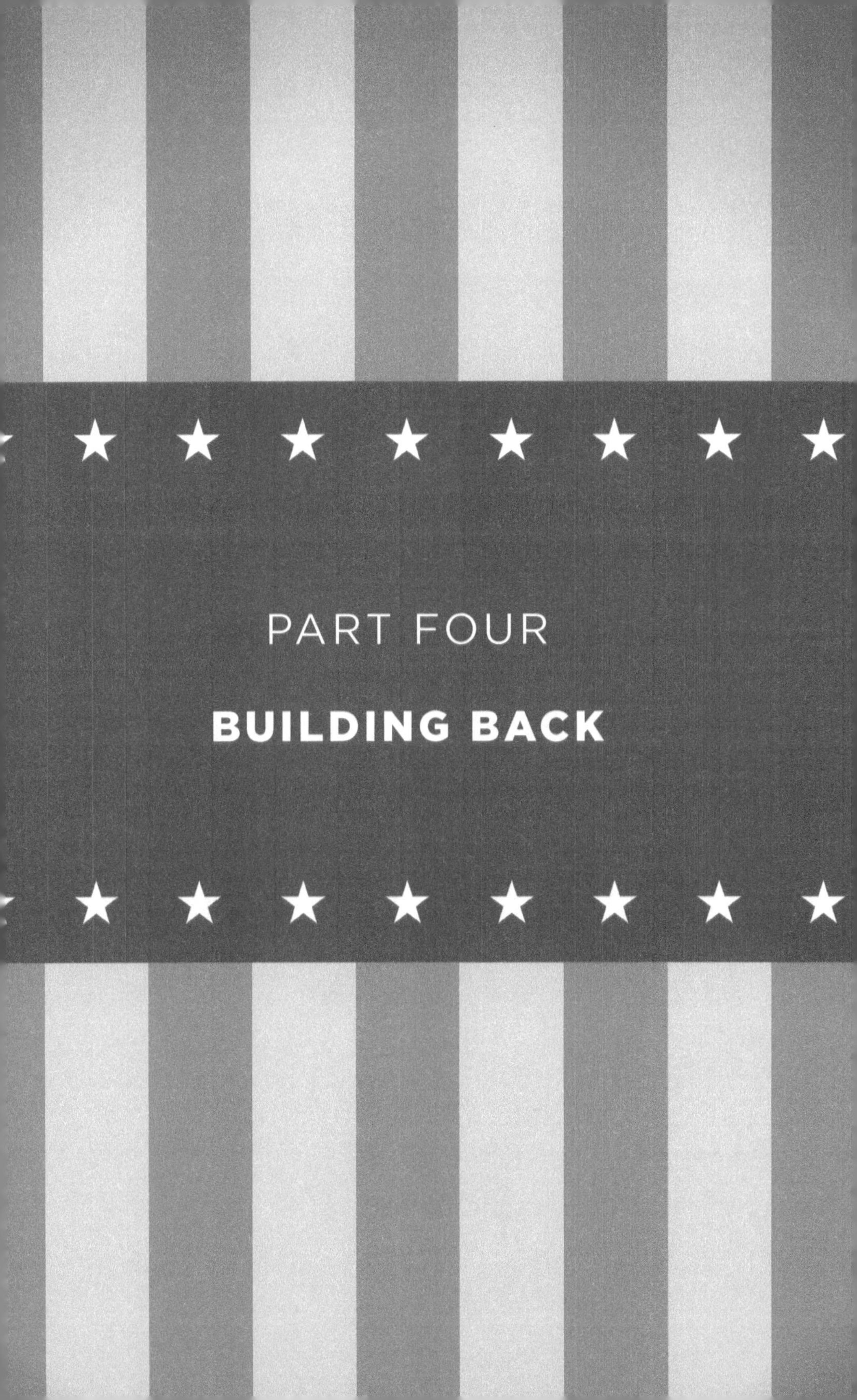

PART FOUR

BUILDING BACK

CHAPTER FOURTEEN

I THINK I CAN SWING IT

In 1961, the new president summoned us, "Ask not what your country can do for you, but what you can do for your country." JFK, Johnson, Nixon, Ford, Carter, and George H. W. Bush, the youngest fighter pilot in the war, followed in taking the oath. All served their country during World War II—with wide disparities in combat experiences. But it's been generations since that tradition, with Clinton, George W. Bush, Biden, and Trump not having served in Vietnam while Obama came of age after the draft ended.

HARDSCRABBLE SERVICE

The George H. W. Bush Presidential Library looms at the end of Barbara Bush Boulevard on the impressive campus of Texas A&M. The visitors are invited to sit in the presidential chair and have their pictures taken. I'm told that something is not a replica if it's under glass, as is the Russian ship model, a gift from Mikhail Gorbachev.

This and other presidential libraries are shrines to public service. Born into wealth in an era when "to those who much is given, much is expected," the elder Bush served his country from World War II through the end of the Cold War, with a brief stint as head of the post-Watergate GOP, in a string of extraordinarily prominent positions.

The Calvin Coolidge Presidential Library in Northampton, Massachusetts, is a more modest affair, befitting the man, his time, and the casualness with preserving presidential papers before the Presidential Records Act of 1978.

Coolidge was not born into privilege but in hardscrabble Vermont, where you had to get your hands dirty in the public service as well as the flinty soil. His father served in a number of local offices, including Justice of the Peace, which would come in handy at a critical time.

Coolidge was lieutenant governor of Massachusetts when John F. Kennedy was born in Brookline in 1917. The Yankee duty of public service, participatory local government where it met the people where they lived, was becoming quaint even then at the end of the World War I, purportedly the war to end all wars, as President Woodrow Wilson and America assumed leadership status on the international stage.

The Greatest Generation of George H. W. Bush and John F. Kennedy asked not what their country could do for them. Isn't that quaint? Few people would dispute that Mitt Romney sought to serve in this spirit, first in a failed attempt at Senate in Massachusetts, then winning the governorship there, failing in 2008 and 2012 presidential campaigns, and winning again in 2018, this time earning a Senate seat in Utah. When he retired, critical of Donald Trump as an elected official and, well, as a person, he seemed baffled by the state of politics.

Our Republic's resilience has withstood historic assaults, defended by public servants responding to the call Kennedy spoke out loud in 1961. I pull into Dallas with the sole purpose to visit Dealey Plaza, the spot where our American experiment was tested, a profoundly sad place, but also one signifying defiance of the terror and evil that threatened the civic order.

Robert Caro's volumes on Lyndon Johnson recount the moments he, too, travelled through Dealey Plaza on that day in November 1963 to become the tragic star of an altered historic arc.

One hundred years ago, in an August visit to his father's farm in Plymouth Notch, Vermont, Coolidge and his wife helped prune some trees and retired to bed. President Harding was on a western swing and had arrived in San Francisco, a continent away from the vice president he ignored and considered dropping from the ticket the following year.

In the middle of the night, a contingent of newsmen arrived at the house and roused the senior Coolidge, informing him that Harding had died from a heart attack. He woke his son and daughter-in-law to tell them. The Secretary of State wired that the oath of office should be administered as quickly as possible by any qualified magistrate, which includes Justices of the Peace.

Calvin Coolidge is the only president to be sworn into office by his own father, and after such a poignant moment, the new President and First Lady returned to bed.

The following morning, he bid his father goodbye and told him the front stoop needed some tending to. As he got into his car, beginning his journey to Washington, sworn into his high office by the man who raised him largely alone after his mother died and who taught him about public service, he thought:

"I think I can swing it."[1]

THE GREATEST GENERATION

I'm speaking about the state of politics, one month after Donald Trump reclaimed the Oval Office, in a boardroom-like space at Maplewood at Mayflower Place, an independent living community in West Yarmouth, Massachusetts, on Cape Cod. The thirty or so attendees are prompt for the 4:30 invitation, some early, the promise of wine and cheese before the dinner bell at 5:30 a draw to mix with the anxiety a lot of them feel about the state of the union.

The audience before me, settled at roundtables of six, sipping on libations in sweet remembrance of a democracy they helped steward, or perhaps saved, haven't checked out of their personal responsibility of stewardship to that democracy or become numb to its peril, as one is arguably entitled to in retirement. The torch of leadership may pass, but not that of citizenship. My host reminds me, in confirming the details, that most in the room will be over eighty. "No," she corrects herself, "*everyone* is over eighty."

The Allies sustained 34,000 casualties in the Battle of Anzio, Italy, in January 1944, the amphibious landing in "Operation Shingle" that eventually liberated Rome and the whole country.

---

1   Amity Shlaes, *Coolidge* (HarperCollins, 2013), 253.

I'm asked if service matters any more. The veteran, who fought at Anzio—perhaps the key battle of the Allies' Italian campaign, resulting in the liberation of Rome—is now 104 years old, his service identified by his neighbor at the table in the back where he is sitting. He would have been twenty-three years old when he hit the beach, three years older than George H. W. Bush and Jimmy Carter, and four years younger than John F. Kennedy.

There is a lot of disconnection in our understanding of what should be and what is: the reverence for military service and the careless care for returning servicemen and women. But there are a lot of disconnections and contradictions in our politics. We value service to the country differently today. There used to be a lot of connection between military service and public service, one flowing into the other, starting with George Washington to those listed above who held public office after World War II.

The Greatest Generation is celebrated, Tom Hanks or Tom Brokaw hosting tributes in our minds' memories. The GI bill honored the returning soldiers who literally birthed the Baby Boom generation.

It's the disconnection from their hard-won victories that makes a veteran from the Battle of Anzio scratch his head; he can't understand where that went. He wasn't asking for hero worship for his service—and he came from a generation where that service, that experience, and those learned skills transferred nicely, both in people's minds and in practice, to public service. He wants to know what happened to *that*.

A few years ago, I chaperoned a trip of Stonehill College students to Washington, DC. College students are technically adults, but they followed me like a line of ducks around the city. It was a bit exhausting. The Honor Flight Network was scheduled to have a group of World War II veterans, from Illinois, I believe, visit the Memorial on the Mall. Their mission is "to celebrate America's veterans by inviting them to share in a day of honor at our nation's memorials."

For many, this visit to the Memorial will be their last visit. The buses pulled up, and volunteers unloaded wheelchair after wheelchair. Getting the heroes off the luxury coach took some time, but once complete, the group of thirty or so veterans from both the Atlantic and Pacific theaters of the war, the details of their service indicated on their caps, were wheeled or otherwise guided, some in walkers or with canes, toward the entrance: the oval plaza ringed by fifty-six granite pillars, each decorated with a bronze laurel wreath.

We watched from a distance as they reached it, when each stood from their chairs to walk in, some with assistance. But they were going to pay their full respect, standing, to their fallen friends, with whom they saved the free world.

We honor military veterans by our words but not always by our deeds as a nation. It's been almost fifty years since World War II veterans were both parties' nominees. And the old-fashioned, put-your-body-on-the-front-line service has also taken a hit.

When I helped Seth Moulton run for Congress in 2014, we held a focus group of voters to test what in his "résumé" would resonate with Democratic primary voters. Moulton is a Marine veteran with four tours of duty in Iraq and two Bronze Stars. I will always remember one participant who asked if there was something wrong with him. "Why would he go back so many times?" Democratic primary voters in Massachusetts didn't necessarily see military service as a qualification for Congress—though the final results could serve as evidence to the contrary. Seth's Massachusetts colleague Jake Auchincloss is also a veteran, but they are members of Congress primarily for other reasons than that line on their résumés.

Donald Trump—who told Howard Stern that dodging sexually transmitted diseases was "my personal Vietnam," a war he avoided due to a "bone spurs" diagnosis that has drawn skepticism—has questioned why anyone would serve in the military, and he's proved himself pretty disdainful of civil servants as well.[2]

I hear these doubts about the merits and value of public service echoed broadly and specifically out there. And this skepticism was a factor in 2024. "I didn't think Harris was ready" or "up for the job" was a typical reaction I heard about the first female vice president and former United States senator, California attorney general, and San Francisco district attorney.

---

2   Ale Russian, "Trump Boasted of Avoiding STDs While Dating: Vaginas Are 'Landmines ... It Is My Personal Vietnam,'" *People.com*, October 15, 2016, https://people.com/politics/ trump-boasted-of-avoiding-stds-while-dating-vaginas-are-landmines-it-was-my-personal- vietnam/.
Leo Shane, III, "Trump made up injury to dodge Vietnam service, his former lawyer testifies," *Military Times*, February 27, 2019, https://www.militarytimes.com/news/ pentagon-congress/2019/02/27/trumps-lawyer-no-basis-for-presidents-medical-defer- ment-from-vietnam/.

CHAPTER FIFTEEN

CONSPIRACY THEORIES

In his novel *Underworld,* **Don** DeLillo offers a page-and-a-half scene about the Zapruder film. The book is about baseball, garbage, nuclear tests, graffiti, Lenny Bruce, nuns, the importance of knowing the exact words for things like the sheath at the end of your shoelace, J. Edgar Hoover—so, America in the second half of the American century, really. But the bit about Abraham Zapruder's footage is memorable because it takes place in the summer of 1974 at a screening of "a bootleg copy...and almost no one outside the government had seen it. It was completely new," DeLillo's narrator notes.[1]

In January 2025, President Trump ordered the release of the files on the assassination of President John F. Kennedy in November 1963 in Dallas, Texas. The event was captured best by Zapruder's 8mm color motion picture camera, filmed while standing on the infamous "grassy knoll" that features prominently in the assassination, or at least the widespread beliefs that the Warren Commission got it wrong—very, very wrong, and perhaps not through honest error.

Nothing counters a good conspiracy theory like sunlight, as the theory goes. The American people deserve to know, after more than sixty years, the truth of the assassination of the president. And that of his brother, Senator Robert Kennedy, gunned down in Los Angeles in 1968, as well as Rev. Dr. Martin Luther King six weeks before. But when more information is put out there, it leads to both clarity and more to conspire about.

---

1   Don DeLillo, *Underworld* (Scribner, 1997), 488.

This document dump, though, lands with a thud. The biggest revelation seems to be the inadvertent publishing of Social Security numbers of congressional staffers from the '70s, many of whom are still alive. New scandal!

When I worked for President Kennedy's brother Edward on his Senate staff in his Boston office during the 1990s, I would, from time to time, be asked to meet with a constituent with a new theory on who killed his brothers. I would listen politely, then recite the company line: The senator accepted the findings of the Warren Commission report that concluded that Lee Harvey Oswald acted alone. On one occasion, this was apparently unsatisfying, and I was told, "Scott, you say that, but you say something else with your eyes."

We expect things to make sense. There is a lot about the Kennedy assassination that doesn't make sense, such profound senselessness at the hand of an inconsequential loser in Lee Harvey Oswald. How can a nonentity affect world events? Oswald, or John Wilkes Booth. Or Thomas Matthew Crooks?

On July 13, 2024, when Crooks attempted to assassinate Donald Trump, I was in Ocean Beach, a bohemian neighborhood in San Diego, California. I was standing near the Municipal Pier, closed and structurally precarious, watching the surfers sitting on their boards riding the rhythm of the swells waiting for a good one, while several people were talking about the news.

Harry and Annie were out walking after a birthday lunch celebrating him. They retired to Mission Hills and have a small apartment on the first floor that they rent to vacationers.

Mike moved here from the farm he owns in Hawaii, where he relocated years ago to help his son manage his business. Hawaii may have been his adopted home, but he has a seemingly congenital laid-back island feel about him. Ocean Beach is pretty laid back too, the smell of weed always wafting in the air.

Harry, Annie, and Mike are Harris voters, and they aren't buying the narrative of a lone gunman getting off a shot that grazes the once-and-future president's ear, producing an impressive amount of blood and a defiant exit from stage. "Now he's a martyr!" says Harry, and not in a celebratory way. I'd put them in the highly skeptical category, and it seems it would be harder to go further than that, the gunman and a spectator dead, lots of eyewitnesses. But it seems too convenient for Mike.

In the late '70s and '80s, conspiracies swirled around the Trilateral Commission, an NGO founded in 1973 by David Rockefeller aimed at "fostering closer cooperation between Japan, Western Europe, and North America,"[2] which sounds like a positive thing until one starts to question the real motivations behind it and assigns conspiracies to a favorite villain.

Just before the 2012 presidential election, I was speaking with a friend of mine, Steve Coltrin, who ran a prominent public relations firm in New York. He was a Romney supporter; I was for Obama. We were both convinced our chosen candidate would win. He was terrified that if given a second term, Obama would then become General Secretary of the United Nations and impose a global order on the country.

The first time someone suggested to me that the 9/11 attacks were an inside job, it was mentioned so casually that I almost missed it. The notion still comes up from time to time, usually from someone who was very young or not yet born in 2001. Conspiracy theories are as old as human life, and our susceptibility is baked into our DNA. When we can't believe something in front of our eyes, we look for something that explains it. Buildings don't just come down because planes fly into them. Seven million extra people don't just show up to vote when they haven't voted before. Presidents don't get shot with rifles peeking out of sixth-floor book depository windows by ideologically incoherent loners who are then murdered themselves two days later by a nightclub owner with mob ties.

The digital revolution is the conspiracist's best friend. In my youth, if I wanted to immerse myself in the Trilateral Commission theories, maybe after listening to The Clash's "Washington Bullets" in my headphones several hundred times, I would need to go to the library or an underground magazine store. It's so much easier today.

What does this mean as we approach the midterm elections and the 2028 presidential election year—an election some think Trump will try to suspend or amend by some contortion of the Constitution? If speculation of a conspiracy can hide the lie and the liar thinks the end justifies the means—of saving the country, or saving the country from those trying to destroy it (the Democrats, in this case), by lying about saving it—how will that inform behavior of those in power moving forward?

Anne Applebaum defined our particular time in "The New Rasputins" in the

---

2   Nadia Batok, "The Global Elite: Power and Influence," Meer, January 15, 2025, https://www.meer.com/en/85275-the-global-elite-power-and-influence.

February 2025 *Atlantic*, explaining that the threads of disconnection and technology and evil actors are meeting in this moment:

> The philosophers of the Enlightenment, whose belief in the possibility of law-based democratic states gave us both the American and French Revolutions, railed against what they called obscurantism: darkness, obfuscation, irrationality. But the prophets of what we might now call the New Obscurantism offer exactly those things: magical solutions, an aura of spirituality, superstition, and the cultivation of fear.[3]

This presented as populism here and around the globe in 2024. The author Yuval Noah Harari spells it out in his book *Nexus: A Brief History of Information Networks from the Stone Age to AI*: "In its more extreme versions, populism posits that there is no objective truth at all and that all persons have 'their own truth' which they wield to vanquish rivals."[4]

On Inauguration Day 2017, when Press Secretary Sean Spicer so botched an exchange with the press over the size of the inaugural crowd that he was rewarded with being played on *Saturday Night Live* by Melissa McCarthy, counselor to the president Kellyanne Conway came to his defense in an appearance on *Meet the Press* by saying that Spicer was presenting "alternative facts."[5]

Harari explains the power in the strategy: "Whenever and wherever populism succeeds in disseminating the view of information as a weapon, language itself is undermined. Nouns like 'facts' and adjectives like 'accurate' and 'truthful' become elusive...any talk of 'facts' or 'truth' is bound to prompt at least some people to ask, "whose facts and whose truth are you referring to." Truth becomes detached, he writes, and "the question to ask isn't 'What is being said? Is it true? But rather, 'Who is saying this? Whose privileges does it serve?'"[6]

---

3   Anne Applebaum, "The New Rasputins," *The Atlantic*, January 7, 2025.

4   Yuval Noah Harari, *Nexus: A Brief History of Information Networks from the Stone Age to AI* (Random House, 2024), xxiv.

5   Eric Bradner, "Conway: Trump White House offered 'alternative facts' on crowd size," CNN, January 23, 2017.

6   Harari, *Nexus*, xxiv.

CHAPTER SIXTEEN

COIN FLIP

A half hour west-northwest of Atlanta, Austell—at different times in history called the New York of the South *and* the Chicago of the South—is home to the Frog Rock Brewing Company, sitting next to a turn-of-the-last-century-style building bearing the incongruous sign "Cincinnati Junction."

Back then, Mark Twain and Teddy Roosevelt and the Vanderbilts would roll into town on the since-refurbished rail line, drawn by the waters of the nearby Lithia Springs and its advertised Fountain of Youth–like qualities. More recently, they're still recovering from the 2009 flooding of Sweetwater Creek, in what the National Weather Service decreed the equivalent of a 10,000-year event. Straddling Cobb and Douglas counties, the small city has a sleepy feel and friendly faces at the South Cobb Diner.

At the brewery, they use Lithia Springs mineral water to craft their products, and Ben the bartender hasn't heard that Vice President Harris is coming to the big city just down the Old Town Road, made famous by country trap pioneer Lil Nas X, who grew up nearby. It's mid-September 2024, and both campaigns are focusing on Georgia as the potential decider. Needlessly, as it turned out.

Sporting a flat-brim ball cap emblazoned with an "A" for the Atlanta Black Crackers of the Negro League and a yellow dish towel tossed jauntily over the left shoulder of his "Beerituality" T-shirt, Ben has no use for either party. He likes his customers and his coworkers, but he doesn't see them in the mirror that the media purports to hold up to society.

"We all have disparate, crazy views, but we all enjoy each other's company," Ben says. "And then, if you listen to the media, we all fucking hate each other and 'you're an asshole and your family is trash'...It's 'my team versus your team, is gonna kick your ass.' It's bullshit."

Gray-bearded with a peripatetic background—North Dakota, Maine, California, Iowa, Florida—Ben is an independent with libertarian leanings, suspicious that the game is rigged and that the putative standard-bearers aren't the ones truly calling the shots. It seems unlikely that either Harris or Trump will be catching Ben's support when Georgia, which factors into most versions of both candidates' winning scenarios, hand counts its ballots and, along with North Carolina, issues the latest round of tea leaves for the trajectory of the perpetually New South.

"You couldn't have two bigger jokes, either side. If we didn't think it was a puppet system when it was Joe...c'mon. No, man. The left is a fucking sham and the right is a fucking sham. They both have broke my confidence. Why would I vote for either one of them?"

Harris is due at Atlanta Cobb Energy Performing Arts Centre in a few hours, where she'll deliver an emotional appeal on abortion rights, including the excruciating stories of two Georgia women who died shortly after enactment of the state's abortion limits, which Harris hung on Trump due to the overturn of *Roe v. Wade* under the Supreme Court Trump stocked with conservatives. "Will abortion be a deciding issue?" reads the morning's *Atlanta Journal-Constitution* front page, along with "Georgia and other swing states pledge fair elections,"[1] spotlighting two issues that hadn't played determinative roles in American presidential elections the last few decades. The *AJC* distributes its Sunday edition on Saturday, meaning less hard news and more in-depth features on the front page, so Harris misses out on a two-day wallop, but probably enjoyed the paper's lead story, "Ga. voters more upbeat on the economy,"[2] and the *Marietta Daily Journal* fronted her visit with "In Cobb, Harris blasts 'Trump's abortion bans.'"[3]

Trump, who hasn't stopped in Georgia in nearly two months, is expected to make a series of Peach State appearances between now and November, per the

---

1   Greg Bluestein and Maya T. Prabhu, "Will abortion be deciding issue in Georgia? Kamala Harris hopes so," *Atlanta Journal Constitution*, September 20, 2024.

2   David Wickert, "Georgia and other swing states pledge fair elections," *Atlanta Journal Constitution*, September 19, 2024.

3   Annie Mayne, "In Cobb, Harris blasts 'Trump's abortion bans,'" *Marietta Daily Journal*, September 20, 2024.

AJC,[4] before he attends the game between the Bulldogs and the Crimson Tide in Tuscaloosa the following Saturday.

The issue of free and fair elections is particularly salient in Georgia, whose Republican governor, Brian Kemp, famously withstood pressure from Trump not to certify the state's 2020 election results, finessing the Trump minefield in a way few Republicans have. The state's elections board is considering mandating hand counting of the state's ballots, a measure opposed by county elections officials but praised by Trump.

A veteran creative who has logged time at the Cartoon Network and the Disney Channel, Ben knows Kabuki theater when he sees it and has adopted an ironic, detached, nearly fatalistic view of the nation's state of political play. "CNN, Fox, MSNBC, they're all the same shitshow...It's funny how the two different sides say the exact same thing about the other side." At Disney, he recalls, "If you had a view that was remotely considered to be kind of conservative, then everybody had you pegged as a goose-stepping Republican."

In Trump, he sees, in part, what one half of the country sees: a charismatic figure who might say and do the uncouth at times, but brooks no bullshit and instills in the national id a little of the swagger it may have surrendered in the face of an onslaught of political correctness and self-editing, to the detriment of geopolitical and economic considerations.

"He at least is anti-establishment," Ben says, drying the mineral water from his hands onto the towel. "They hid [Harris] from the public when she was VP. You didn't hear a peep out of her. She did a shit job on the border...and now she's a genius" in media portrayals.

Who would be his ideal candidate, Ben is asked. "Nobody who has presented themselves. I'd vote for Dave Chappelle. He calls it like he sees it, either direction."

WE WILL DISOWN YOU

Different generations project their dissatisfactions in different ways. Baby Boomers burned draft cards and occupied college administration buildings

---

4   Greg Bluestein and Maya T. Prabhu, "Will abortion be deciding issue in Georgia? Kamala Harris hopes so," *Atlanta Journal Constitution*, September 20, 2024.

while Gen X settled on angst and grunge. Today's young people seem to have opted for "all of the above," breaking the traditional molds of ideology and manifesting this age's unhappiness with the system by casting a pox on all houses, with a healthy lack of what those older would call loyalty.

For Natasha, a twenty-six-year-old waitress from Lawrenceville, Georgia, who dabbles in day trading, Barack Obama's 2008 election was "a huge thing for my family" because, like him, she is "half-Kenyan, half-American." And, like generations of African Americans, her family has practiced loyalty to the Democratic Party.

"My grandparents told me: 'Do not become a Republican. We will disown you.' They didn't tell me why. They said, 'That's just what we do,'" Natasha recalls over spicy hummus and pickled vegetable snacks at a table in an alcove at Mac McGee's in Roswell, Georgia. It's late June of 2024, mere days before Biden incinerates his reelection campaign on the debate stage. About sixteen miles to our west is a memorabilia shop, Wildman's Civil War Surplus, which sits in downtown Kennesaw, its storefront festooned with the Stars and Bars. It's Father's Day, three days before Juneteenth.

When asked who they'd vote for if the election were held that day, neither Natasha nor her boyfriend, thirty-two-year-old David, a mechanical engineer and fellow day trader, hesitates before answering: "Trump."

She recalls an "awkward tension" while bartending a 2020 Trump-themed Election Night party she was staffing. Patrons assumed she was anti-Trump because she is African American. The sentiment was unspoken, she said, but palpable.

"Especially with color on your skin, people assume you don't like Trump," echoes David, who grew up Black in Detroit. "It isn't that I don't like specifically him; I don't like any fucking president."

Both got plenty of peer pressure to vote Biden in 2020. But when asked who's urging them to vote—if not for the Democrat, at least against Trump—David responds, "My white friends." He says, "I think more people are waking up to the fact that just because we were told for decades that Black voters should vote Democratic, we shouldn't vote Democratic. We should vote for Trump. That's why you're seeing things like Blacks for Trump."

Like many—perhaps a majority of Americans—Natasha and David consume a great deal of information, but broadly for most and deeply for their work and interests, and their ideological leanings defy easy description under any hidebound political rubric. David thinks he has heard that Vice President Harris takes an excessive amount of vacation time, but he's unsure where he heard it or whether it's true. Natasha, despite planning to vote for Trump, picks Stacey Abrams, a Democratic firebrand and two-time gubernatorial nominee in Georgia, when asked about her ideal presidential candidate.

Posed the same question, David fumbles before naming a movie character, then finds the actor's name on his phone: Morgan Freeman (not a bad choice, given that he has, indeed, played a US president multiple times, as well as God in *Bruce Almighty*, which is how Dave knows him). "That guy. Something different. Something else. When I voted for Trump the first time, I did it sarcastically. I thought it was a joke. It was like, here's a TV guy, of course I'm going to vote for him."

But now in their twenties and thirties, working, they have grown more politically attuned. Natasha says she wants to get more involved in local government. She calls Biden "a puppet," and both fret about behind-the-scenes meddling in the markets that could influence the election, espousing various theories about how and why "the system" is so easily manipulated. They're upbeat, optimistic people, but there's an uneasiness with how things are run and those who run them and an ineffable sense that whether it's the S&P 500 or the Electoral College, the system is not working for them.

After Biden drops out, Natasha emails with a more ambivalent tone about her decision. "This election, whatever comes out of it, this is a checkpoint and we're about to go into the serious unknown because there's so much going on," says Natasha. Regardless of the outcome, she says, her dread of the unknown will not be alleviated. "I'm feeling very heavy."

Her mood does not brighten after the votes are in. "Feeling very heavy still," she emails in November.

THE POWER IS OURS TO USE OR NOT

Before 2016, David Wainscott, sixty-two, didn't know which "team was red and which team was blue." Since then, "it's just been thrown in your face all the time." He wonders, "Was it always like this?"

We're having lunch at the Hard Rock Casino in Cincinnati, Ohio, in March

2025, and Dave is figuring out how to stay occupied during the first year of retirement. He still teaches occasionally as a substitute, but it's not the same, and the kids are different. He likes the vibe of the casino, he likes being around people, and has put his name in at the sportsbook lounge, steps away from our table, if there's any job open there.

And, with the newfound free time, he can't help but notice that, alongside the seemingly constant flow of political news, there's political noise, and it's not always easy to distinguish. And the last few years, he's been teaching kids during COVID, and things have changed with them too.

It's hard to know where to get accurate information. "I'll see one network and I'll say, 'That can't be true,' but then I'll go to the other one and say, 'Wait a minute, that can't be true either.'" He's questioning the validity of the news he gets, as a late baby boomer accustomed to reliable news sources, perhaps of Walter Cronkite caliber, or at least Brokaw.

A math teacher for thirty-six years, including AP statistics, he calculates his reasoning for never voting, once, ever, in his life, though his wife dogs him for it. "The odds of me getting killed on my way to the voting booth are way higher than my vote deciding the outcome of an election." He means this as a deflection, a bit of a joke, and in all seriousness. He's never found a compelling reason to vote, and it's more that, by the math, his vote won't count more than concern for his safety while driving.

He really felt that Biden was cognitively impaired, and "I don't think we're going to see a whole lot more of him." He coached basketball for thirty-four years. He can teach, and he can call X's and O's with anyone, but he finds it hard to watch two of his friends, who used to go to the track and have a good time, cut off communication because of politics. "It just makes no sense."

His wife voted for Trump, and she thinks Dave's more conservative than he thinks he is, which might be true. She's "very strong-willed" and responds to candidates who exhibit that quality.

Dave thought Hillary Clinton was really smart, but he never thought that about Kamala Harris. He was less certain about any politician's ethics; they all seem pretty suspect. He reacts to prices, inflation. "That's what affects me"—gas and food. I ask if he made different choices when he was shopping as he saw his grocery bills rise. "No." He didn't have to adjust his grocery buy, but he did note the price hike.

Dave is not too ideological, though he agrees with his wife that he is "more right than left," and remembers when he was younger finding himself annoyed that political happenings like the State of the Union would intrude on preferable television like *Charlie's Angels*, starring Farrah Fawcett, dream girl of (at least) one generation of American males. Nobody buys State of the Union posters.

"I want Farrah, I don't want this dumbass State of the Union thing," Dave recalls thinking. Dave seems to me less left or right, more in the very clogged lane of the turned-off and slightly apathetic, and his non-voting history may be driven by his numbers-oriented, logical mind. He wants things to add up, and if they don't, he'll stick to coaching his X's and O's and the students in front of him, where the statistics are in black and white and always make sense.

And if Dave is not persuaded by either party or any candidate, at any level of government, if a candidate or a party were to make their pronouncements and platform add up to him, maybe he would take the risk to drive to the polls or, maybe, vote by mail.

He doesn't know if DOGE's out-of-the-gate criticism of federal spending is "really true or not, or if [Musk] is just making that shit up. If it's true, how can you not be in favor of that?" He expected Musk and Trump to split "because Musk was gonna take some of his shine." And a few months later they did, so maybe Dave should be on the other side of the sportsbook window from the ticket takers, laying down shrewd bets.

Trump has "never done anything to me. I listen to what he says, and I just laugh. He is crazy. I believe he does want good things for the country. He's an egomaniac." He sits back, "He does think pretty highly of himself."

Driving away from the Hard Rock I think about Dave's parting words. Trump hasn't done anything to him. Yet so many voters do feel assaulted by an "egomaniac" who more than "thinks pretty highly of himself," who is willing to sacrifice our democracy. They don't think it's a laughing matter. They agree "he is crazy" and they think democracy shouldn't be decided by a coin flip.

Dave is exercising his Constitutional right to vote. Or not. And the Democrats are playing their own game of chance of who to ignore and who to engage. Dave might not ever vote, but he might be a good person to help run the numbers to calculate the best odds of winning with nonvoters like himself.

CHAPTER SEVENTEEN

AN APPRENTICE NO MORE

Driving in Vermont reminds me that 40 percent of the US is farmland. And here, 70 percent of the state's agricultural economy is dairy. There are, in fact, more people in Vermont than cows, contrary to an old canard, though if you're driving through the lush hills from the state's Northeast Kingdom down to the capital, you will definitely see more cows. The state beverage is milk.

Vermont's state capital, Montpelier, is the least populated in the nation with even fewer residents than Pierre, South Dakota. But the bar at J. Morgan's Steakhouse in the Capitol Plaza Hotel Montpelier is packed with the legislature in session in May 2022. The representatives seem in disguise to me. I ask a man in his thirties wearing a dress shirt and coat if he's a member. No, he's with Ace Hardware, cycling through his territory of New England and New York, supervising dozens of stores. He tells them to order Christmas lights now, at the end of Vermont's mud season, just as the trees leaf out, given the supply chain shortage the previous year. I ask if Ace adjusts to events. He says yes, and they anticipate a move to batteries and away from gas-powered yard tools this year, given the war in Ukraine.

Almost three years later, one month into Donald Trump's second term, I'm having lunch with a colleague at the counter of Henry's Louisiana Grill in Acworth, Georgia, the town that had once mandated each household own a rake, an impish revoke of neighboring Kennesaw's firearm ownership mandate. It's my second trip to town and my second to Henry's, the best Cajun fusion food outside of New Orleans, in my opinion.

Drew works in finance for the American Honda Motor Company. Although he's lived in Tampa, Florida, with a detour to New York City, he tells us he's originally from Dogtown, Illinois, a place so small and rural, as a young child if he needed to pee, he would just do so outside wherever he happened to be. This habit required some adjustment after moving to Tampa, when it was pointed out to his mother by neighbors. He is Norman Rockwell earnest and polite. He introduces himself to those to his left and right and offers a hand. He marvels that he found this amazing place, a random selection, as he decided to stop in Acworth for lunch on his way back home to Cartersville.

I ask if he's concerned about the threat of tariffs. "Absolutely. A hundred percent." Even though American Honda is a subsidiary of the parent company with its own leadership, when something warrants it, "the Japanese come." This is that time.

A lot of Trump voters I have talked to, while concerned about the impact of tariffs and the threat of inflation spiking, are willing to give the President the benefit of the doubt and to trust that the actions are part of a larger strategy. Robert Pitcherski, the Marietta Hilton bartender who remembers repeat customers' drinks, voted for Trump and gives me an analogy as he watches Trump's first month in office. "If you release a lot of animals at once into the backyard, you're only able to catch a few." Flooding the zone with executive orders makes it harder to catch them all, as it were, to block them using the checks and balances in the system that slow things down, that inhibit bold change, that cause the problems people find themselves in. The threat of and implementation of tariffs must be part of a larger strategy.

If a voter I talk to doesn't like a position or program, he or she tends to attach a name to it. People like the Affordable Care Act, but if you're opposed, it's Obamacare. You can even love the first and hate the latter and think you are being consistent.

If you hate the border wall, it's Trump's Wall. Barriers built before and after his first administration have no name. Bidenomics is a moniker Biden first liked but backed off only months later. Going way back, there were Hoovervilles, an unflattering term for the shantytowns of the Great Depression. Remember Hillarycare? Like most observations, this one isn't perfect. The ultimate marketer, Trump is happy to have his base refer to his wall.

In February 2025, Denny's and Waffle House announce that there will be a premium on egg dishes, while Costco limits purchases to a dozen per customer. Democrats cry that Trump promised to lower prices "day one," not later, and as the clock continues to tick, they wonder when his voters will revolt. Where Democrats take his words literally, Trump voters like the bold assertions and have long made peace with discounting his supersizing of numbers, his fantastical predictions of timelines.

Two years before, in February 2023, Joe Biden stood in the well of the US House of Representatives to deliver an address on the State of the Union, as prescribed by the Constitution. This was familiar ground for Biden, his attendance welcomed every year since Richard Nixon's address in 1973, save the four years of the Trump Administration when he held no federal office.

By the time of Nixon's speech, just after his landslide reelection victory, Lyndon Johnson's war in Vietnam had become Nixon's. The Cold War raged. Nixon was forced to adjust international monetary policy. He said that the threat to the environment needed to be addressed, "Now or never." And of course, Watergate loomed.

Jimmy Carter also felt the weight of our existential national threat in the third year of his presidency and disappeared to Camp David in 1979 to ponder this, emerging to call us to renewed purpose as a nation. He said: "The threat is nearly invisible in ordinary ways. It is a crisis of confidence. It is a crisis that strikes at the very heart and soul and spirit of our national will. We can see this crisis in the growing doubt about the meaning of our own lives and in the loss of a unity of purpose for our nation."[1]

Initially, the reaction to Carter's speech was positive. He had struck a chord, spoke a truth we couldn't ourselves articulate but knew to be true. We had to reflect on our values, as citizens and as a country. The spark was the energy crisis, but the charge to examine our values challenged us to a higher public purpose.

But once you yell "charge" and point the way to the promised land, you have to keep running for the people to follow. Carter paused, pondered, and continued his self-reflection, shuffled his cabinet, lost the moment, and his call became the "malaise" speech. Eventually his administration wore it as a cloak of moral judgment of all of us.

Ronald Reagan seized the call and told us he could deliver us to the promised land of our hopes and dreams as Americans. Carter may have told us the truth of

---

1   American Experience, PBS, "Crisis of Confidence," *American Experience | PBS*, March 20, 2019, https://www.pbs.org/wgbh/americanexperience/features/carter-crisis/.

our crisis of confidence, but Reagan provided the quick answer that satisfied the supermajority of voters in 1980.

A half century after Nixon, from the same rostrum, Biden said he was asked all the time to sum up America in one word, and that word was "possibilities." That word appeals to our sense of the best of America, where we tell our children that anything is possible. But is that true for all of us? Are we all equal in the quest of the American Dream?

If Donald Trump was as surprised as anyone to find himself elected in 2016, an embedded hatred of Hillary Clinton exposed among enough Americans to decide the Electoral College, in 2024 he struck a chord. Here in Georgia in late February 2025, voters believe he is taking steps to remake both the federal government and the country's place on the national stage. Where the first Trump term seemed chaotic from the starting gate, the second, while still a bucking governmental bronco, is undeniably more focused, with four intervening years to plan for real change. And change is hard for people, which is why the reins of our system have, in the past, calmed nerves. Trump's second term is raw, seemingly untamable. Some are all in, some are praying the wild horse settles down, while some are strapped in against their will for the ride, terrified and white-knuckled.

Donald Trump stormed Washington in 2017 pledging to "drain the swamp" and left it four years later just as swampy but with the country exhausted. Joe Biden tried to stir us to imagine future possibilities, which fit his seeming pledge to be a bridge president, but, in a traditional democratic framework of a first-term president running for reelection, sounded more like Jimmy Carter. Donald Trump's second term, at least in the first few months, sounds a bit like Ronald Reagan's first in its bold action to his voters, and like his, thrilling the faithful and terrifying the opposition.

History has shown that voters want bold pronouncements of leadership, and then they want follow-through once in office. If the electorate feels betrayed, or tires of the direction, or refocuses, they will respond to new calls of leadership.

THROUGH THE LOOKING GLASS

A month after Trump's second inauguration, Hamp & Harry's in Marietta Square, Georgia, is bedecked in an *Alice in Wonderland* theme and offers dinner and a showing of various movie adaptations of the Lewis Carroll classic during February. I sit down with Robert Pitcherski over a lunch, which does not seem so themed, of fried artichokes and chicken caprese sandwiches sans bread.

Robert has served as a political barometer of sorts on my trips over the past two years to Marietta. He has a bit of a wide-eyed curiosity that serves him well overseeing the restaurant and bar at the Marietta Hilton; his go-to answer to any request is a cheery "absolutely."

"He's doing a lot, all at once.... It's pretty concerning, particularly the tariffs," he tells me when I open with a question of how President Trump is faring so far. "It's never pleasant to go on a budget. No family's like, 'Hey, let's cut our budget a third.' Nobody likes it, right? But it's got to be done."

Robert was born in New Jersey and moved to North Carolina at a young age, where his grandmother ran an "herb shop" focused on holistic healing and natural medicines. Some would call it "alternative," but Robert would counter with "if someone takes 2,000 years working on anything and isn't good at it, then something is wrong. I'm third-generation alternative medicine."

He has a degree in psychology from the University of Georgia and has worked in hospitality and movie production. In 2000, he worked on the movie *Road Trip* and got to stand in for actor Tom Green. But hospitality and movie production have taken hits here. He was laid off from the Congress Center when COVID first hit but kept his job at the Palm, commenting that Nicolas Cage, lunching there, "is a nice guy."

The state of Georgia invested time and money luring movie production into the state, and Robert had a good run, but that has dried up with the industry increasingly controlled by the whims and ROI of venture capital, which seeks low-cost production all over the world.

From our first discussion about the state of affairs in the nation, when I chose to hang out in the key county of Cobb in the swing state of Georgia in early 2023, Robert has voiced concern over the country's debt and also his own, working to bring it back under control after his pandemic layoff. I was impressed with this, the sense of responsibility for both his finances and the nation's.

And he has thoughts about how to get control of the debt, and it partially informs the reason he voted the way he did in 2024, for Donald Trump, as he did in 2020. Not the first time, though—"the 2016 campaign was just wacky."

"It looks like there's already some whining in foreign policy and whatever, but at the end of the day, we kind of don't owe them anything. It's not like, 'Oh, we promised you.' Every government has to be self-sufficient in its own right, and we shouldn't just be spending money keeping everybody afloat."

Robert is talking generally and not specifically about funding for Ukraine, but he does find Trump's rhetoric on Greenland and Canada to be troubling. Ukraine would rocket into focus the week after we spoke with an explosive Oval Office exchange between Presidents Zelenskyy and Trump, fueled by Vice President Vance, and Trump continued to poke the Canadians, even after the election of a new Prime Minister.

He's talking about cuts to USAID—months before the highly public falling out between Musk and Trump. He has heard about money being wasted on programs in Zimbabwe, which perhaps involve money laundering that makes no sense, and he thinks a review of spending is a great first step.

"One of the things I like about Elon is that he'll go in and get it done, and he says it straight, and he surrounds himself with some of the smartest people out there. And that's one of the things they say you should do if you really want to be successful." But Musk has no experience in government, I point out. "I've talked with a lot of engineers out there, and they have their methodology of solving a problem.... I wouldn't hire these guys for PR, but for problem-solving—I mean, that's their job. They take a problem, and they break it down," he says. "The country needs businesspeople to equalize the budget."

A year prior, just as the primaries were getting underway, with Minnesota Congressman Dean Phillips mounting a quixotic primary challenge to President Biden, talking about a "new generation" of leadership, Robert asks me about Robert F. Kennedy Jr. also running for the nomination—largely on the name of a storied family that people of a certain generation think invented that phrase.

Where Phillips's challenge to Biden seems largely based on the President's age—a canary-in-the-coal-mine warning unheeded by party leaders but of concern to most voters I speak with—Kennedy has an actual agenda, grounded in his focus on health, and it has caught Robert's attention.

"I was going to vote for him originally before he folded his campaign. I'm like, you know what? He has a certain integrity about him that I really appreciate." Robert understands Kennedy's skepticism of vaccines. He's never railed against them in conversations, but over lunch, when asked, said his family got "minimal" vaccines. "Didn't go to a doctor, really, when I was sick. Western medicine is excellent at diagnosing stuff, but there's a huge conflict of interest when it comes to executing the healing process, if one wants to call it that."

It's Kennedy's Make America Healthy Again (MAHA) agenda that most interests Robert. Robert is single and fit and looks well younger than his forty-seven years, has a positive outlook, is a devotee of Tony Robbins, and reads a lot of self-improvement books. "I really do think there needs to be some major reforms in the health industry. Drug companies are running amok. All the medical schools are funded by the drug companies, so what information are they going to get? They're going to get the information the drug companies want them to get. They're not going to get natural medicine. There's no money in that," he says.

While Dean Phillips was brushed quickly to the curb, Kennedy feints at a third-party run after being muscled by the Democratic establishment and then endorses Trump. Robert tracks the journey. "I'm like, you know what? I don't think he's just going to recommend somebody who's not about doing the right thing or at least going after what he says he's going to go after," he tells me. Kennedy's endorsement of Trump was a "turning point" for Robert.

He thinks every person, after thirty years of age or so, should have one US cause and one global cause that you support "actively." "If you don't, you aren't adulting right. If you're making most of your decisions strictly for yourself, you're doing it wrong." His personal domestic cause is a healthier United States. Globally, he supports Amnesty International. "I'm very much into humanitarianism. I think everybody deserves certain rights and respects…. If everybody had at least one domestic and one international cause—like, everybody in the world—that's a pretty good world right there!"

And if he knows Trump, voting both for him and not, Kennedy tipping his vote this time, what of Kamala Harris? "I thought she wasn't a bad candidate. I just thought she wasn't prepared…[a] deer in the headlights."

Harry Truman was thrust into the presidency three months into his tenure as vice president, a product of the Kansas City political machine who had been kept out of the loop on everything: the war, the atomic bomb, everything. But when Eleanor Roosevelt summoned him from the Capitol, where he was lazily presiding over the Senate, to the White House to tell him that FDR was dead, and he asked if there was anything he could do for her, she replied, "Harry, is there anything we can do for *you?* For you are the one in trouble now."[2] At least when he ran for his own term, Truman had already been president for three years, unlike Biden's understudy. Harris was handed the reins for the nomination, but not the reins of government, and for a lot of voters it proved too hard to close the deal.

The deal was closed for Robert with Trump's focus on cutting government, trimming what he thinks is an overreach in foreign assistance as well as his appointment of Robert F. Kennedy Jr. to curb the excesses of the food industry. But the first month "seems like a lot." Donald Trump being Donald Trump, one never knows where he might focus next.

"In a way, I find myself leaning more libertarian than anything in my perspective, in that I just think the government should not—you have this certain freedom that government shouldn't overstep," he says. The risk of "overstepping" is a distinct possibility in any administration.

On election day, his top decision made, he sat in his car and reviewed the candidate descriptions of down-ballot candidates in the voter guide before heading into the voting booth. For one local office, after reading about two opposing candidates and finding himself impressed with both, "I actually had to choose the one I liked more. I haven't had that experience in so long!"

TILTING AT WINDMILLS

The view from the veranda of Bryan Hambley's 1872 Victorian "The Hermitage" takes in his expansive lawn sloping down to the tree line that runs toward the "historic" downtown of Loveland, "the Sweetheart of Ohio." Spring is in the air, and we've pulled a variety of dusty chairs around a coffee table to eat a lunch of quiche, salad, apples, bananas, and a sleeve of Girl Scouts Thin Mints.

Ohio is home to the front porch campaign, a strategy made famous back in the day by William McKinley in 1896 up in Canton, Ohio. That porch, and the house it was attached to, are sadly gone, but this one could accommodate quite a crowd, and I imagine red, white, and blue bunting hanging from the railing,

---

2   David McCullough, *Truman* (Simon and Schuster, 1992), 342.

prompting Bryan to quip that "you'd need a lot of people" to create a politically imposing tableau.

Sitting outside for me, leaving eighteen-degree weather in Massachusetts the day before, and for weeks before that, stirs a little giddiness about what might be possible, even for a Democrat running in a state that just rejected the last one standing, US Senator Sherrod Brown. I picture the scene—people drawn to someone new to politics, filling the lawn, the smell of hamburgers grilling nearby, paper cups of punch laid out by volunteers, each of them new to working on a campaign. Ohioans feeling hopeful about someone running for office for the first time in a long time, some who came just to see what all the buzz is about, skeptical that there can be someone running for office that they would be proud to vote for, and not just against.

Political operatives may consider Bryan a little giddy himself, thinking that he can run as a Democrat for the office of Secretary of State in one that, its "swing" status for much of my adult life notwithstanding, has gone fully aggressively red. Brown's loss the previous November left Ohio without a statewide elected Democrat. And if you can't reelect Brown, a proven champion for middle- and working-class economic interests, what Democrat can be elected?

Both houses of the state legislature and a majority of the congressional delegation are controlled by the Republicans. And the courts. A few weeks before our luminous repast, two MAGA Republicans even announced intentions to challenge the incumbent Democratic mayor of nearby Cincinnati, one of them coincidentally the brother of the vice president, who was briefly a senator from Ohio.

But Bryan is a leukemia doctor, accustomed not only to facing daunting prognoses, but in guiding others through them. I imagine him thinking that long odds are surmountable and figuring out how to beat them in a clinical manner might just work here as well.

The year 2026 seems a long way off in the first week of March 2025, even if the past month and a half have seemed like several years, and anything can happen, given the fast pace of events. The first-time candidate, who forayed onto the political stage at the Republican National Convention in Cleveland, Ohio, in 2016, organizing a group of doctors supporting their Muslim brothers and sisters in medicine against calls for a ban on "Muslim countries," has consistently increased his activism, most recently in the failed ballot initiative to ban gerrymandered districts.

After lunch, but before Bryan discusses campaign tactics with his hired consultants while simultaneously washing dishes, he produces a clear plastic baggy and it appears briefly as if he may inquire about our vaccination status, with remedy at hand. But the baggy contains cards for a game of Dutch Blitz, a rapid-fire contest whose difficulty is heightened by the mid-afternoon wind that occasionally sweeps cards off our lunch table and onto the veranda floor.

Accustomed as I am to the calculated—some might say cynical—campaign-trail gimmicks and figurative card tricks of seasoned, hardened politicians, the notion flickers that Bryan may be attempting to make a larger point with the game. Or perhaps readying a heartland bromide to impress an East Coast political consultant, using a children's game to impart some folk wisdom underpinning his plans to upend the Buckeye State's political order and put us in our places besides. But it is a guileless gesture. He wanted to feed us lunch and then play a quick game of cards. And despite his intentions, a lesson is learned nonetheless.

His in-state consultants are young but with experience and success working on local races; one was a candidate herself, but this is the first statewide race either has managed. They think that the campaign must, as we say on successful insurgent efforts after the fact, "throw out the playbook." It's a status-heightening and potentially career-making statement if it works—"we were smarter than the playbook." But the reality is more frequently darker, that the playbook wasn't available or the money that comes with it, the access, the attention, wasn't made available. So, you have to find your own way, and maybe circumstances out of your control align for the campaign, and the candidate wins.

They know that running a "traditional" campaign from that Democratic playbook will not win. It is said the definition of insanity is doing the same thing over and over and over and over again and expecting a different outcome. In the formerly swing state of Ohio, the two operatives have watched losing campaign strategies. And the party elite, the elected Democrats who remain in lower offices, haven't been quick to reach out in support. Ohio has term limits, and term-limited Democrats, like their more numerous Republican counterparts, are assessing their options if they've reached the limit. The field for Secretary of State may grow and potential endorsers don't want to buy in, particularly on behalf of an outside unknown.

But each industry also has its rules, its norms, its conventions. And political consulting is a business. When Bryan's consultants ask about running a campaign that is more aggressive, that calls out, for instance, Vivek Ramaswamy's pronouncements as his expected gubernatorial campaign ramps up, they are told by the powers that be in the state's Democratic Party: "That's not the way we do it."

To me, this speaks to the business of politics. Play by the rules and you too can make a career in this quirky business. The money flowed even before the 2010 Supreme Court decision in *Citizens United*, geysering since, and there is room for lucrative, long careers, win or lose. And I think this is increasingly true. Politics is big business.

Being a doctor is a profession, but it isn't just a job. And even when lucrative, it is a calling, and led Bryan and his wife, Jana, also a doctor, to stand with fellow caregivers, even when under assault by the Republican nominee for president. Bryan thinks, perhaps quaintly, that running for office is a calling too.

The breeze that upended the playing cards kicks up, and the possibilities seem, well, possible in the warm spring air. Bryan has a few business-keeping questions for me, someone who graduated college the year he was born, about how he should spend his time and where to focus. One is if he should pay someone to conduct a poll. I say yes, that he should pay me $30,000 and I will tell him that nobody in Ohio knows who he is. He has an infectious and genuine laugh that I think would carry well across his lawn, rippling toward the historic downtown, should anyone be listening.

CHAPTER EIGHTEEN

THEY HATE US

The rain following the snow had frozen the town field solid. But Willa hadn't been there in a while, with the snow and rain, where she could chase a ball and hopefully steal one from another dog, so we suit up and head down. We live in New England for the seasons, but there is no upside to February in Massachusetts that I can think of.

The minute I fired the Chuckit! stick, Willa was off, and my feet, both of them, left the ground at exactly the same time and I came down, cartoon style, on my back. I did not hit my head or twist my body, but stuck the landing perfectly horizontal, briefly rearranging my internal organs. I felt fine that day, but not the next. Over the next two weeks, the rain continued and it started to warm, but the town had closed the fields to dogs to let the grass recover, time that allowed me to do the same. I told Willa you couldn't fight city hall, but she didn't understand.

And the geese came.

They particularly liked the baseball field, and I wonder if an enormous flock of Canadian geese pooping on America's pastime was deliberate. Everything looks political these days from the dog park. Each day brings a new outrage. If the rule of law were not under constant assault, our military orders carried out over unsecure platforms, targeted vindictive actions against law firms the President personally hates, the policy decisions that defy logic, the blanket tariffs, attacking our friends and praising our enemies—would things be different, calmer, or the same? If Harris had won and the Republicans controlled both branches of Congress, would every decision, declaration, action, or executive order come under withering fire from the loyal opposition? Have we crossed the Rubicon, tweeting, X'ing, Truth Socialing, TikToking, and podcasting all the way? It's hard for me to imagine that a Republican Congress with a Harris Administration would extend the olive branch of cooperation. Was there even a hint at a honeymoon in Trump 2.0?

Some brave dog parents take it upon themselves to clean up the Canadian carpet-bombing, and the dogs return. I've just come back from the road trip from Ohio, through Oklahoma to Dallas, Texas. Surely, I must be hearing concern out there, or maybe regret, the long-awaited scales falling from Trump supporters' eyes with the prospect that their carburetor or washing machine, which they had no idea came from Canada, now cost three times as much? Even though the states I drove through voted for Trump, they have to view his actions the same way we do, right?

And in the dog park in Belmont, Massachusetts, those brave enough to check their investment accounts or 401k plan hope against hope that there might be this olive branch of concern and dismay that will bring all of us closer for the future of the republic.

If I answer yes, that Trump voters I encounter are repentant, then the rampant Constitutional crimes that greet us every morning are based on their ignorance. But the answer is no. I don't hear regret from Trump voters for their support, three months into his term. He's done a lot, everyone agrees, and some things are not going to work. But they voted for action, and he hasn't done anything that he didn't promise he would. In fact, Trump and Harris both told us that he would do these things, and he is doing them.

A lot of Democratic voices spent Trump's first term, where he seemed obsessed with the ups and downs of the stock market, explaining that most Americans aren't dependent on it, confident he was speaking over the heads of his base. Now Trump seems not to know that a stock exchange exists, and his gaze is on the golden horizon of a new age in America, while Democrats refresh financial updates every few minutes.

"They hate us," someone tells me. "But we hate them," someone else says broadly about Trump voters. I've clocked a lot of miles going around the country, and it's too much to ask that everyone I speak with reveal their true feelings about "us," but I don't think that the people I speak with hate Harris voters, or Democrats or progressives, or even those from the northeast. I am all of those and worked for Ted Kennedy to boot, and I feel my conversations have always informed me of how one approaches politics from where one lives.

A lot of Trump voters I talk to do think that the people like those in my dog park probably do hate them, or look down on them, or question their reasons for supporting such a "loathsome" individual. Donald Trump isn't the first politician to elicit such venom. Hillary Clinton still makes people's eyes narrow in contempt when her name comes up in certain circles or is brought up in my travels. But I never heard such hate for Harris, and even though I know it's out there, it's far short of the animus toward Hillary Clinton or Trump. Biden gets more of a sympathetic pass now that he's not in office and battling a serious cancer diagnosis.

Elizabeth Currid-Halkett asked people she interviewed for her book, *The Overlooked Americans*, whether there was a divided America. She writes about talking to voters in rural America: "While I listened to folks answer …one thing was clear; whatever division they perceived in America, they did not feel divided from other Americans." She points out that the educated urban dwellers did think this. She asked a man in Missouri if he felt left behind. He replied, "The truth is, Elizabeth, we don't feel left behind. We want to be left alone."[1]

THE BALLAD OF EAST AND WEST

Earl has seen the changes in East Greenwich, Rhode Island, over the thirty-four years he's manned the chair at the Town Barber Shop on Main Street. If he has indeed been there for that long, he couldn't have changed much himself; he doesn't look a whole lot older than thirty-four. He explains proudly that he was, and believes he still holds, the record as the youngest barber to be licensed in the state, at fifteen. A popular truism in politics holds that a week can feel like an Ice Age, both in terms of how quickly things can change and how cold and isolating it can feel. By that logic, thirty-four years isn't an Ice Age; it predates the Big Bang.

The pandemic was the hardest blow to Earl's business, of course, grinding

---

1   Elizabeth Currid-Halkett, *The Overlooked Americans* (Basic Books, 2023), 31.

everything to a halt, and the barber business was particularly slow to recover. Customers who would come in every four weeks before now come in every six or so, not needing to look so neat working from home in their pajama bottoms, Zoom camera turned off.

It has upset his TV routine in the shop. For decades, the pattern was so predictable he knew when to turn the channel. The morning was a stream of the retired, the TV turned to local news or one of the networks, the talk politics, usually of the local variety. In the afternoon, he would turn on *SpongeBob SquarePants* for the kids while the parents chatted, or more recently got lost in their phones. Then he'd put on the sports channel for the after-work crowd.

COVID ruined his "process." Retirees got used to having their wives give them a trim of the wisps at home, and there is no predictability to when others come in. There is more money in the town since COVID, East Greenwich being a prime relocation destination, with not a lot of seasonal rentals. In the winter, it's easy to find a parking space downtown, but year-round the city maintains that New England upscale but unpretentious vibe.

More money brings change, and more detachment. He used to know all the business owners on Main Street, but not now. A local broker confirms the trend: the location—close to Providence, and Newport, and T.F. Green Airport, on the water, with the top-rated school district in the state—is attracting those who fled bigger cities during the pandemic and young families alike. By some metrics, East Greenwich is the wealthiest town in Rhode Island.

New people expect things they think should be at hand, amenities, a level of service, and they get involved in local politics too. The faux cobblestone crosswalks they wanted deteriorated very quickly. Snowplows will always win that battle. This is a small community and it's hard when newcomers couple sharp elbows with a lack of understanding of the place, of how things are done.

I've come on this windswept day in spring, sleet hitting my window as I made my way down from Massachusetts, to investigate what might be a tale of two cities, or small towns: East Greenwich and West Greenwich. One of the earliest incorporated towns in the state, in the late 1600s, the once united town stretched from Narragansett Bay to the Connecticut border. With the end of King Philip's War, militia from Connecticut made feints at what they thought was unsettled land, so Rhode Island quickly settled and populated it.

But by 1740, traveling for town meetings from the west part of town proved hard, and the state split the town into the two roughly equally populated ones that are there today. Since West Greenwich had two-thirds of the land, it settled into farming. Meanwhile, the population grew in the less rural, coastal East Greenwich.

Almost two centuries later, the makeup of the towns remained largely the same, but though there is a clear "city/country" divide, the voting at the national level was in sync. In 2012, Mitt Romney edged Barack Obama in both towns. But since then, a chasm has opened between sibling municipalities, and in 2024, East went for Harris 60–40 percent and West split the same for Trump.

This was news to Earl and to everyone else I spoke with on Main Street. A couple of Trump voters on the eastern side know that the town leans pretty heavily "Democrat," one whispers under her breath. Her coworker, who has just finished notarizing a document says, "All I know is I voted for Trump," in a bit of a triumphant singsong. They agree there isn't a whole lot they can do about it in East Greenwich. I ask why, and one grabs two envelopes sitting on the counter and puts one on either side of her head. "Blinders," she says.

They think the electoral divide, which they were also not aware of, is due more to the rural vs. rich nature of the towns. West Greenwich votes "like the farmers they are" she says sympathetically, and since she lives in the east, a little wistfully. East and West do not share a school system, for instance, one that might have exposed political divides in the discussion of hot-button issues, particularly schools. The five town council members, the executive branch in each town, are all Republican in one and all Democratic in the other. One Republican Councilor in West Greenwich, a teacher, submitted a letter in testimony opposed to a state bill on mask mandates. One Democratic councilor in East Greenwich wrote a letter to the editor raising the issue of gender bias in reaction to unanimous council decisions, the two female members getting more criticism than their male colleagues.

Driving out of the historic East Greenwich downtown, parallel to the highway on Division Road, you wouldn't notice when you entered West Greenwich—there is no sign. But if you come from west to east, it's easy to know you've crossed the town line because you're immediately met by expensive wood and stone fences, horse farms, tasteful street posts announcing named estates, and a fair amount of lawn signs urging protection of open space and reminding us to slow down—children live there. East Greenwich to West Greenwich, the population just dribbles away, as it does all over America when you head out of "town."

I did google "barber shop, West Greenwich" but was directed to West Warwick, and there is no downtown. But there is Tavern on the Hill, ominously located on Nooseneck Hill Road, a "casual, backwoods bar" with live music daily and very friendly staff. The owner comes in to check on things, to make sure the chili he made the other day is still holding up. He feels the weather ever since he broke his back a number of years ago and is hoping it'll get warm soon.

The in-house event planner stalks the place at noon, hyper-focused, around the big bar moving a chair here, hanging a poster for an upcoming event there. She's particularly concerned with flow, and it can fill up pretty fast at night, the regulars in the big room, and if it gets two-deep at the narrow end of the bar, hard up against the front wall, it makes it difficult to navigate if you come in the back door by the parking lot.

The bartender was born in the area but spent years in Pawtucket, a working-class city bordering Providence to the north from here, starting when she was seventeen. She never liked it there, but it's gotten much worse than it was then. She's happy to be back, where she's more comfortable and people are laid back. I ask about the east/west divide, but she says she's not from West Greenwich. She's from Coventry, the next town over. Rhode Island is small, and geographic identity seems opposite Massachusetts. If asked, I would say I'm from Boston; even though I don't live there, it's close enough, and I'm happy to tell you what Bostonians think.

If you ask a plumber in the Boston area what his territory is, it might be a few nearby towns. I ask Bob, a plumbing contractor, what region he covers. He says "Rhode Island." Both answers speak to the varying intimacies of their states.

We live in deeply divided political times, and East and West Greenwich have grown apart in their politics too. But it's not battled out on the football field on Thanksgiving Day, since both high schools are matched against other rivals, and if the rhetoric isn't flying in a joint school district arrangement, the division isn't noticed much in either place. Of course, the downside to this divided harmony is that there isn't an opportunity to hear others' perspectives from their experiences.

Rudyard Kipling's poem "The Ballad of East and West" begins its famous final stanza, "Oh, East is East, and West is West, and never the twain shall meet,/

Till Earth and Sky stand presently at God's great Judgment Seat." Born and raised in British colonial India, he viewed things through the lens of his time and station. And you can read the line this way: east is east; west is west.

The story is of an unlikely friendship, of enemies turned, well, not only allies but with a conversion of one to the other side. And the poem ends with this line: "But there is neither East nor West, Border, nor Breed, nor Birth, When two strong men stand face to face though they come from the ends of the earth!" Theodore Roosevelt liked the last stanza so much he used it on campaign posters in his 1912 "Bull Moose" campaign for the presidency.

We seem a nation divided, each holding blinders up to the side of our faces when describing the other side. In the Greenwiches, the blinders are there. I suspect that both towns are largely happy where they are presently. I also guess that if I quoted the Missourian Elizabeth Currid-Halkett spoke with, that they would "just like to be left alone," I might get nods in the Tavern on the Hill. I'd also be surprised if they ever have had a discussion about installing faux cobblestones.

When one has little interaction with those who disagree with them politically, you can start to question what motivates them to their positions, not from a disagreement of facts or goals, but of beliefs, and it is a short leap, when encouraged by social media or tactics of dark forces, to get to a place where they hate us, but maybe because of that, we hate them.

In Kipling's poem, it is the hatred that brings the two men into initial contact, a battle for the return of a stolen horse. Both respond so honorably to the resulting confrontation that each sees the other differently, and they become brothers. Today, east is east, and west is west, and the toxic nature of politics makes all of us want to keep to our geographies or hide in the one we're in, so as not to face "the enemy."

MANCAVE MUSEUM

There is a ridge of Republican-leaning communities that run up the I-15 corridor in California, north of San Diego heading to Los Angeles. Temecula, Murrieta, Menifee, and Corona would give Donald Trump enough votes to overcome Democrat-heavy Palm Springs and Cathedral City to pull Congressman Ken Calvert over the top with just over 51 percent of the vote in his swing district.

Just off the Grand Boulevard Historic District in Corona, "Crown" in Spanish, two antique stores square off across the street from one another. The Antique Gallery anchors an open-air mall, in that it's the only business left standing, everything else boarded up long ago. Jeanne, the proprietor, is playing detective. In a collection of dolls, all looking about the same, one is labelled $3.95 while all the others are listed for $13.95. Where some shop owners, those who house dozens of vendors, might assume there has been a printing mistake, she wants to be careful. Maybe there is a reason one is deeply discounted?

I say I'm browsing, and she tells me they charge for that. It's a smart move when you're located in a business district that looks abandoned, I tell her. And it is. Jeanne, kidding about the browsing charge, is serious about the threat to her livelihood. The city has been planning to make Corona beautiful by leveling the shops and several blocks around this key intersection. Only the public library would remain, it seems.

She doesn't know what the plan is, just that leveling it all, including her shop, has been in the plans for over a decade. Recently, talk has started again. But fate has worked in her favor before. A public-school teacher by profession, she was looking for something different to do when she walked into this place. "Swear to God, what I'm telling you is the truth," she says. "The owner looks at me and says, 'Do you want to buy me out of this place?'" They had never met before. Jeanne's school district did not give annual raises but periodically would give teachers bonuses. "A pretty good bonus," she says, which she had just received, and here she is.

I can imagine it's a tough business, and Jeanne needs a few more years until retirement, and she hopes fate stays on her good side. I'm constantly struck by the passivity when under assault by a government of any level. I don't even ask if Jeanne is fighting city hall. She says the jeweler on the corner lot owns the whole complex, and she can't imagine he will sell. But it also strikes me that no one from the local government has ever reached out to Jeanne, who invested her work bonus to keep a local business up and running for over a dozen years.

It gets to the heart of the role of government, particularly at the local level, where participatory democracy should be the purest. Our local elected officials are neighbors. Their finger on the pulse should count the beats better than any other. Later that evening, checking into my hotel in Cathedral City, in the Coachella Valley, the proprietor wonders how Jeanne could be unaware of such a momentous public undertaking. There must have been years of hearings and notices and opportunities to weigh in. California is a highly regulated state. Maybe her landlord has not kept her informed?

I'm traveling by myself on this leg of the trip, and so I am genetically obligated to check out the Mancave Museum back in Corona in the strip mall next to Jashua Liquor. I tell John he's a master marketer, coming up with that name. It drew me in. He had a couple of good years a couple of years ago, but the past few have been really slow. His bread and butter is vintage neon signs, but to meet the downturn in sales, he will take custom orders.

Most of his customers were repeats, given license perhaps to outfit a personal man cave, but how many neon signs can one paneled basement support? He's seen a lot of change here, and an explosion of growth. He flipped houses in the '70s and '80s, bought an office building or two, and "got greedy." His block is coming down at the end of the year. "This one and the next one," he says, that houses a boarded restaurant and parking lot. He also doesn't know what the plan is, just that his end of the road is certain. He has nowhere to relocate, like Jeanne, and will probably just fold up or take the neon sign business online.

He's not surprised that the lineup of communities from Temecula to here voted for Trump. His customers are almost all Trump voters. Maybe I'm the only Harris voter to walk through the doors of the Mancave Museum. But these are up-and-coming bedroom communities where the houses cost a lot of money. Families sacrifice to live here, and budgets are tight. "Things cost more these past four years." He explains this: "This should have happened forty years ago. Government got too big." I explain that back home, people think too much is happening too fast, with disregard for the laws on the books. "Yeah, well they all get their news from the same place. I know people who have lost friends here because they voted for Trump. It's crazy."

"And this week, the only thing they keep showing about JD Vance is that he fumbled the trophy," he adds. It's true. Memes labeled, "See the moment JD Vance dropped the Ohio State College Football Championship trophy," fill my inbox.

I ask him who his member of Congress is and tell him that most people I ask don't know or confuse one of their senators. "Ken Calvert," he tells me, correctly. Impressive enough, but the newly redrawn districts have no geographic logic. He's never seen him, but he knows who he is. I say, conversely, people here knew

Kamala Harris when they walked into the voting booth in November. "No one knows Kamala," he says.

The Grand Boulevard Historic District will need a lot of work to be grand again, if it even was at one time. The decision process to approve the leveling of several blocks and the construction of something that would "make Corona beautiful" certainly goes more smoothly without Jeanne chaining herself to her front door when the bulldozers show up. City leaders expect a certain level of civic awareness, and if you missed every single opportunity to participate in the public process, well, maybe that's on you.

And I think back on the county-elected official in Congresswoman Marjorie Taylor Greene's district, who told me, correctly, that she would comfortably win her 2022 primary. Running for County Commissioner was his first foray into electoral politics. He was pretty apolitical, and then there was a notice to put a big-box store across the street from the elementary school. He thought this was madness—there wasn't even a traffic light there—and marched down to city hall to inquire how this had gotten so far. He learned such matters were handled by the county, not the city, and he wasn't even sure he understood the division of responsibilities. He got involved, learned his way around the process, got a light for the intersection, ran for the county commission, and won.

There is a uniformity to antique stores across the country, an anthropological dive into Americana, shoppers finding the nostalgic gem amid general chaos. Each is a small business—each pays taxes and wages and plays an important role in recycling items and each keeps a storefront occupied. But I get the sense they are generally unloved by the communities where they are located. No one thinks a store that sells what a lot of people have cast aside is the preferred anchor of a revitalization effort. Ignored, at best, they quietly tell the story of America.

CHAPTER NINETEEN

THE BATTLE OVER DEMOCRACY

DOES MY BASE MAKE
ME LOOK RACIST?

Much was, and is still, made of Donald Trump's base. Those who find Trump unqualified to be president because of his personal behavior or his policy pronouncements also dislike his personal base, finding them, well, base. The "basket of deplorables," Hillary labeled them, clinging to their "guns and religion," as Barack Obama said in 2008. To them, these hardcore MAGA voters, the ones waving the flags even if they weren't actually the ones storming the Capitol—and some of them certainly were or would have been if they could have taken the time off from work—are racist, and a good percentage of them are probably white supremacists.

The America these diehard Trumpers consider to have been great, was and would be again, according to his detractors, segregated and with women who stayed home and raised kids. They respond only to the call of an authoritarian figure and stand ready to be deputized to deport anyone who doesn't look like them. They care little for democracy and hate that the government assists anyone but themselves.

When I'm talking to progressive voters, they tell me about a MAGA aunt or Uncle So-and-So who wasn't always this way but now sits in front of the TV watching Fox, thinking the January 6th participants were populated by Antifa or infiltrated by the FBI. And at the same time that Fox has brainwashed Uncle So-and-So, the Left's view of Trump's base has been cemented by left-leaning media.

I did not set out on this journey in search of "the base." There is no need to do so when one just needs to flip on the TV, as they seem to be moths to a flame. And late-night comedy reporters love to talk to the MAGA base, to mock them simply by giving them oxygen and letting them go on and on, encouraged even, creating bits that get shared and go viral the next day.

It reminds me of the opening lyrics from Randy Newman's "Rednecks" where he uses an appearance of segregationist Georgia Governor Lester Maddox on The Dick Cavett Show to expose elite hypocrisy. Before Pixar and "You've Got a Friend in Me," Newman wrote of the raw, if vulgar, political truth, holding a mirror up to expose the ignorance and bigotry of the wealthy, well-educated, and white elite.

And while the Trump base both repulses and frightens those on the left, through his first term, it seemed that it was contained. Polls showed that his favorability ratings were always underwater. He was speaking only to the base, they told themselves, and that was reflected in the ten million fewer votes he got in his first two elections, losing the popular vote in both.

Trump voters I talk with generally don't consider themselves Trump's base. And there are a fair amount of Obama-to-Trump voters. Or Trump-Biden-Trump voters. There are a lot of party-fluid voters out there.

There are traditional Republican voters who might have preferred DeSantis or Haley but couldn't bring themselves to vote for a Democrat. In 2024, "the base" became a shiny distraction, a convenient one for the media to focus on. The base voters were portrayed in a lump group, wearing their support for Trump, literally, on their chests, tattooed if shirtless, and logoed if covered, or both. They would stand in front of the cameras all day long, their pride apparent, some saying he was chosen for this mission by God, a particular draw for those reporting.

The glare from this distraction hid the shift beyond the base, both with the thin layer of swing voters in the seven crucial battlegrounds and with the vast depth of ignored voters in the other forty-three states.

It's the Des Moines effect. Back in the gymnasium in the Theodore Roosevelt School on a cold February morning in 2016, when neighbors gathered to vote in the Iowa caucus, no one spoke for Donald Trump, but he won anyway. The Des Moines effect wasn't confined to Iowa, of course. It was no snapshot in time; it was a tectonic shift in American politics and culture, and much of the real, durable movement occurred below the surface.

Everyone knows someone—a friend, family member, coworker—they're astounded to learn voted for Trump. For the lucky ones, politics doesn't interfere with the preexisting relationship.

Polling for a ballot initiative in Massachusetts in 2022 to allow undocumented residents the right to have drivers' licenses was not doing well, from the advocates' perspective. The pollster characterized the profile of the "no" voter who would decide the election as "someone with a Black Lives Matter sign in their living room window." The campaign adjusted strategy, and law enforcement voices pointed out the benefit of having only licensed and insured drivers on the state's roads, which helped the initiative pass.

We all stand before our ultimate judge, be it a higher authority or the mirror, and hope to see the better angel of our nature. But we often vote our fears and rationalize that one is not connected to the other.

The Trump voters I talk to like that he just does things. Old-school, stick-to-the-standard playbook in foreign and personal relations where opponents can disagree but do so agreeably doesn't appeal to this expanded Trump base. They would not like to sit down across the table from him in a negotiation. Who would? But he is the type of person the base wants negotiating for the United States.

Let's take the American embassy in Israel. The Jerusalem Embassy Act of 1995, overwhelmingly passed by Congress, called for the embassy to be moved from Tel Aviv. Polls showed significant public opposition to this move, and there were dire predictions that if it did, the delicate Middle East balance would take a hit. Twenty-three years after the Act was signed by President Clinton, Donald Trump moved it, largely because mega-donor Sheldon Adelson wanted it to happen.

Democrats have known for a long time that they need to send a "better message" to red states and to the broader Trump base that wants bold action, which may upset the delicate checks and balances that preserve the status quo.

The talk of the need for better "messaging" raises my blood pressure. On the one hand, the condescending one, it sounds to me like it might be something you would employ with children to explain finances or good nutrition. On the other hand, the one that misses the point, is that there is great benefit to not leading with a "message" we think those we are not connecting with would like to hear.

When Democrats listen to what people tell them they are looking for, then the Democrats could propose initiatives and solutions, and the message might take care of itself. A lot of the Trump expanded base likes, and voted for, Bernie Sanders.

In early March 2025, AOC proposed a cap on credit card interest rates of ten percent. This was the first nonresistance initiative proposed by a Democrat elected member of Congress, though she has also been vocal on fighting the administration.

And in late March, Health and Human Services Secretary Robert F. Kennedy Jr. issued a ban on pharmaceutical advertising on TV. Reporting is fairly silent on both initiatives, and I think, in a bi- or nonpartisan way, there might be a connection between the two, both potential good policy decisions that hit the monied interests, the elite…"the regime."

O-K-L-A-H-O-M-A

As you approach the State Capitol in Oklahoma City, Oklahoma, even in the late winter, the sun can hit you. You search for a tree to stop under briefly, but there is none. I've walked from my hotel downtown, and the lack of shade, plus the lack of sidewalks in certain sections, sends me out into the lawns of the business park on my route. I wonder if this is snake country. Safely reaching the parking lot, also treeless, I pass the working oil derrick out front and enter the fortress-like structure of limestone and granite, which was domeless until 2002.

The inside, extensively renovated, glows; its new hat fits the rotunda well. Some fiddle players are serenading not only the busy capitol but also the legislature in session, the tourists during this school vacation week, and even a few couples who are doing the Texas two-step around the perimeter.

I find the portrait of Carl Albert, the highest-ranking Oklahoman to serve in the federal government, Speaker of the House from 1971 to 1977, some fairly turbulent years in Washington. When Vice President Spiro Agnew resigned in 1973, Albert became second in line to the presidency. With Richard Nixon embroiled in the Watergate scandal, Albert could be forgiven for briefly measuring the Oval Office drapes in his mind. When Agnew resigned, Albert's Secret Service protection increased.

But Carl was a modest man, and I can't imagine him getting too far ahead of himself with the Oval Office decor. He was an old-school pragmatist, and his portrait is discreetly displayed in an alcove in the Capitol building. Albert couldn't get elected as a Democrat today in Oklahoma, and maybe he wouldn't be one. He said, "I very much disliked doctrinaire liberals—they want to own your minds. And I don't like reactionary conservatives. I like to face issues in terms of conditions and not in terms of someone's inborn political philosophy."[1]

A cap on interest rates and a ban on pharma ads on TV don't sound particularly doctrinaire liberal or reactionary conservative to me, and I wonder if Speaker Albert would agree. In late April 2025, President Trump asked the IRS to revoke Harvard University's tax-exempt status, causing outrage and panic in academia. I'm old enough to remember when it was Democrats who called for a reexamination of tax-exempt institutions.

But things look different through the looking glass.

---

1   Martin Weil, "Ex-Speaker Carl Albert Dies at 91," *Washington Post*, February 5, 2000.

CONCLUSION

Democracy was on the ballot in 2024. Election day came and went, the integrity of the vote across the country worked as it should and had for over 240 years, including 2020. The Electoral College met in the various state capitals in December 2024, voted and reported the results to the Congress of the United States in Washington, DC, as it had every four years since 1788. On January 6, 2025, Vice President Harris supervised the opening of the envelopes and declared Donald J. Trump and JD Vance the victors, and on January 20, they were sworn into office. The powers of the government were handed over, in a peaceful transfer, from one political party to another, just as intended by the Founders who codified them in the Constitution.

And this is the brilliance of our experiment. John Adams woke early on March 4, 1801, walked out of the White House, and took the stagecoach to Baltimore, Maryland, then went home to Braintree, Massachusetts, abandoning the city and the federal government to his bitter rival, peacefully, for the first time in history.

In 2025, the fight over democracy, after the swearing-in, expanded from Article One of the Constitution, which lays out elections, to Articles One, Two, and Three of the document, focusing on how the government works day to day. The Constitutional Convention of 1787 listed them in order of importance: Legislative, Executive, Judiciary.

Our history is rich with examples of how, over two and a half centuries, the checks and balances written into each have worked in real life, through geographic expansion, slavery and civil war, the rise of political parties, civil liberty and civil rights struggles, modernization, and the revolutions of the steam engine in the country's first century, foreign entanglements and conflicts in its second, and technology and terrorism in its third. And throughout, social upheaval.

The Executive, held by one person—unlike the other two, now 535 in the legislative branch and nine on the Supreme Court—has to answer to no one within its designated branch, save the voters, every four years. As the United States grew into a world power, the Executive was given additional powers, assuming additional authority when allowed to do so or in the face of inaction by Congress.

And late in Joe Biden's term, the Supreme Court gave the Executive unheard-of power, removing checks on his authority to make decisions he deems legally necessary. Suddenly, Richard Nixon's statement to interviewer David Frost in 1977, that "when the President does it, that means it's not illegal,"[1] was case law, and the battle for democracy, having survived the election, moved to the administration. If Nixon, so backed by the Supreme Court, had burned the Watergate tapes in the interest of national security, he would have, in all probability, finished his second term in 1977, working through his enemies list for an additional two years.

If you go to the National Archives and reread the Constitution, the checks and balances remain, the implied and enumerated powers given to the Legislature, the narrower running-of-the-government powers of administration given to the President, and the vague you'll-have-to-figure-it-out-on-your-own powers of review of statutes passed to the Supreme Court.

And the first few months of the second Trump Administration could certainly have been a masterclass of our checks and balances in action. Trump dipping into Congress's authority to set tariffs, or make border policy and immigration, or maneuvering around their advise-and-consent authority of key appointments, or of not honoring approved spending would historically result in a sharp rebuke from the legislative branch. In our democracy, a constitutional republic, Congress would be expected to exert its authority, its power of the purse, its oversight function, to fight for its first-in-the-lineup place in the hearts and minds of our Founders, and as the branch nearest the people.

---

1   David Frost, *Transcript of David Frost's Interview With Richard Nixon*, interview, *Frost/Nixon: Behind the Scenes of the Nixon Interviews* (Harper Perennial, 1977), https://docs.house.gov/meetings.

CHECKS AND BALANCES

The first year of Donald Trump's second nonconsecutive term might have been filled with that kind of high political drama, one that would make every political scientist dream of appearing on CNN or Fox News to explain the intricacies of the battles of the branches. Take the War Powers Act. Congress is given the power to declare war. The President is the Commander in Chief of the Armed Forces. President Harry Truman sent troops to Korea in 1950 without asking for a Declaration from Congress.

In 1965, President Lyndon Johnson did the same in Vietnam. In both instances, during very different unwritten rules of comity and bipartisanship in Washington, Congress let these actions go largely unchecked. The conflicts in Korea and Vietnam were by any definition war, except in the eyes of the federal government in Washington, DC. But in 1973, when President Richard Nixon bombed the country of Cambodia, Democratic Congressman Clement Zablocki introduced a resolution requiring that the president notify Congress within forty-eight hours after a military action, and such action could only last for sixty days without congressional approval.

The resolution passed both houses of Congress, sending it to President Nixon, who vetoed. With Nixon beginning to bleed out over Watergate, Congress overrode, and the War Powers Resolution became law in 1973. But laws on the books, or enumerative powers given the legislative branch, do not guarantee that the unitary executive will always comply, particularly in areas presidents think are theirs to handle alone, and no one, Republican or Democrat, was a fan of complying with the War Powers Act. Our system of checks and balances requires an always active and attentive Congress, or laws become merely gestures.

UNCHECKED AND OFF-BALANCE

But Congress stood, cheered Trump, and returned to focus on its more public-facing oversight hearing strategy, where political points could be made to the folks back home, content to leave the work to Trump. It had long ago watched its power diminish in both Republican and Democratic administrations, except that of their impeachment power. Congress left tariffs to presidents decades ago. They have been unable to update our immigration policy for nearly half a century. Spending increases and tax cuts proposed by administrations are agreed to, holder of the purse and the ballooning deficit be damned.

If democracy was on the ballot in 2024, its practical function is under assault in 2025 and 2026. Abraham Lincoln, in his second inaugural address in March 1865, stated that while the North and South both dreaded war, "insurgent agents were...seeking to destroy it without war," and ultimately, "the war came."[2]

During the campaign, divisive voices warned of the coming war if Trump lost, dark implications that if "they" wouldn't let Trump win, the country would face grave and possibly violent consequences. In July 2024, Heritage Foundation President Kevin Roberts said the country was in a "second American Revolution." It didn't have to be an actual war, though the language seemed to carry the threat, but would be bloodless "if the left allows it to be."[3]

Civil War or Revolutionary, take your analogy, but the battle over democracy is engaged. Donald Trump, his forces breaching the ramparts of the Capitol in 2021 but rebuffed, triumphantly claimed his domain in his first return joint address to Congress—functionally but not technically a State of the Union. The resistance has been reduced to screaming from sidelines, with one martyr, Representative Al Green of Texas, removed from the chamber as he spoke, just to make an example. Others lamely held up what looked like ping-pong paddles with trite messages of dissent written on them. Nearly a decade into what can only be candidly called The Trump Era, the opposition party is still struggling with how to, you know, *oppose*.

As the juggernaut rolled forward, the resistance took to the airways to, well, fight among themselves. The Senate votes to stay and defend the government, the House votes to fight. Battle cries abound, but where is the battle plan?

Guest speaking in a political science class at the University of Massachusetts-Lowell in March 2025, I ask the students what the Democratic platform is on

---

2   A Spotlight on a Primary Source by Abraham Lincoln, "President Lincoln's Second Inaugural Address, 1865," President Lincoln's Second Inaugural Address, 1865 | Gilder Lehrman Institute of American History, accessed May 25, 2025, https://www.gilderlehrman.org/history-resources/spotlight-primary-source/president-lincolns-second-inaugural-address-1865.

3   Associated Press report, "Leader of the pro-Trump Project 2025 suggests there will be a New American Revolution," *Politico*, July 4, 2024.

housing, immigration, the border, or the economy. The students, mostly life science majors fulfilling their general studies requirement, stare at me in silence. I can hardly blame them. Kamala Harris had the makings of a platform, inherited and of her own invention: the outline of an "Opportunity Economy," $25,000 down payments for first-time homebuyers. Codifying *Roe*. Standing up to Vladimir Putin. But when your leader leaves the scene, the plan, which for the Democrats under Harris never had the time to be fully written, goes *poof*.

If the Republican battle plan was spelled out in their Heritage-sponsored "Project 2025," the Democratic plan is to fight and recognize that there needs to be better messaging. This is unsatisfying to almost everyone, but there is no leader to blame or urge to action. So rank-and-file Democrats and liberal monied and special interests take aim at any leader they can find, in Congress, in the party, in Joe and Jill Biden. Meanwhile, Trump is well through his playbook in his first few months.

Where to start? Democrats might start with this: "In recent decades, members of the House and Senate discovered that if they give away that power to the Article II branch of government, they can also deny responsibility for its actions. So today in Washington, most policy is no longer set by Congress at all, but by the administrative state. Given the choice between being powerful but vulnerable or irrelevant but famous, most Members of Congress have chosen the latter."[4]

Congress was designed to be the branch of government closest to the people, and conveniently, the next federal contest is over control of it. The Senate seems lost to Democrats for the foreseeable future, and despite the hope that corrupt regimes fall under sustained resistance, which some have pegged at 3.5 percent of the population or so, the term of office of president in this country remains four years. The Democrats might take the above indictment of Congress to heart and beat the Republicans and Project 2025 at their own game, since the above quote comes directly from the Project 2025 manifesto, which seemed to manifest itself with remarkable efficacy in the early months of Trump II.

If Speaker Mike Johnson took offense to the characterization of Congress in the Project 2025 report, he has accepted it as he has every other belittlement of the body he controls, including the pardoning of those who stormed the

---

4   "Mandate for Leadership: The Conservative Promise," edited by Paul Dans and Steven Groves, The Heritage Foundation, 7.

chamber he leads and threatened its members on January 6th. In fact, Republicans are fine with this constitutionally neutered state. The hollowing of congressional action, and the power shifted to the administrative state headed by Donald Trump, is something to be celebrated.

This is an opportunity for Democrats if they can resist taking the hard truth of the state of affairs personally, which is a tall order. The decline of congressional power has been long and not the responsibility of current members. But it is their responsibility to rebuild, and soon, or perhaps now. There will be a desire to primary Democratic incumbents or to pour millions into campaigns of candidates that do not reflect their districts, rather than what *is* needed, a unified counter to Trump's Project 2025 agenda. And there is a lot to counter.

REIMAGINING DEMOCRACY

The Constitution of the United States is the operating manual of the country, if you will. It's pretty dry stuff, except for the preamble: "We the People, in order to form a more perfect Union..." It spells out how things work. And it's worked well, to the extent that the country is still here as the oldest living democracy in the world.

But in the same way one can read the Bible and take lessons for a more inclusive world or not, one can see what it wants in the Constitution. It's an expansive framework flexible enough to grow with the country, or it's one written by white men of property for white men of property, with the accommodation of others by the grace of white men of property.

This battle over inclusion and exclusion, of equality and competing visions of what that means, is engaged by the rarified few who go by different pejoratives, depending on where you stand—the elites or the regime or the oligarchy, take your pick. This separates out "We the People" from those who hold bipartisan power, and that power has divided the people, too simple a division when you talk to people in real time, but one promoted by media of all stripes. One side storms the gates, fully MAGA, and one side provides hard resistance but secretly thinks they might need a gate storming of their own. And Trump has both captivated his acolytes, with his Liberation Day of Tariffs and targeting of liberal universities, and utterly exhausted the opposition with his antics, self-absorption, and constitutional violations—even when he's not intermittently tuned out. On one side, there are loyal foot soldiers in the cause; on the other, people are searching for someone to lead the charge against dictatorship.

The word "democracy" has been weaponized, as Joe Trippi found out through the effort of The Lincoln Project, the effort of mostly disillusioned Republicans, the Never Trumpers, who feared for the future of democracy. When volunteers knocked on doors of Republicans and Democrats in Pennsylvania, the unenrolled and the unregistered, in an effort to promote participation in our democracy, in T-shirts with "Democracy," just that word, written on it, he says they knew the minute the door opened if they would be hugged or spat on.

Perhaps the Democrats should thank Donald Trump for the opportunity to think differently about how the government should work. The checks and balances that underpin the norms of engagement and interaction in the running of the government, that make change difficult if not impossible, have been blown up. Trump and the Heritage Foundation have an agenda that would prove destructive to the social safety net that has benefited so many in this country. But those who voted for Trump, and some who voted for Harris, were ready, some for a long time, for a reset in addressing critical systemic issues facing the country. The next Democratic administration should look to Trump 2.0 as a model to follow for its drastically redirectional bent—but toward a very different, and inclusive, vision for the future of America. If "democracy" has been weaponized, Democrats can engage in that battle and infuse it with meaning in the Jeffersonian tradition of reimagining democracy.

REWRITING THE OWNER'S MANUAL

Project 2025 wants to take the judicial philosophy of strict constructionism and dial the United States in 2025 as far back in Constitutional interpretation as it can. As I travel around the country in the first few months of the administration's slash-and-burn actions, most are taking a wait-and-see attitude. Robert Pitcherski in Marietta, Georgia, a Trump voter, says, "It seems like a lot." But this notion, relentlessly hammered on CNN, that people are outraged at the cuts is just not the reality on the ground.

Robert signed up for bold action, but would he agree with a Constitutional ban on abortion? Or would he be OK with jailing those who distribute pornography? Is he OK with a robust protection of the tax-exempt status of churches, but not of Harvard, or maybe his alma mater, the University of Georgia? Does he agree with this statement from Project 2025: "In essence, our deficit problem is a Medicare and Medicaid problem"?[5] Does Donald Trump? If so, and he moves to cut benefits or eligibility to either, what will the Democrats do? Is Robert OK with banning birthright citizenship and deporting the undocumented mother of children who are citizens, who get deported with her?

But those I talk with aren't familiar with the underlying game plan. And Project 2025's plan for the Constitution is right there, on their website: "Project 2025 actually represents an attempt to restore Constitutional governance, not terminate it. Bringing the administrative state more firmly under the control of the president, whose authority traces directly from the Constitution, could not be further from terminating this quintessential found document."[6]

The line, "Bringing the administrative state more firmly under the control of the president, *whose authority traces directly from the Constitution*" makes me think of Jenna Ellis's argument during her appearance on Alex McFarland's *The Truth & Liberty Show* that our rights come not from nature, or the nature of mankind, but from God, and it is the government's responsibility to carry out His will.[7]

The Heritage Foundation and Project 2025 want to restore Constitutional governance in the same way that some reactionary fetishists might want to return women to corsets. To this end, the Trump Administration has focused on reordering the first three Articles of the Constitution in functional practice, maybe to: two, three, one, the Executive over the Judiciary with the Legislature bringing up the rear. And it's not clear if they think the Legislature is needed, particularly if the Judiciary allows or rubber-stamps all actions by the Executive. Of course, what is left unsaid is whether the Supreme Court would feel the same way about a President Harris Administration or an Ocasio-Cortez

---

5   "Mandate for Leadership," 315.

6   Van, "Faith without Integrity," *Values in the Golden Age* (blog), April 30, 2025, https://www.valuesinthegoldenage.com/p/faith-without-integrity.

7   "The Alex McFarland Show, Episode 152-God and Government with Guest Jenna Ellis," Apple Podcasts, March 11, 2025, https://podcasts.apple.com/ng/podcast/episode-152-god-and-government-with-guest-jenna-ellis/.

Administration. The high court likes to pretend it isn't a political body, but Franklin Roosevelt could tell them different.

RENEWING POETRY

When Abraham Lincoln spoke at Gettysburg, he pinned four score and seven years not to the date of the ratification of the Constitution but to the signing of that earth-shaking, history-making Declaration. The way forward for Democrats might be right there: "We hold these truths to be self-evident, that all men are created equal, that they are endowed by their Creator with certain unalienable rights, and that among these are life, liberty, and the pursuit of happiness."

Personally, I'm a big fan of happiness, a more expansive and sunnier take on our British forebears' version: life, liberty, property. Imagine living in a country where happiness is an unalienable right. And we do! How lucky for all of us!

We may need to focus on the disconnect people have with politics and government. If the benefits of government are obvious to you, you might ask those who do not see it, *how can the government work for you?* But if MAGA is focused on the original quill markings on the Constitution—the Articles at least, if less so the Amendments of inclusion—perhaps the Democrats should embrace the poetry that framed the reason for the separation from Britain, so novel an idea it had to be spelled out on paper for all the world to read and breathe new life into that promise. The Founders told us, in the Declaration of Independence, that:

"Governments are instituted among Men, deriving their just powers from the consent of the governed, that when any form of government becomes destructive of these ends, it is the right of the people to alter or abolish it, and to institute new government, laying its foundation on such principles and organizing its powers in such form, as to them shall seem most likely to affect their safety and happiness."

It is the right of the people to alter or abolish it. Of course, we know who they meant. But are those words living? I believe Jefferson thought so. Many of the Founders might marvel that we're still here. Not John Adams, though. I'm guessing he was pretty sure we would be, and he'd be in favor of not only a robust Executive, but also the enforcement of the Alien and Sedition Act.

But if Donald Trump's vision (and by that I mean the vision of his vice president and the Heritage Foundation) for the future is a retrenchment and rollback to the world of a strict constructionist reading of the Constitution, can the alternative be a fierce embrace of our Declaration of Independence? Once you jolt the words "alter or abolish" to life, you run the same risk Dr. Frankenstein did. But he had never loosed such power before he did so with his creation. He was winging it. Americans have a history of losing powerful ideas.

Another power of a declaration is that, to be effective, you need others to stand with. Ours concludes, "And for the support of this Declaration, with a firm reliance on the protection of divine Providence, we mutually pledge to each other our Lives, our Fortunes and our sacred Honor." They were all in if they were asking others to do the same. Would elected Democrats today put the same skin in the game? Hopefully it doesn't have to come to putting one's life on the line, but certainly their fortunes, no? Maybe it's time to prove participating in politics isn't meant to enrich oneself, or at least to have the courage to push it all in for the prospect of betterment for those left out or left behind.

What of honor? The use of the term has become devalued in politics, if not derided or discarded altogether. It reminds me of a Ralph Waldo Emerson story, where he remarked about a house guest, "The more he spoke of his honor, the faster we counted our spoons."[8]

Project 2025 argues that Democrats are anti-family and anti-community and fill the void they hope to create by this hatred for traditional understandings of each with "government." And certainly, voters would agree that the Democratic Party views the government as expansive: Obamacare, Build Back Better, and of course Medicaid, Medicare, and Social Security. You know, the things people like even when the connection to Democratic policies isn't front of mind. Political parties used to be essential to one's community, but not so now. A focus on strengthening community, and by strengthening I mean welcoming others in, is key to countering this misleading positioning of Project 2025.

But Democrats have done so before and helped power the remaking, through waves of immigration and expansion and workers' rights and civil rights and renewal of purpose with Franklin Roosevelt's Four Freedoms and Johnson's

---

8   Ralph Waldo Emerson, *The Conduct of Life: By Ralph Waldo Emerson* (University Press of America, 2006).

Great Society. Today, it needs a fresh effort, the same process of remaking the Republicans have gone through, whether you agree with them or not. The vision of the advancement of democracy, one of inclusion and progress, happens when you include everyone in the coalition who's willing to join. It's not a further-left or further-right fight. For Democrats, that has never been a winning strategy. I remember a cartoon from the 1930s, I think, maybe Herbert Block, of a coal miner with his head lamp shining toward the entrance of the mine, exclaiming, "It's Mrs. Roosevelt!" During the Great Depression, those left out and left behind felt they had a champion in the White House. A couple of them, in fact.

The wringing of the hands over this idea that Democrats have a messaging problem and need to figure out what people want to hear needs to end. This is both condescending and proof that the party remains out of touch with a lot of America, an America that is foreign to them. The message is the easy part if you find out what matters because the message always flows from ideas to address what matters.

Amanda and Don in Cleveland, Tennessee, would be happy to help since they've manned an abandoned outpost without air or, more importantly, ground support or hopes for reinforcements. Bryan Hambley, too, stepping up to run for office as a Democrat without any prospect of institutional backing in the abandoned battlefront of Ohio. But also the patrons of the Twin Peaks bar in Independence, Missouri, including "Let's Go Brandon" and her husband, and the convenience store clerk in Cartersville, Georgia, who needs to find a more stable place for his family, and an apartment where his kids can be safe. Mayor Santini there too, who is just trying to do well on the local level, where most people get their services.

Teri and the Baptist minister in Springfield, Ohio, who don't rise to the noise about dogs and cats being eaten. The guy in the truck in Texas with the "Don't California my Texas" bumper sticker. John in Mt. Vernon, Illinois, who is frustrated and wants to move his generational car dealership to Tennessee. The barber with the John Wayne shrine in Taylor, Texas. The armorer in Reno, Nevada. The women from the "Wild Horse Preservation League" in Carson City.

The director of the Eugene V. Debs Foundation in Terre Haute, Indiana, and blocks away Ann, originally from Philadelphia, now working at the Copper Bar, and her son, the engineering student. The barbers in Denton, Texas, Eli and Libby, who now has one man's haircut on their resume. Tiffany and Calvin in

Rockford, Illinois. The veteran of the Battle of Anzio. Max and Emma at the Radisson in Charleston, South Carolina. The young couple expecting a baby in Miami, Florida. The four guys who work in the movement of cargo. James Rabun who sells guns in Kennesaw, Georgia. The bearded guys who line up nightly at the small bar at the Sunset Grille in Belgrade, Maine. The range safety officer at the Texas Gun Experience and the regional manager for Ace Hardware in Vermont.

Drew from Honda, and Robert Pitcherski and Steve Fischer, and the folks who gathered, in the proud tradition of our democracy, in the gym of the Theodore Roosevelt School on the west side of Des Moines to participate in the Republican caucus and shocked me by voting for Donald Trump.

I think they all would be willing to tell Democrats what's on their minds.

And this is the pivotal difference between Donald Trump's MAGA movement and what the Democratic Party might become. Trump has figured out what people want, and he tells them what they want to hear. Democrats and independents, who seem to care about democracy enough not to try to overthrow it, and even those who *want* to care but are too dispirited right now, might take up the hard work and find out how that democracy can adapt to include those it has left out, not just historically, but today.

The Democrats don't need to figure out what people want to hear.

The Democrats need to listen to what people want.

ACKNOWLEDGMENTS

This book is the result of eight years of travel and countless interactions with people in thirty four states. I am grateful to those who joined me in listening and reporting: John Warner, Tim DeLouchrey, Barbara Brown, Eric Chast, David Sullivan, and Kerry Walls. Lila Guzowski and Connor Murphy took the pulse of voters in their age cohort, from which I am numerically distanced. And I am particularly grateful to Jim O'Sullivan for his reporting and editing. Jeannette Schlaeger and Betty Reed were kind enough to apply their editing skills and Judy Rakowsky, colleague and author, was invaluable throughout. Special thanks to Scott W. Berg who took time away from his own writing and teaching to guide me through the pitch process.

This would not be a book without the great advocacy of my agent Jane Dystel and Miriam Goderich at Dystel, Goderich and Bourret, and Amanda Chiu Krohn and Ashlyn Inman and the team at Turner Publishing.

Thank you to my family, my friends in Belmont, and my colleagues at the Liberty Square Group, who indulged this need of mine to understand this time in history.

Finally, I want to thank everyone who spoke to us and whose stories were told here. I hope I have done so with the respect those folks—my fellow Americans—deserve.

ABOUT THE AUTHOR

SCOTT FERSON has watched and worked in politics for forty years, from the John Anderson for President campaign while in High School, as a press secretary to the late Senator Edward M. Kennedy, a chief strategist for the insurgent congressional campaign of Seth Moulton (D-MA) and advisor to dozens of candidates for office at the local and state level. He is the President/CEO of the strategic communications shop, the Liberty Square Group, and runs a political incubator, the Blue Lab, that trains young people how to run campaigns. He is an adjunct professor of Political Science at Stonehill College in Easton, Massachusetts.